The Politics and Dynamics of
HUMAN RIGHTS

The Politics and Dynamics of
HUMAN RIGHTS

by

MOSES MOSKOWITZ

1968

Oceana Publications, Inc.
Dobbs Ferry, New York

By the same author:

HUMAN RIGHTS AND WORLD ORDER

Library of Congress Catalog Card Number: 68-21376

Oceana Book No. 360

MANUFACTURED IN THE UNITED STATES OF AMERICA

Table of Contents

Preface

I welcome this opportunity to pay tribute to the Officers and Members of the Governing Board of the Consultative Council of Jewish Organizations (CCJO), which I have had the honor to serve as Secretary-General since its founding in the autumn of 1946. Their personal dedication to the cause of international human rights; their imaginative grasp of the problem; their uncompromising intellectual integrity and their insistence on essential conviction and authentic interest encouraged constant questioning of commonplace assumptions and invited suggestions of new themes and new theses. This book had its beginnings in the intellectual atmosphere which has prevailed in the CCJO and in its striving to transcend the historical and juridical arena of discourse for a more philosophic and universal expression of international concern with human rights.

I have shared in full measure the advantages that accrued from an association so rich in challenge and experience. I wish to express my appreciation to Professor René Cassin, Honorary Chairman; the Hon. Mr. Justice Harry Batshaw, Co-Chairman; M. Jules Braunschvig, Co-Chairman; Mr. Harold Sebag-Montefiore, Co-Chairman; Mr. Marcel Franco, Vice-Chairman; Mr. Alexander E. Salzman, Deputy Vice-Chairman; Professor Norman Bentwich, O. B. E., M. C.; Mr. Allan Bronfman; Mr. Robert N. Carvalho; Mr. Edgar Cohen; Dean Maxwell Cohen, Q. C.; Mr. Seymour W. Harrison; M. Jean Jaudel; M. Pierre Kahn; Mr. Milton Klein, Q. C.; M. P.; Mr. Clemens N. Nathan; Mr. Albert I. Polack; the Hon. Mr. Justice Manfred Simon; Mr. Philip Vineberg, Q. C.; Professor Prosper Weil, and M. André Wormser.

No one who has had the privilege of close contact with Professor Cassin has escaped the impact of his greatness. I have also had the good fortune to enjoy the wise counsel of Messrs.

Franco and Salzman, who have been shouldering special responsibilities in the Council. Their understanding and diplomacy and their preference for substance guaranteed the pursuit of a reasoned course of policy and action. And I cherish the friendship and loyal cooperation of my colleagues and associates, at home and abroad; Mrs. Helene Kadane, who for the past fifteen years has volunteered her services to the CCJO as its representative at UNICEF, and Mr. David K. Kadane, attorney and counsellor; M. Eugene Weill, Secretary-General of the Alliance Israélite Universelle; M. Gérard Israel, Assistant Secretary-General of the Alliance Israélite Universelle; Mme. I. Kowarski; Mrs. Gabrielle Cairncross, Secretary of the Anglo-Jewish Association; M. François Brunschwig, Honorary Representative of the CCJO at the European Headquarters of the United Nations; Mr. Saadiah Cherniak, Executive Director of the American Friends of the Alliance Israélite Universelle; Mr. Marc Lithman; Miss Estelle Lugen, and M. Armand Himy, Permanent Representative of the CCJO in Europe.

I owe a special debt of gratitude to my wife for the spaciousness of her perspective and to our children for their sense and sensibility and their consuming, but not uncritical, interest in my work.

Moses Moskowitz

New York, September 1967.

Introduction

International concern with human rights, especially in the larger setting of the culture and the historical currents and forces of the times, is nearly an untrodden area of systematic inquiry and research. Yet there is secreted in this concern a dynamic force for the conciliation between nations, regions, ideologies and groupings, that awaits only the firm hand to release it. A great ethic surrounds the idea. Elevated to an operating principle of international relations, international concern with human rights has the quality of a sovereign answer to the many questions that torment the world. It is at once capable of rekindling the fires of idealism and of satisfying the demands of practicability. As the foundation for international cooperation in the broadest reaches of policy and action, the concern of the community of nations with the fate of the human individual gains a deep sense of connection with the world of great achievement.

The theme of this book is international concern with human rights striving for ascendancy as an idea which suggests the transcendance of the fixed framework of international relations in the search of solutions to the problems of the human condition. Once it is recognized that the nation-state is no longer the sanctuary which can shield the citizen against the perils that threaten to bring man's fondest hopes to naught, there is only international concern with the fate of the human individual to rescue people trapped by ancient loyalties and to bring a fresh sense of purpose and dedication to the world. If myth and legend are not to move close to fatal error, human rights must be established as an obligatory pattern of thought everywhere and serve as a criterion for essaying the policies and goals of government.

Generations of men have borne the burden of the nationalist creed, reluctant to abandon so deeply an embedded myth. Nationalism is a faith which is still the life and strength of peoples around the world. But as long as the basic goal of the state is the defense of its own interests and the power methods by which they are ensured, there can be no disinterested nation concerned with the welfare of other nations. As long as the state is more concerned with exploiting immediate advantages rather than with long-range plans of interest to all states, nationality will come between man and his neighbor. This places severe limits upon cooperation between nations, be it within an ideological group or military alliance, within regions or within international organization. Just as fundamental changes in man's attitude are needed to avoid ecological disaster, so there is need for a fresh relationship among nations for humanity to continue to coexist with itself. Such a relationship must spring from the requirements of the age and accord with the basic realities and deepest aspirations of peoples.

Man is the ultimate reality and his deepest aspirations find most authentic expression in the Universal Declaration of Human Rights. Their satisfaction is the supreme guarantee of change for the better in all realms of life and society. The rights and freedoms enunciated in the Declaration provide the only enduring framework in which particular policies can be cast, with no confinements to halt their forward march and no horizons to limit their imaginative thrust. The advancement of the rights and freedoms of man as the subject and object of all international cooperation and its transformation into norms of political action is no bid in the void. The reorientation of the world toward human rights is an eminently practical proposition, both as an end and as a means to an end. Moral sensitivity, historical perspective, and psychological and social awareness are its dimensions. It not only commands power to stir the emotions, but conveys an exquisite sense of direction, with specific referents in time and space and capable of generating thought and action of the highest order.

In an age in which the curtain has fallen on so many utopian hopes and didactic pronouncements have only served to mask confusion, it might be the better part of virtue to avoid creating the illusion of a new dawn and forego the temptation of setting loose a euphoria of unattainable goals. But there can be no doubt as to the validity of the principle of human rights as the one point of concurrence where the best interests of the individual, the community, the state and the world converge. Only the triumph of this principle will bring us peace and chart right public policy for dealing with the formidable problems of the century.

Among these problems are many which can never be properly attacked, let alone resolved, within the framework of an international system which recognizes the state as the sole unit of international organization and the subject of its principal concern. Such, for example, is the problem of the population explosion on an already crowded planet; the problem of the hundreds of million people around the world who constitute minorities of one kind or another and whose survival is forever periled by the intolerance of the nation-state of diversity; the problem of the color bar, which comes between men and nations as a primordially subjective experience; and the problem of poverty and social stagnation, of frustrated aspirations and unspent talent, whose insidious touch is felt everywhere.

For reasons that should stir the interest of publicists and arouse the curiosity of historians, the idea of international concern with human rights has not become a theme of extensive development. It lies dramatically inert. Its excitement has not been communicated to the public, nor have its qualities attracted the attention of the politician. To prosper and flourish, this high-souled idea needs more than the frail support of casual assent. It needs profound conviction and consistent action. Until it enters into the mainstream of national and international politics at the apex of the power structure, its potentialities for creative initiative will remain dormant. The good will of individuals cannot substitute for action which lies in the field of government.

To place international concern with the fate of the human person on the commanding heights of international diplomacy, there must be challenge, innovation or protest. Without them, there can be no persuasive public discussion. And there must be pervasive interest to allow for a settled vision of an issue that is so deceptively simple in basic moral terms, yet so highly complex and so fundamental in its implications. A splendid opportunity for authentic debate is opening up to the peoples of the world on the occasion of the International Year for Human Rights and in the years ahead as the nations are asked to pronounce themselves on the two international covenants on human rights and their enforcement. These are the International Covenant on

Economic, Social and Cultural Rights, the International Covenant on Civil and Political Rights and the Optional Protocol to the Covenant on Political and Civil Rights which the United Nations General Assembly opened for signature and ratification at the close of its twenty-first session in December 1966.

The three documents, which had been more than eighteen years in preparation, provide the politico-juridical foundations for translating international concern with human rights into a concrete program of action. These international treaties give a new definition to governmental purpose and objective and they reach out for goals of unsurpassed generosity. Whatever their failings as texts, the Covenants are cast in broad perspectives. Great human aims and desires underlie them, which hold together minds widely scattered in geography, culture and doctrinal loyalties. Yet, a superlative virtuosity is called for to overcome the linguistic and conceptual barriers which bar a fruitful dialogue in many places high and low, and formidable talent and energy must be mobilized to fight off the pretenses, evasions, diversions and crudities on many sides, to win weary allies, to appeal to indifferent audiences, to cut through the stubborn constraints of thought and interest and to break the deadlock which seems to have settled on so many hopeful things in so many parts of the world. These efforts must be pursued with force and authority equal to the task lest the Covenants drift in an isolated orbit into an inconclusive climax.

CHAPTER I

The Burden
of the Nationalist Creed

A world of sovereign, independent nation-states working not
against each other but for the common good of all is a snare
and delusion. Either we discover a new framework of international relations which transcends all national boundaries, or we
shall continue to reap the bitter harvest of international strife
and lawlessness. What stands in the way of an enduring peace
and world order today is the preemption of international relations by the sovereign state, whose power ultimately arbitrates
on all occasions when differences regarded as vital to the national
interest arise among nations. The traditional framework of international relations, in which the interests and advantages of
the state, real or imaginary, determine a nation's foreign policy,
cannot bring forth the kind of international cooperative effort
which is necessary to cope successfully with the formidable problems of the age. As long as irrational motives and false loyalties
blind us to the realities of human existence, the world will never
rise above differences of nationality.

These differences are a basic feature of the modern world
and the decisive factor in international intercourse. All the verbal
pieties mouthed in praise of internationalism cannot disguise
the intense national rivalries that keep men apart. All the im-
passioned evocations of the interdependence of the world cannot
hide the universal quest for national self-aggrandizement. Where
national interests are involved or national advantages at stake,
neither racial nor ethnic kinship, nor religious community, nor
cultural affinity, nor ideological fellowship, let alone moral and
humanitarian considerations, carry weight on the opposite scale
in the balance.[1] Until the barriers raised among men by the

forces of nationalism are conquered, nothing will hush the imperious and decisive voice of national pride and prejudice.

The quest for peace and world order must begin by an active search for realities external to the existence of the sovereign state and immune to the blandishments of the nationalistic creed. There is danger in reliance on evolution in the affairs of men. The upward growth and progress which Turgot proclaimed two centuries ago as the law of human life commands little historic respect today. It has been discredited by the tragic ironies of history, the momentuous miscalculations, and all the good intentions gone awry.[2] Too many wastelands of illusion and cruelty and betrayal already dot the earth and we must not add to their number. One of these illusions is that nationalism and its excesses are destined to dwindle gradually and to ultimately disappear in response to essentially the same forces which first set the stage for its emergence—common interests and attitudes, living together and working together, and sharing experiences and memories. It is a crude belief that world peace and international justice will grow out of the cooperation among peoples and nations in the arts and sciences, in economics and culture and in the host of other areas of peaceful pursuit among men. The indications are that the world will continue to spin in a vicious circle of nationalism, until it comes to realize that only the transcendence of nationalism will set it free.

Nationalism, John Stuart Mill observed in commenting on the events of 1848 in Europe, "makes man indifferent to the rights and interests of any portion of the human species, save that which is called by the same name and speaks the same language as themselves."[3] Behind the term nationalism lies a most complex interplay of human factors which is beyond the range of any one social discipline to lay bare. But whether we conceive of it as a composite of the deepest human beliefs, sentiments and emotions, or as an abstraction compounded of other abstractions, the fact remains that nationalism stands supreme in the center of all existing networks and interests which unite or divide people everywhere.

The roots of nationalism[4] strike deep into the past. By the time of the Renaissance, the mass emotions known today as nationalism had emerged triumphant. It was as much a revolt against the medieval notion of a universal state as broad as the frontiers of Christendom, as against the localism and particularism of the feudal barony. But it was not until the French Revolution that the concept of an all-inclusive national political community entered into the experience and imagination of the masses. It was the French Revolution, with its stirring battle cry of Liberty, Equality and Fraternity that created that self-conscious nationalism which has since become the greatest single dynamic force in the world. It was the French Revolution that had swept away most of the feudal encumbrances that impeded the process of national unification and crystallized the notion of nationalism into a conscious aspiration towards nationhood, one and indivisible, living within fixed boundaries under a common sovereignty, and loyally sharing a common destiny.

A child of the humanism and cosmopolitanism of the Enlightenment, the nationalism which was borne aloft by the French Revolution carried with it a great and generous message of a new liberty and a new dignity to all men and all peoples. It proclaimed the optimistic cosmology of the eighteenth century, with its triple doctrine of popular sovereignty, progress and the perfectability of man. The rights of man and the notion of national sovereignty were an organic whole and the nation was regarded but as the link between the individual and humanity. But the nationalism which gained momentum as it swept across the face of the earth was totally different. As it engulfed ever larger areas of the world, the new nationalism shed its early liberalism and humanitarianism and changed into an aggressive exclusiveness. The glorification of the national collectivity took the place of the dignity of man, while the autonomy of the individual gave way to the exaltation of the state. Instead of a link between the individual and humanity, nationalism barred all loyalties outside its own frontiers.

From a predominantly political movement to limit governmental power and to ensure political rights and personal liberties, nationalism rapidly evolved into a metaphysical dogma embodying the supreme ideal of human self-expression and the highest incarnation of the collective will. Its symbol became the nation-state, guardian of the supreme ideal and executor of the collective will. In time the symbol itself came to be worshipped as an idolatrous end in its own right, with patriotism as its religion. "Midway through the twentieth century of the Christian Era," Arnold Toynbee tells us, the Western Society was manifestly given over to the worship of a number of idols that had been the bane of other civilizations in the past; but, among these, one stood out above all the rest, and this was the cult of the institution of Parochial Sovereignty embodied in parochial states that were being worshipped by their respective subjects as very gods and that were demonstrating their demonic power over their devotees by exacting from them human sacrifices of ever greater enormity in cycles of fratricidal wars of a violence that was increasing in geometrical progression.[5]

The postulation of a national, supra-personal will served to obscure man's relation to his fellow-men; the assertion by the state of internal and external sovereignty absolved the citizen from his duties to mankind. Whether man is considered the servant of the state or the state the servant of man, all states share alike a doctrinaire rigidity as to their fundamental prerogatives. They all demand the subordination of all purposes and all loyalties to their own and the unswerving and undivided allegiance of their citizens. Their preocupation with their own sovereign rights and interests leaves little room for the development of an international community-consciousness and of a common loyalty to the human family.

It is this national egocentrism that leads governments to judge issues of world-wide import wholly by their effect on the nation's welfare and to subordinate the general interest to the destiny of the state. To the sovereign state its own needs and concience are the ultimate criteria of right and wrong and of law and justice, and the realization of national interests and aspirations stands above all virtue and morality. With a blindness that afflicts those whom the gods would destroy, nations cling to the illusion that they can forever escape the consequences of a morality which sanctions abroad the very things they reprove at home.

All states, without exception, are bent upon the realization of national interests, which more often than not derive from the unreasoning acceptance of the nationalist creed, with all its ineluctable and tragic consequences. For behind the generality of national interests lies a deep myth. It is a myth created by the makers of national policy in response to a world of their own imagination and nurtured by distorted pride in nationality and narrow-minded personal, class and sectional interests. It is the same myth which has toppled thrones, razed empires and levelled nations; which twice in this century brought disaster upon the world and which today threatens the human race with extinction.

No nation can any longer cope unaided with the probabilities and possibilities, as well as with the certainties, of modern existence. Yet the state invariably claims its own interests to be the center of its moral universe. However much the presumption may be in favor of the pursuit of the welfare of all peoples and all nations as the surest guarantee of the welfare of any one people and any one nation, national interests are seldom asserted in the wider setting of the general interest. However self-evident it may appear that in the present state of the technical arts it is no more possible to defend the national interest without defending the interests of the whole of the human family than formerly it was possible to defend one's home without defending one's country, it does not avail to dissolve the concrete ambitions of the state. And however widespread the comprehension may be of the incompatibility of national sovereignty with the steadily increasing interdependence of peoples, the great problems of war and peace, economic development and social progress remain essentially matters of national attitudes.

As long as the assertion of the interests of the national community is regarded as the highest good, nationalism will remain an armed doctrine and national sovereignty an aggressive force. When the promotion and defense of the national interest is the be-all and end-all of national policy, power becomes the supreme good to which a nation can aspire. It is only by the use of power, be it by inducement, persuasion or force, that the state can hope to achieve its ends. The greater the power of the state, the greater the influence or control it can exercise over the policies and actions of other states whose cooperation, compliance or tolerance it must secure in order to advance and safeguard its own interests. The massive strategic reality of international relations is the struggle for power—not necessarily power for its own sake, but power to defend or to change the *status quo*. Any other state which balances or limits this power is an actual or potential enemy.

The forces which seek to free man from the insularity of nationalism's influence are no match for the phantasies which are entrenched in the popular imagination. In the fierce, competitive struggle for persuasion convulsing the world, nationalism yields to none in its concentrated impact on the course of events. Nationalism has become the universal faith of mankind, with all its glories, frustrations and aberrations. The clarion call of nationalism reverberates with explosive intensity, as the ripening seeds all-too successfully planted by the imperial powers bear fruit throughout the world. Its onward march has kindled fires which today burn fiercely in the remotest corners on earth, among the Bemba tribesmen along the Zambezi, the Chaga on the slopes of Kilimanjaro, the warring Lulua and Baluba in the Congo, and the displaced Herrero and Ovambo in Southwest Africa.[6]

Since the end of World War II, more than three score countries in Asia, Africa, Oceania and the Caribbean have emerged into independence.[7] In all, more than a thousand million people have come into the fullness of their political personalities.[8] They include old civilizations and ancient cultures, greater or lesser aggregations of social groups and tribal structures, and scattered communities cut off and isolated from each other and from civilization. Their emancipation has vindicated the democratic ideal, which since the French Revolution has been committed to national freedom and independence. It has redeemed the promise of Woodrow Wilson made half-a-century ago and reaffirmed in the Charter of the United Nations as a fundamental principle of international relations. And it has upheld the right of man to associate himself with his fellow-men in nationhood and to create the juridical organs of state sovereignty to carry out their appointed mission.

The social experiences through which men identify themselves with specific groups and nations are historically real and culturally dynamic. Nationalism appears to be perfectly congruous with the most important elements of modern group life and consonant with the basic scheme of the universe. The material setting for the exultation of the state is the citizen's increasing dependence upon it. The enormously enhanced power of the state in response to the combined effects of increasing numbers and the refined techniques of modern science, as well as its inexhaustive capacity for service, makes it the primary agent for ordering man's social context. In the face of the ever-growing complexities of modern life, people turn ever more confidently towards the state for the satisfaction of their wants and the solution of their problems. It is not alone the quest for the realization of national aspirations and for collective unity and power that makes the state the focal point round which center the ambitions of men; the state has become the sole agent responsible for creating the conditions without which the citizen can realize neither his internal capacities nor his external opportunities.

There is not a single state in the world today, old or new, that is not to a greater or lesser degree a welfare state. Whether it derives from doctrinaire theories or is the result forced by the conditions of life, the state everywhere has shed its traditional role of umpire to become an agency ministering to the economic, social and cultural needs of the nation. Even the most conservative elements are now committed to some form of governmental intervention in the national economy and to a measure of social legislation. It has come to be almost universally recognized that it is the government's responsibility to adopt measures looking towards full employment and to strengthen the national economy to sustain it; to offer relief to the unemployed and to provide economic security for the ill, the aged and the dependent; to establish minimum standards of compensation and working conditions; to protect and insure the health of the citizen against the hazards of accident and disease; to guarantee a minimum of education to children and to encourage the growth of secondary, technical and higher education and training; and, in general, to foster the economic, social and educational conditions that make for equality of opportunity for all.[9]

In the new countries, nationalism is not only the most potent vehicle for lifting the masses from the abyss of human misery and degradation to the heights of human dignity and equality, but seems to provide the only common idiom capable of articulating the diverse visions of the future which animate people in various stages of civilization and development. When former President Kwame Nkrumah of Ghana thundered, "Seek ye the political kingdom and all other things will be added unto it," he only gave voice to a deep-seated conviction that a people which is unable to express itself by means of its own free and independent national institutions can neither fullfil its aspirations nor contribute to the common civilization of the world. Nationalism is the seeming force able to provide the stimulus necessary to redress the imbalance between the will to national independence and the insuficiency of the political, economic and social development of vast regions acrros Asia and Africa.[10]

Moreover, nationalism appears to be the sole social and political framework broad enough to contain within it all the inner tensions and outer contradictions to which so many of the new countries have fallen heir, and to oppose all the separate orientations and divisive tendencies which have their roots in the traditional loyalties to caste and religion, to tribe and community. Whatever their integrative capacities may be, all the states which have emerged into independence since the end of World War II have placed their hopes on nationalism to overcome the racial, national, linguistic, religious, ethnic, tribal and cultural diversity of their populations. Nationalism has become the matrix of Asian and African culture and civilization and their acknowledged leaders and recognized spokesmen have quickly grasped its essence. They are all committed to national unification in politics, industrialization, and secularization in thought and in juridical and social organization.[11]

In all, the unquestioned belief of people that their most cherished individual and collective values are inextricably bound up with the sovereign independence of their own state heightens the sense of nationality. Their dependence upon the state in a thousand ways for their physical security, their standard of living, and their way of life charges all nationalist claims with intense mass emotion. The pressure for survival among states competing for national advantage, unbridled and unrestricted by law or morality, only enhances nationalism's aggressive quality. The compulsion states must meet in preserving internal order and external security and the need to equip themselves for a successful role on the stage of international politics requires that the national spirit be kept in perpetual fervor. The nature of modern war demands the permanent indoctrination of the people into national unity. As the areas of conflict and power politics increase, the weight upon every state to strengthen itself grows heavier. Thus, the intense stimulation of national patriotism induced by war or the threat of war and fear for political and economic security springs eternal from the very conditions it has helped to create—international anarchy, lack of security, competition for national advantage, and the ever-present danger of war. When the organized forces of nationalism remain locked in a permanent acrimonious duel, the state can no more tolerate a common loyalty to mankind than it can suffer a divided allegiance within its own borders.[12]

The weight of historic evidence and contemporary political realities lend no comfort to the idea of an international order which remains at the mercy of shifting national sentiment or interest. Sovereign nation-states are incapable of cooperation for the common welfare. They cannot wage an honest and sustained campaign for a just and lasting peace, when they have yet to renounce the right and freedom to defend what they regard as their national interests, by force of arms if necessary. They cannot come forward with a genuine affirmation of a common humanity, when they have yet to awaken from the dreams of their own grandeur and come to terms with their roles as members of a community of nations. And they move along too narrow trails to rid themselves of their fears and prejudices of the past and to recognize the forces which speak with the persuasiveness of a long yearning. Common interests and cooperation for mutual advantage may produce an alliance between nations for the purpose of common policies through a common effort, varying in intensity and purpose from issue to issue. Eventually, however, such alliances, whether in the form of bilateral, multilateral, regional or universal agreements, reach a point beyond which their cooperation becomes too attenuated and too elastic to provide cohesiveness or sense of purpose. National interests are not static and issues change with the times. Sooner or later, all international cooperative ventures founder on conflicting national interests.

CHAPTER II

The Limits of International Cooperation

The rejection of the requirements of the general interest of the human family for the sake of national advantage is expressed in an infinite variety of words and deeds. They are chronicled daily around the world and are deeply etched on the face of the earth. It is very rare that international cooperation is inspired and guided by principles which transcend all immediate considerations of national interest and of political and material advantage. This explains why all the grand designs for international peace have failed to blunt the sword and why all international organization has brought us no nearer to world order and justice.

There was a time, for example, when the conviction that war could be exorcised by professions of peace was widespread. It was a dream as deep as myth. That myth finally exploded with the Kellogg-Briand Pact of 1928. "The High Contracting Parties," Article 1 of the Pact of Paris reads, "solemnly declare in the names of their respective peoples that they condemn recourse to war for the solution of international controversies, and renounce it as an instrument of national policy in their relations with one another."[1] The High Contracting Parties included nearly all the sovereign and independent nations of the world at the time. Their solemn renunciation of war as an instrument of national policy was hailed everywhere as heralding a turning point in human history. But the ink had hardly dried on the paper on which the Pact was written, when one act of aggression followed in swift succession upon the other, beginning in 1931 with the Japanese aggression in Manchuria and ending on September 1, 1939, with the Nazi invasion of Poland.

It was not merely that the forces of peace proved too feeble to overcome the forces of aggression. Behind the collapse of the Kellogg-Briand Pact lay the chasm of implacable faith in incompatible ideals—the ideal of universal peace and the ideal of national greatness and glory. The High Contracting Parties united in their renunciation of war as an instrument of national policy, but they did not renounce the right to be judge in their own cause and the freedom to act in accordance with their own judgement. It did not prevent Great Britain, for example, to virtually nullify the Treaty by asserting freedom of action in certain regions without explicit geographical limitations. In a note dated May 19, 1928, to United States Secretary of State Frank B. Kellogg, British Foreign Secretary Sir Austin Chamberlain stated:

> The language of Article 1, as to the renunciation of war as an instrument of national policy, renders it desirable that I should remind Your Excellency that there are certain regions in the world the welfare and integrity of which constitute a special and vital interest for our peace and safety. His Majesty's Government have been at pains to make it clear in the past that interference with these regions cannot be suffered. Their protection against attack is to the British Empire a measure of self-defense. It must be clearly understood that His Majesty's Government in Great Britain accept the new treaty upon the distinct understanding that it does not prejudice their freedom of action in this respect...[2]

The understanding postulated by Great Britain, which asserted the primacy of the national interest, was reinforced and broadened by Secretary of State Kellogg himself. In a statement on June 23, 1928, in which he gave America's official interpretation of the Pact, Mr. Kellogg declared:

> Every nation is free at all times and regardless of treaty provisions to defend its territory from attack or invasion, and it alone is competent to decide whether circumstances require recourse to war in self-defense...[3]

Commenting on this statement, Professor F. P. Walters writes:

> The official interpretation given to the Pact by the American Secretary of State was that it did not forbid war. "Every nation," the Secretary of State wrote, "alone is competent to decide whether circumstances require recourse to war in self-defense," and it was plain that under self-defense he included the defense not only of the national territory but also of vital interests and policies such as the Monroe Doctrine. Similarly, the British Government formally announced that it regarded the maintenance of peace "in certain regions of the world" not under British sovereignty as a measure of self-defense. Since, therefore, each signatory was the sole judge of its own self-defense and since the greatest among them proclaimed an extensive interpretation of that word, the way was open, as far as the Kellogg Pact was concerned, to military action which would certainly not be consistent with the Covenant. And indeed when Japan undertook the conquest of Manchuria, she claimed the benefit of the right thus recognized, declaring that Manchuria was no less vital to her self-defense than the Suez Canal to Britain or the Panama Canal to the United States.[4]

Great reliance had been placed on the development of instruments for the pacific settlement of international disputes. Pacific settlement of such disputes rightly boasts of steady progress. Ever since its intrusion into the realm of practical statesmanship following the Hague Peace Conferences in the beginning of this century, the peaceful settlement of international disputes has undoubtedly contributed to the peaceful relations among states.[5] But they could never substitute for war as the final arbiter in disputes among nations. War is not just another means of settling international disputes. War is an instrument of national policy whether for aggression or defense, for the maintenance of the *status quo* or its destruction, for honor, profit or glory. The conflicts of interest which lead nations over the rim of the abyss are rarely susceptible to arbitration, conciliation or peaceful settlement.

Over a period of thirty-five years, we are told,

> the United States entered into ninety-seven international
> arbitrational and conciliative contracts. To what practical
> effect? The permanent engagements for arbitrations so
> elaborately worked out with great public eclat have proved
> relevant in a few claim adjudications of no moment what-
> soever and, if memory serves, in the settlement between
> ourselves and other states of two issues of substance. One
> case, adjudicated about forty-five years ago, involved the
> interpretation of a treaty between the United States and
> Great Britain with respect to fishing rights in the North
> Atlantic. The other, adjudicated about twenty-five years
> ago, related to a dispute with the Netherlands over title
> to an unimportant island. Not by even the widest stretch
> of the imagination would either issue be considered to have
> involved danger of hostilities...One may ask whether
> harm was done by all this effort so meagre of measurable
> good results. Only the harm—a considerable one, I believe,
> of encouraging and protecting an illusion. This illusion sees
> great world political issues as susceptible of being trans-
> lated into questions solvable by legal and judicial means.
> It entertains the futile belief in strenghtening peace by
> pretending that the factor of force in the image which na-
> tions cast on the consciousness of other nations is not
> really present.[6]

The instruments for the peaceful settlement of disputes among
nations which would substitute for war or the threat of war have
yet to be forged. Neither the International Court of Justice, nor
the many agencies of arbitration, conciliation and mediation have
been able to intervene successfully to right injustices, to set the
facts straight, to revise old settlements and review past agreements, to compose differences of view and interpretation, or to
conciliate conflicts of interest. Nations have consistently shied
away from the International Court and resorted to political settlement of even their minor disputes.[7] Their reluctance to appeal
to the organ of international justice is but another manifestation
of the basic characteristic of the state, which refuses to compromise its freedom of action. It derives from the same sources
and from the same spirit as, for example, the so-called Connally
reservation to the optional clause of the Statute of the Inter-

national Court of Justice, under which the United States reserved the right to determine by itself whether a dispute was or was not "essentially within the domestic jurisdiction of the United States of America," and retained the freedom of action in the matter of referring any dispute to the Court.[8] The ever-growing number of unresolved international disputes, from Kashmir to Cyprus, from South Africa to the Middle East, from South Tyrol to the frontiers between Somalia and Ethiopia attests to the unwillingness of states to entrust what they regard as their vital interests to the judgement of third parties. Nations are never more self-righteous than when they are in anger.

Collective security and disarmament continue to occupy the center of the stage in the search for peace. In its true meaning, collective security implies an absolute and unconditional recognition of the indivisibility of peace and presupposes an identification of interest which only a common loyalty to the world community can sustain. But as long as considerations of national interest and distinctions between traditional friend and inveterate foe impede the "rigorously objective and anonymous operations of collective security," it remains a snare and delusion. The same is true of disarmament.

Like war iself, arms are but instruments at the disposal of national policy. Their explosion is neither automatic, nor a direct and inescapable function of their size and power. What is decisive is the political consequence of military power. As long as armed might underwrites the security of nations and as long as it constitutes the measure of national power, the limitation, control, let alone the total prohibition of arms are beyond the reach of contemporary statesmanship. The solution to the problem of armaments, whether nuclear or conventional, cannot be sought in isolation from the solution of the basic problems of international organization.[9] Neither the portends looming large on the horizon, nor the apocalyptic visions of the prophets of doom have been enough to persuade nations to dismantle their forces or to surrender their military advantages. The existence all over the world in massive quantities of weapons of unimaginably destructive power has not deterred nations from adding to their number, nor halted the search for even more potent instruments of mass destruction. Power politics remains the principal factor of disarmament and as long as the interests of the most powerful members of the international community diverge, little progress is

in the offing. Disarmament will enter into the realm of the practical when arms become superfluous as a guarantee of national
security and military superiority irrelevant to a nation's greatness.

The efforts to dent the armor of war and to promote international cooperation range over the totality of human activity, from
personal contact among citizens of the different countries of the
world to the most elaborate schemes of international organization.
Anything that is calculated to reduce the areas of tension and
conflict among nations and everything which serves to promote
mutual understanding among peoples are weapons in the arsenal
of peace.[10] The notion that international cooperation, at all levels,
for the promotion of economic and social progress is a most potent
instrument for peace has come to be accepted as self-evident.
One of the principal purposes of the United Nations is to "achieve
international cooperation in solving international problems of an
economic, social, cultural or humanitarian character."[11] One of
UNESCO's principal objectives is to maintain, increase and dif-
fuse knowledge among the peoples of the world,

> by encouraging cooperation among the nations in all
> branches of intellectual activity, including the interna-
> tional exchange of persons active in the fields of education,
> science and culture and the exchange of publications, ob-
> jects of artistic and scientific interest and other materials
> of information.[12]

Yet, while all these efforts are indispensible to the promotion
of a positive sense of international community and are no doubt
essential to the ultimate solution of the fundamental problems of
international relations, their immediate impact on the questions
of war and peace, international solidarity and national self-assertion appears to be so remote as to be negligible. For the most part,
international cooperation, whether in the political, military, economic, social, cultural or humanitarian spheres, takes place at
various levels, at different times, among different countries, for
a variety of reasons, for diverse ends. These cooperative activities
are rarely integrated in a way as to reinforce each other or pursued with a view to changing the conduct of states in the international arena. All the varied and complex institutions and procedures of international cooperation do not even remotely add up
to an international sharing of responsibility or to an international

division of labor. The test is their ability to forestall that moment of fury in which the best works of man are laid waste and to provide permanent relief to the problems of the human condition. Given the experience in war in the twentieth century and the nature of modern weapons, the unreasoning acceptance of the functional approach to international peace and world order is morally disastrous and materially futile.

Nothing could be further from the truth than to construe the proliferation of multilateral organizations and agencies[13] as an expression of a cosmic tendency toward integration, or as a conscious effort to hasten the coming of a world-state. These international agencies and organizations are in no sense deliberate instruments fashioned by governments to promote the idea of the parliament of man and the federation of the world. They are but methods of cooperation among sovereign states for mutual advantage. More often, they are arenas where nations meet to pursue their national interests. As Secretary-General U Thant has suggested,

> The proliferation of international bodies and meetings, both intergovernmental and private, should not be a cause for concern as such. Their number is a response to the demands which are already evident. What is a matter for reflection, however, is whether in fact the response provided by the international bodies is adequate and whether their structure, their activities and the support given them are consonant with present-day requirements.[14]

Except, perhaps, for the several European Communities, none of the existing international agencies purports to transcend the nation-state system. Except, perhaps, for Western Europe, where the conflicting virtues of loose federal association and close political union have entered the realm of practical politics, international relations remain imprisoned within the mold of yesteryear. In the crossfire of critical assertion and historical debate, those who argue that even supra-national institutions are no more than a collection of public services without will or power, which resides in the nation-state and will remain its monopoly as long as international institutions remain at the mercy of the nations in whose name they function, seem to have the edge.[15]

What the multiplication of international organizations attests to is the growing need for international cooperation and accommodation in ever-widening areas of governmental competence and responsibility. The hundreds of intergovernmental bodies and agencies that dot the five continents and the many more hundreds of intergovernmental conferences and meetings convened each year with increasing regularity spring from the more permanent imperatives arising from the complexities of contemporary civilization, as well as from the exigencies of the moment. No country, however large and powerful, is sufficient unto itself. No country, however small and unobtrusive, can live and thrive in isolation. The traditional dividing lines which distinguish between internal and external problems have grown increasingly thin. The problems themselves have come ever more to depend for their solution upon a common course of action.[16] Human interference with the environment and man's increasing control over natural forces are producing effects that not only cross national boundaries and sectional frontiers, but reach ever more from continent to continent. Nuclear energy is but the most dramatic illustration of the reverberation of a sovereign act like the detonation of a nuclear device throughout the world.[17]

But a recognition of common interests is not a strong enough base upon which world order can be erected, even if only because the centers toward which the interests of states gravitate are widely diffused, shifting and often contradictory. It is as rare for national interests to run parallel, as it is for nations to have identity of purpose. Even when national interests run parallel and purposes are identical, differences in approach and divergencies in pursuit of them arise to corrode the relations between like-minded states and loyal allies. This is eloquently attested to by the disarray in recent years in the Atlantic Alliance.

This alliance,[18] which has been represented as a fundamental fact in the existence of the peoples in its embrace,[19] has no more than other alliances in history yielded the recognition of common, long-term objectives and the gradual accommodation of national interests and ambitions to the interdependence of its members. The fact is that the interests and ambitions of the nations of the Western alliance have come into conflict with one another and with the whole system of international groupings in the West developed after World War II, of which the North Atlantic Treaty Organization (NATO) has become the core and backbone. Neither the imperatives of the long term Soviet challenge, nor the basic propositions which may dictate the unity of the North

Atlantic Treaty states have been able to overcome the resurgent nationalism among the Alliance's members. The grand design for Atlantic Community and all the larger plans and longer goals looking far beyond the requirements of collective defense have been too feeble to stem the centrifugal forces generated within the Alliance. As long as the tentacles of Soviet power immediately threatened to spread over Western Europe, broad purposes and distant goals could be agreed upon in uncritical harmony. Once the Marshall Plan had wrought its economic miracle; once the military void which had existed in Western Europe at the end of the war was filled; and once the tidewaters of Communist expansion were stemmed, each member of the Alliance tended increasingly to determine its policies and actions independently and in accordance with its understanding of its own best interests.

Like the Delian League of ancient Greece, which Aristides of Athens organized to bar a new Persian expedition from the East and which steadily grew weaker as the immediate danger of such an expedition receded, so the Atlantic Alliance, founded at the initiative of the United States after the absorption of Czechoslovakia into the Eastern camp, lost much of its ardor as the military threat to the West perceptibly diminished. Although the purely military aims of NATO have almost from the very beginning come to be regarded as essentially a shield behind which larger plans might develop for the close cooperation among the partners of the Alliance in the realm of politics, economic and social policy, and science and technology, the stated purpose of such cooperation was the need of confronting the infinitely more supple policies and methods employed by the adversary to subvert the resistance of nations to his lures and blandishments. When the nations of the West felt strong enough to resist the temptations offered by the adversary and when the adversary's power to entice and to cajole lessened with time, much of the logic of Atlantic Community was obscured.

President Charles de Gaulle has been the first to challenge openly the most fundamental assumptions on which the Alliance has been erected. Basic to the Alliance has been the acceptance of the indivisibility of Western Europe's military defense and its organization on an Atlantic basis under the decisive voice of the United States as the paramount source of military power in the West. It has demanded the unification of Western Europe as an essential pre-requisite of Atlantic strength and the accommodation of national interests and ambitions to the requirements of Atlantic interdependence.[20] The President of France has not only challenged the need of the Western European nations to subordinate their political, military and economic independence in the interest of the defensive unity of the West; he has denounced the Alliance as an instrument for the perpetuation of American military, scientific and economic preponderance and as an obstacle to European unity.

On February 21, 1966, President de Gaulle summed up his conception of NATO in perspective and prospective as follows:

> Nothing can make a law enforceable, without amendment, when it no longer agrees with the ways of the times. Nothing can make a treaty wholly valid when its object has changed. Nothing can make an alliance remain as such when the conditions in which it was concluded have changed. It is therefore necessary to adapt the law, the treaty and the alliance to the new factors, failing which the texts, emptied of their substance, will, if circumstances so require, be nothing more than useless papers in the archives, unless there is a harsh break between these obsolete forms and the living realities.

> Well! If France considers, today still, that it is useful to her security and to that of the West that she be allied with a certain number of States, particularly with America, for their defense and for hers in the event of aggression against one of them; if the declaration made in common on this subject, in the form of the Atlantic Alliance treaty signed in Washington on April 4, 1949, still remains valid in her eyes, at the same time she recognizes that the measures for implementation taken subsequently no longer correspond to what she deems satisfactory, with respect to herself, in the new conditions.

> I say, in the new conditions. For it is quite clear that, owing to the internal and external evolution in the countries of the East, the Western world is no longer threatened today as it was at the time when the American protectorate was set up in Europe under the cover of NATO. But, at the same time as the alarms were dying down, there was also a reduction in the guarantee of security

—one might say absolute—that the possession of the nuclear weapon by American alone gave the Old Continent, and in the certainty that America would employ it, without reservation, in the event of aggression. For Soviet Russia has since that time equipped itself with a nuclear power capable of striking the United States directly, which has made the decisions of the Americans as to the eventual use of their bombs at least indeterminate, and which has, by the same token, stripped of justification —I speak for France—not the Alliance, of course, but indeed integration.

On the other hand, while the prospects of a world war breaking out on account of Europe are dissipating, conflicts in which America engages in other parts of the world—as the day before yesterday in Korea, yesterday in Cuba, today in Vietnam—risk, by virtue of that famous escalation, being extended so that the result could be a general conflagration. In that case Europe—whose strategy is, within NATO, that of America—would be automatically involved in the struggle, even when it would not have so desired. It would be so for France, if the intermeshing of her territory, of her communications, of certain of her forces, of several of her air bases, of some of her ports with the military system under American command were to continue much longer. Moreover, our country, having become for its part and by its own means an atomic power, is led to assume itself the very extensive strategic and political responsibilities that this capacity involves and that, by their nature and by their dimensions, are obviously inalienable. Lastly, France's determination to dispose of herself, a determination without which she would soon cease to believe in her own role and be able to be useful to others, is incompatible with a defense organization in which she finds herself subordinate . . .[21]

Whether President de Gaulle is isolated in his views or is the authentic voice of Europe is immaterial. The fact is that the national interests of the United States and its partners in the Alliance diverge at many points, whether they relate to Europe's defense and control of nuclear weapons;[22] the polarization of the world between East and West;[23] the relations of the Western

European nations to one another, to the rest of the continent and to the wider world;[24] their economic progress and trade policies, and their inward bends and outward concerns.[25] It stems from America's overwhelming preponderance of military and economic might and the interests, commitments and responsibilities which flow from such preponderance of power. The basic differences between the United States and the Western European allies spring from different historical experiences, traditions and conceptions of themselves and the world and their needs. These cannot be overcome by appeals to Atlantic Community. The essence of community is the equality between its members. The overpowering posture of the United States precludes such an equality—a fact which has from the very beginning militated against the success of every effort to forge closer military, political and economic links across the Atlantic.

At no time since the end of World War II was the United States prepared to set up institutions for joint decision-making that would have limited America's freedom of action. Throughout the years various members of the Alliance have expressed misgivings over the tendency of the leading power to take vital initiatives and make important decisions affecting the interests of all the Allies without consulting them. Much has been made, for example, of the fact that during the Cuban missile crisis, the United States made the almost ultimate decision of taking the Allies to the brink of nuclear war without having consulted them. In the spring of 1964, former Supreme Commander of NATO, General Lauris Norstad, was moved to point out that,

> our allies are demanding more than merely to be kept informed about decisions over which they have no control, more also than 'consultation' in which their views carry weight only if they conform with United States preconceptions. What they want is real participation, a true share in the process by which decisions vital to all are reached. This is what they have every right to demand.[26]

Perhaps the clearest and most straightforward explanation was given by former Under-Secretary of State George W. Ball, in a speech to the Center for Strategic Studies at Georgetown University in Washington, exactly one month after General Norstad had spoken. Mr. Ball stated:

...Most of the nation states which form the membership of NATO are not large enough by themselves to play roles commensurate with the requirements of the present age. Clearly, this is true with regard to atomic weapons. The defense of the West requires not merely that an individual nation have the ability to mobilize vast resources of men, money, material, industrial plant and technology, but also that there be unity of control of the life-or-death decision of nuclear destruction.

...Here is where the political organization of Europe becomes relevant. If Europe were sufficiently far advanced toward political unity that it could itself manage and control an atomic deterrent, we could hopefully look forward to an effective and integrated Atlantic defense founded on a true nuclear partnership. But this is not the case today, nor is it likely to be for some time.

...We Americans have few national interests outside our territory, but we have assumed vast world responsibility. The result is an unequal allocation among the Atlantic nations both of responsibility and of the burden of decision that goes with it. This imbalance derives from the imperatives of history—not from deliberate American choice. We are aware that policy and responsibility must not be divided. We recognize that no nation can be expected to share one without the other...[27]

The Western European nations can no more surrender their freedom to decide their own future for the sake of Atlantic unity, than the United States is able and willing to surrender its freedom of action to accommodate Europe's quest for parity in the military and political spheres. The United States has rejected the idea of relinquishing ultimate control over the deployment and use of atomic weapons in the defense of the West. Europe, on the other hand, has not been prepared to entrust its fate to an ally without sharing in the perils and responsibilities of supreme power. The United States has committed vast resources to the reconstruction of Western Europe in order to establish the absolute triumph of the Western world over its rivals in power. In the

fulfilled grand design for Atlantic Community, the partnership of
North America and Western Europe would possess decisive military, economic and political superiority over any actual or potential challenger anywhere in the world. But Western Europe
has been reluctant to become hostage to United States commitments in the wider world and to accommodate itself to the all-
pervading contest between America and the Communist world.[28]
The United States has urged the economic and political integration of the Western European nations as indispensible to Atlantic
strength and as a means of redressing the imbalance in size and
power between the two partners in the Alliance. But Western
Europe's economic and political union, though it was nurtured
by the United States and made its initial progress under the
protective shield of America, could not mature tied to the apron-
strings of Atlantic Community. It has had to follow its own
inner logic.

No combination of sovereign states, whatever its form, constitution or persuasion, can produce more than fleeting coalitions
and unstable alliances. All states, without exception, are bent
on the realization of their national interests. Whatever inhibiting
or selective influence moral, humanitarian and ideological considerations may have on a nation's foreign policy, they do not
alter its essential character. More often than not, these considerations become a force behind a nation's policy when they prove a
handmaiden to the process of extension and consolidation of
national power. Appeals to ideals and ideologies purporting to be
of universal interest and application have almost invariably been
annexed to the enhancement of the power of a particular state
and have frequently proved an ideal instrument of national
policy.[29] The Messianic pretensions of Soviet Communism, for
example, are in the tradition of a long succession of Providence's
appointed agents for executing improvements in the lot of man.
In reality, however, they postulate in universal ideological terms
Russia's national goals and interests and seek to transform what
is essentially a competitive struggle for national advantage into
an ideological conflict involving the destiny of many peoples and
many nations.

"The socialist camp," we have often been told,

> is a social, economic and political community of free and sovereign peoples united by the close bonds of international socialist solidarity, by common interests and objectives, and following the path of socialism and communism. It is an inviolable law of the mutual relations between socialist countries strictly to adhere to the principles of Marxism-Leninism and socialist internationalism. Every country in the socialist camp is insured genuinely equal rights and independence. Guided by the principles of complete equality, mutual advantage, and comradely mutual assistance, the socialist states improve their all-round economic, political and cultural cooperation, which meets both the interests of each socialist country and those of the socialist camp as a whole.
>
> One of the great achievements of the world socialist system is the practical confirmation of the Marxist-Leninist thesis that national antagonisms diminish with the decline of class antagonisms ... There are no objective causes in the nature of the socialist system for contradictions and conflicts between the peoples and states belonging to it. Its development leads to greater unity among the states and nations and to the consolidation of all the forms of cooperation between them.
>
> Under socialism, the development of national economy, culture and statehood goes hand in hand with the strengthening and development of the entire world socialist system, and with an ever greater consolidation of the unity of nations. The interests of the socialist system as a whole and national interests are harmoniously combined. It is on this basis that the moral and political unity of all the peoples of the great socialist community has arisen and has been growing. Fraternal friendship and mutual assistance of peoples, born of the socialist system, have superceded the political isolation and national egoism typical of capitalism.
>
> The common interests of the peoples of the socialist countries and the interests of peace and socialism demand the proper combination of the principles of socialist internationalism and socialist patriotism in politics. Every Com-

munist Party which has become the ruling party in the
state, bears historical responsibility for the destinies of
both its country and the entire socialist camp...

Solid unity of the Comunist and workers parties and of the
peoples of the socialist countries and their loyalty to the
Marxist-Leninist doctrine are the main source of the
strength and invincibility of each socialist country and the
socialist camp as a whole...[30]

But the facts stand arrayed in massive opposition to the claim
that the "socialist camp" has succeeded, where the capitalist world
has failed, in establishing harmony where there was discord and
in reconciling the irreconcilable. The monotonous regularity with
which the states members of the "socialist camp" have until
recently dutifully repeated the same slogans and invoked the
same incantations was never convincing proof that the conflict
between nationalism, self-determination and sovereign independence and the demands of proletarian international solidarity have
been resolved. Just as Marxism is wholly inadequate to define and
explain the Communist movement, so the relations between the
states members of the "socialist camp" are not truly described by
an appeal to Communist doctrine. Recent events in the Communist
world have confirmed that socialist solidarity is neither a bar to
the assertion of national self-interest, nor a guarantee of im-
munity against power politics. All the lumbering rhetoric of
Marxist disputation enveloping the doctrinal disputes which have
been convulsing the international Communist movement cannot
conceal the underlying struggle for power and dominion among
states.

For a long time, the position of the Soviet Union as fatherland
of the world's working classes, entitled to their allegiance and
the disciplined duty of Communists everywhere to serve the interests of the first socialist country,[31] had masked the fact that
the "socialist camp" was in reality what Martin Buber called
fellowship by domination. It was a monolith which obeyed the
will of an uncontested leading power and which was subjected to
an iron discipline imposed by an absolute authority. When the will
relented and the heavy hand of Moscow lightened, the erosive
effect of Tito's nationalist independence proclaimed in 1948[32]
became increasingly apparent. The spread of nationalism in the
Communist world attained contrasting heights in Yugoslavia and

China and exploded in Poland and Hungary.[33] The continued power of nationalism over the minds of the people in the "socialist camp," however manifested, has put the modern concept of proletarian internationalism to unprecedented tests. The bonds of common ideals and the articles of faith of a common philosophy have not been enough to prevent national traditions and interests from re-asserting themselves against the international creed. Apparently, too, "socialist patriotism" has proved as much a threat to proletarian internationalism, as "bourgeois nationalism" has proved an obstacle to international solidarity.[34]

The struggle within the "socialist camp" and in the broader arena of international politics has all the earmarks of the classical quest for expansion or consolidation of national power. Communism, like so many other ideological movements which played such a tremendous role in the development of the internal structure of states, has had little effect on the external activities and objectives of the governments concerned. The Soviet Union has not only exercised the prerogatives of the strong everywhere, but has consistently and persistently pursued a foreign policy laid down by its Tsarist antecedents. It has emerged victorious from a great war and today stands sentinel over an alliance of nations in Eastern and Southeastern Europe which bears a close resemblance to the imperial dreams of Pan-Slavism of old, both in the grand design and in many of the details.[35] This is neither a coincident, nor an inescapable consequence of the dialectic of history. The Soviet bloc is the product of a deliberate policy of permanent Russian national interests which fortuitous circumstances have brought to fruition at the hands of the Soviet Union. It is a policy encumbered with an historical liability, which the ideological ties between the regimes of the Eastern and Southeastern European countries cannot readily remove. The same nationalist forces which in the past stood in the way of the czarist pan-Russian political plans are arrayed against Soviet hegemony. They cast a shadow on all plans to consolidate the "socialist camp" into a permanent brotherhood.

The disarray in the once monolithic Communist bloc is not necessarily to be construed as a challenge to the Soviet Union's political, diplomatic, military and economic preeminence in Eastern and Southeastern Europe. But it does attest to the fact that the Communist world, too, is being harried by conflicts of national interest and that Communist ideology is still very far from vic-

tory in its battle against the "survivals of bourgeois nationalism
and chauvinism." A resurgence of suppressed nationalism, conflicts of interests, and a persistent pressure for greater national
freedom are corroding the mold of uniformity fashioned by
Moscow. Roumania's recalcitrance, which finds expression in a
variety of ways from resistance to Moscow's plans for the economic integration of the Soviet bloc countries, to the recognition
of the Federal Republic of Germany, is only a dramatic confirmation of the clear triumph of national interest over ideology. Nationalism seems to be winning out over ideology in all parts of the
now fragmented Communist bloc, so much so that the reinstitu-
tion of effective Soviet control over a reunified bloc of Communist-
ruled nations and free-world Communist parties is inconceivable.
A major blow against the restoration of monolithic Communist
unity was struck by the late Italian Communist leader Palmiro
Togliatti. In a *Memorandum on the Problems of World Communism* written just before he died at Yalta in August 1964,
Togliatti noted that:

> ...the diversities between one country and the other are
> rather great. That is why every party must know how
> to act in an autonomous manner. The autonomy of parties,
> of which we are decisive champions, is not just an internal
> necessity for our movement, but an essential condition for
> our development under present conditions...Therefore, we
> would be against any proposal to create once again a cen-
> tralized international organization. We are firm supporters
> of the unity of our movement and of the international
> workers movement, but this unity must be achieved in the
> diversity of our concrete political positions, conforming to
> the situation and degree of development in each country.

Among other things, Togliatti recognized the force of nationalism and declared:

> A fact worrying us and one we do not succeed in explaining
> fully is the manifestation among the socialist countries of
> a centrifugal tendency. In this lies an evident and serious
> danger with which the Soviet comrades should concern
> themselves. Without doubt there is a revival of nationalism.
> However, we know that the national sentiment remains a
> permanent factor in the working class and Socialist move-
> ment a long period, also after the conquest of power.[36]

When these developments are combined with the open and violent outbreak of ideological warfare between China and the Soviet Union, they put an end to one of the great myths of the twentieth century—that Communism could permanently unite peoples of varied national, cultural and historic backgrounds and diverse interests into one fraternal and ideological community.

In their ideological dispute, both China and the Soviet Union have contrived to conceal the underlying clash of national interests between a country still in the throes of revolution seeking to extend its dominance and influence in the world, and a country half-a-century beyond the barricades of revolution seeking to secure and preserve her position "as the most powerful bulwark for the peoples of the world in their struggle for peace, democratic freedoms, national independence and social progress,"[37] with all the rights, privileges and prerogatives appertaining thereto. But the language of controversy employed by Peking and Moscow cannot hide the fact that the dispute between them is a confrontation in world-wide power politics and that China, like Russia, is seeking to exploit the international ties of Communism for national ends.

It becomes clear from a reading of the public pronouncements from Peking that China is bidding publicly for leadership of world Communism and is engaging in an active campaign to win others to her berth. It is equally clear from a reading of the pronouncements from Moscow that the Soviet Union refuses to divest itself of its paramount position as the rallying center for all socialist forces.[38] If China and the Soviet Union confront each other with what appears to be unyielding hostility, it is certainly not in order to preserve the orthodoxy of Marxist-Leninist doctrine. The past fifty years of Communist history teach us that the orthodoxy of today can readily become the heresy of tomorrow, and vice versa. The nationalist independence which President Tito of Yugoslavia has never compromised since he broke with Stalin, to cite a paramount example, is now fully and publicly accepted by Stalin's successors.[39] The Sino-Soviet conflict is at bottom a new expression of historically-rooted national antagonisms and divergency of interest. China's ultimate ambitions and objectives are the subject of worried speculation in many parts of the world. It is generally accepted that they are inherent in a situation which finds a vast, overpopulated but potentially powerful country pressing against the frontiers of her neighbors, including those of the Soviet Union.

Many books and articles have been written to explain the Sino-Soviet dispute and the national interests that come between the two countries. A number of them see Communist China sharing the characteristics of unified China of old, which was always expansionist and imperialist, politically as well as culturally.[40] Be that as it may, the admittedly unresolved territorial issue between China and the Soviet Union may in itself be sufficient to account for the hostility between the two nations. While Chinese theoreticians proclaim the duty to lend active support to rebellion against social inequities abroad, her cartographers raise the spectre of an irredentism unequalled in any other part of the world. The frontier between the Soviet Union and China is the longest land frontier on earth.[41] It is a dividing line not only between two sovereign states, but between underdevelopment and overpopulation and development and underpopulation. This is a formidable combination of reasons and goes far toward explaining some of the developments in Sino-Soviet relations in recent years. China has openly challenged the validity and permanence of nine territorial treaties, including three by which Chinese territory was ceded to Czarist Russia. They have all been condemned as imperialistic, by which old imperialist nations had "annexed Chinese territory in the north, south, east and west, and had leased territories on the seaboard and in the hinterland of China.[42] These and other references to territorial questions have not been ignored by the Soviet Union. They have caused misgivings among Soviet leaders, who see in them further evidence of China's design not only to reduce Soviet influence in the world, but to undermine its whole position in Asia, including its sovereignty over the vast expanses of Siberia. On September 2, 1964, *Pravda* warned:

> We are faced with an openly expansionist program with far-reaching pretensions. What would happen if all states should follow the Peking recipe and start presenting mutual claims to each other for a revision of historically formed borders? There is no difficulty in answering this question. This road would mean an inevitable aggravation of international tensions and would be fraught with military conflicts.[43]

Stalin overhauled Marxism's basic political theory concerning
the future of the state, by assigning it a long-term positive role
in developing socialist society. By doing so he committed the
Soviet Union and all those who follow in its path to pursue their
objectives by the calculating pragmatism of power politics characteristic of the state everywhere. As one authority notes:

> Both Marx and Lenin had taught that while the state
> would persist during the transition from Capitalism to
> Communism, it was a temporary phenomenon and that the
> only question was how long the State would endure. Indeed,
> in the late twenties there was a group in the Soviet Union
> led by Bukharin which maintained not only that the State
> "should wither away," but that the Russian workers should
> be indoctrinated to regard all States, including their own,
> as evil. In 1936 Stalin openly attacked this thesis, when
> he introduced the new Constitution, and he insisted that
> the Soviet State was of a special type which neither Marx
> nor Engel nor Lenin had foreseen. He said that the earlier
> conception was inapplicable to a State like that of the
> Soviet Union, which he said was the servant not of any
> particular section of society, but of society as a whole,
> protecting it from capitalist encirclement and guiding it
> into the "higher phase" of Communism. He stated that
> the "victory of Socialism within the Soviet Union did not
> and could not lead to any relaxation even of the internal
> powers of the State, or Russia could not become the great
> power..."

At the sixteenth Party Congress in June 1930, Stalin
declared:

> We are for the withering away of the State. And yet
> we also believe in the proletarian dictatorship which
> represents the strongest and mightiest form of state
> power which has existed up to now. To keep on devel-
> oping state power in order to prepare the conditions
> for the withering away of the state power—that is
> the Marxist formula. Is it contradictory? Yes, con-
> tradictory. But the contradiction is vital, and wholly
> reflects the Marxist dialectics... Whoever has not un-
> derstood this feature of the contradictions belonging to

our transitional time, whoever has not understood this
dialectic of historical processes, that person is dead
to Marxism...

At the 18th Congress in 1939 Stalin devoted a whole section of his report to the question why the State should
continue, if, as he maintained, "the exploiting classes have
been abolished and there are no more Bourgeois classes."
He explained that when Engels spoke of the "withering
away of the State," it was on the assumption "that Socialism had already been victorious in all countries or the
majority of them"; and that as long as Russia was sur-
rounded by hostile countries the State would not only
have to continue until "capitalist encirclement is liquidated
and the danger of foreign military attack has disappeared."
This, (Stalin added), would continue even if Russia passed
from the socialist to the communist stage.[44]

There is no indication that his successors are proposing to
materially advance the day when the state will wither away. The
process of the withering away of the state, former Premier
Nikita Khrushchev told the Twenty-second Communist Party
Congress in Moscow in October, 1961, will be a long one and will not
reach completion until Communism has emerged victorious in a
grand and final conflict. Until that day comes, the Communist state
cannot, any more than any other state, escape the consequences
of its own ethos. Until the end of that historic period when,
according to Marxian prophecy, Communism will bring forth "a
new man, who will harmoniously combine spiritual wealth, moral
purity and a perfect physique,"[45] the Communist state cannot,
any more than any other state, pretend to pursue power for the
sake of achieving moral objectives.

There exists no simple statement of American purpose, for
example, similar to the concise Communist Manifesto of Marx
and Engels of 1848, which has served the Soviet Union so well
as an instrument of foreign policy. To gauge the aim and direction of American policy abroad is to choose from a bewildering
aggregation of national aspirations and historical commitments;
of public deeds and special interests; and of political pressures
and doctrinaire prepossessions. In essence. however, the operating principle of United States foreign policy, like that of all
other great powers, is to choose the most advantageous course

in accordance with the criterion held to be valid for the purpose, to ensure the peace and security of the realm, to provide for the prosperity of the people, and to promote, defend and protect the national interest. It is part of these interests to identify the United States with the aspirations and interests of those who would follow its leadership on which American prosperity, security and greatness depends. But the United States has been very careful to retain the margin of power which nature's bounty had bestowed upon her, and she did not always turn aside from the ambitions which have historically been associated with great power. Nor has the United States soared above the sordid world of particular interest and scorned the use of its great might for its own ends.[46] In the eyes of the overwhelming majority of the world's peoples, the "cold war," for instance, is not necessarily an ideological conflict between Communism and democracy, nor is America's role regarded as a disinterested attempt to set bounds to a dangerous trend of Communist expansion.[47] The real source of tension between the Soviet Union and the United States is seen as stemming from a more traditional struggle for national advantage. Whatever the issues of the "cold war" may be—and they are often in dispute, they are reduced ultimately to a struggle between great powers for influence and dominion, if for no other reason than that the victory of the ideology of the one or the other may prove decisive.

As already noted, the actions of nations are rarely dictated by considerations of disinterested justice.[48] A country's external policy is almost invariably intended to serve narrow and limited national purposes. But nations, like individuals, have a great capacity for combining conscious avowals of virtue with apparent blindness as to their true motives.[49] Though states may be prepared to concede that in exercising their sovereign rights they are obliged to abide by certain universal principles of right and justice, they insist on the freedom to judge by themselves whether their actions accord with those principles. Thus Soviet Russia's former Premier Krushchev stated categorically that he would refuse to bow to international authority if he conceived it to be contrary to the vital interests of the Soviet Union. In a welcoming address to Ghana's then President Kwame Nkrumah on his visit to Moscov in July, 1963, Premier Krushchev said:

> Even though all the nations of the world adopted a decision that was not in accordance with the interests of the Soviet Union and that threatened its security, the Soviet Union would not only not recognize such a decision, but would defend its rights even to the use of force.[50]

This statement might have been made by any other representative of a sovereign state, large or small. It was in fact made by the late President John F. Kennedy to the Convention of the American Society of Newspaper Editors and Publishers on April 20, 1962, in Washington, D.C. in connection with the situation in Cuba. Said President Kennedy:

> Any unilateral American intervention in the absence of an external attack upon ourselves or an ally would have been contrary to our traditions and to our international obligations. But let the record show that our restraint is not inexhaustible. Should it ever appear that the inter- American doctrine of non-interference merely conceals or excuses a policy of non-action; if the nations of this hemisphere should fail to meet their commitments against outside Communist penetration, then I want it clearly understood that this Government will not hesitate in meeting its primary obligations, which are the security of our nation...[51]

CHAPTER III

The Limits of
Regional Organization

It is quite clear that no act or endeavor of a military, political, economic, social, cultural or technical nature, separately or jointly, is sufficient in itself to overcome the forces of nationalism. There is no alliance among sovereign states which is strong enough to transcend the immediate objectives for which it may have been brought into existence, to harmonize the basic irreconcilables of national interest or to override national ambitions. And there is no universalist doctrine in existence so potent as to bid the waves of nationalism recede.[1]

Cooperation among states for mutual advantage will not of itself produce a system of international relations which move across frontiers of mind and land into new and larger loyalties. Common interests must be joined with bold ideas to produce more than fleeting coalitions and unstable alliances. That unique experiment in integration among six ancient European peoples was brought to its present stage by the willful purpose of people who had gauged the drift of history and measured the tides of events. Were the quest for Western European unity motivated by nothing more than a desire for greater security abroad and prosperity at home, it is doubtful whether the several Communities to which it has already given birth could ever add up to a grand design for a true community of nations.

External and internal reasons of varying degree and urgency in the years immediately following World War II dictated the need for close collaboration among the nations of Western Europe. In particular, there was need for concerted action in the interest of economic reconstruction[2] and to bar the further expansion of international Communism westward.[3] This need was

in large measure satisfied within the traditional framework of
international relations, by the creation in 1948-49 of the Organization for European Economic Cooperation,[4] the Western
European Union,[5] the Council of Europe[6] and the North Atlantic
Treaty Organization.[7] There were no compelling reasons to question the capacity of those and other organizations which were
brought into existence at the time on the Continent to meet the
requirements of economic cooperation, military defense and political agreement, at least for the then foreseeable future. Only
those who had reflected sadly on the frustrations of so many
hopes that foundered on the rock of nationalism were anxious to
rush ahead, resolutely and relentlessly, toward the goal of European integration and political union.

The idea of European unity, to which Count Richard N.
Coudenhove-Kalergi gave modern expression after World War I,[8]
was clothed after World War II with a new substance and given a
new impetus. "If Europe is to be saved from infinite misery,"
Winston Churchill told a gathering on September 19, 1946, at the
University of Zürich,

> and indeed from final doom, there must be an act of faith
> in the European family and an act of oblivion against all
> the crimes and follies of the past,

and he called for a sovereign remedy, which he said was

> to recreate the European family, or as much of it as we
> can, and to provide it with a structure under which it can
> dwell in peace, safety and freedom. We must build a kind
> of United States of Europe.[9]

The disillusionment of defeat, which the ultimate victors shared with the vanquished, bred the need for a new faith and a new
political orientation which the nationalism of old was too discredited to supply and the universalim of new too abstract to inspire.
The idea of European unity eminently filled this need. It inspired
a vision of a resurgent Europe as the center of great expectations
and of a vital and expanding society. Through free trade, greater
productivity, higher standards of living and political unity, Europe would grow into a new composite world power and take its
rightful place with the great power blocs which emerged in the

aftermath of the war. A continent which had known greatness and glory could never reconcile itself to a permanent condition of reduced status and power.

The idea of European unity also satisfied certain concrete realities. Ultimate political federation would bind the nations of Western Europe into an indissoluble unit and thus put a final end to the ancient enmities and historical rivalries which in the past had brought disaster upon themselves and the rest of the world. Total defeat, partition and humiliation could not forever arrest Germany's rise to become in time Western Europe's strongest nation in population, organization and industrial potential. Within a few years after the end of the war, it became clear that West Germany was once more on the road to a position of commanding economic and military power in Europe. This power had to be harnessed before it had an opportunity to sow new seeds of destruction. Only the idea of European union could overcome all the intangibles of sentiment and tradition that stood in the way of reconciliation.[10]

On May 9, 1950, France's Foreign Minister Robert Schuman made the first concrete move toward European integration when, at a press conference at the Quai d'Orsay, he announced a plan for pooling the entire French and German production of coal and steel under a supra-national authority in an organization which would be open to other European countries. Said Mr. Schuman:

> The contribution which an organized and active Europe can make to civilization is indispensible for the maintenance of peaceful relations. France, by championing during more than twenty years the idea of a united Europe, has always regarded it as an essential objective to serve the purposes of peace. Because Europe was not united, we have had war.
>
> A united Europe will not be achieved all at once, nor in a single framework; it will be formed by concrete measures which first of all create a solidarity in fact. The uniting of the European nations requires that the age-old opposition between France and Germany be overcome; the action to be taken must, first of all, concern France and Germany.

To that end, the French Government proposes that immediate action be concentrated on one limited but decisive
point. The French Government proposes that the entire
Franco-German production of coal and steel be placed
under a joint High Authority, within an organization
open to the participation of other European nations.[11]

With surprising speed the Schuman Plan was written into a
treaty instituting the European Coal and Steel Community. It
entered into force on July 25, 1952, and the High Authority in-
stalled itself in Luxembourg to direct the future common destiny
of Belgium, France, West Germany, Italy, Luxembourg and the
Netherlands in a vital sector of their economic life. But its
significance as the first supra-national institution to emerge from
the movement toward European integration far surpassed in
importance the immediate objectives it was created to serve. It
derived from the patently political process upon which the six
European nations had embarked and whose ultimate goal was,
in the words of the Treaty's Preamble:

to substitute for historic rivalries a fusion of their essential interests; to establish, by creating an economic
community, the foundation of a broad and independent
community among peoples long divided by bloody conflicts; and to lay the basis of institutions capable of giving
direction to their future common destiny.[12]

Even while the Coal and Steel Community was still in the
making, the French Government, spurred on by United States
pressure in the wake of the Korean War for the partial rearmament of West Germany, once again took the initiative and
launched a plan for the creation of a European Defense Community. The plan brought the six Coal and Steel Community
nations almost within sight of federation.[13] On May 27, 1952,
their Foreign Ministers put their signatures to a draft treaty
which provided for the merger of the armed forces of the member states under a supra-national authority and envisioned the
establishment of an all-inclusive European Political Community
on federal or confederal lines.[14] The blueprint for such a Community, which would have taken over the powers of the Coal and
Steel and Defense and other Communities created in the interim
and would have exercised powers in its own right in foreign
affairs and economic policy, was contained in a draft of the

Statutes of the European Community completed on March 10, 1953.[15] But changes in the political atmosphere in the world in the aftermath of the Korean War and following the death of Joseph Stalin combined with the fact that the idea of the European Defense Community outran the ability of many people in Europe to accept its implications to deliver what was thought at the time to be a fatal blow to the cause of European integration. After having been ratified by five of the six members of the Coal and Steel Community, the Defense Community Treaty drifted toward an inconclusive anti-climax. On August 30, 1954, the French Parliament, by a vote of 319 to 264, decided to adjourn consideration of the Treaty *sine die*. Inasmuch as the idea of an all-inclusive European Community was an integral part of the Defense Community Treaty, it fell with the latter.[16]

Undaunted by their defeat on the political front, the protagonists of European integration proceeded at once to attack the problem on other fronts. Within little more than two years, the six Western European nations succeeded in hammering out plans for the creation, respectively, of a European Atomic Energy Community and a European Economic Community. The Treaties for the establishment of these Communities were signed on March 25, 1957, in Rome, and they entered into force on January 1, 1958.[17]

Of all the experiments to-date in unity of the oft-warring European continent, the most daring is without doubt the Economic Community, or Common Market. Conceived in broad terms of economic and social policies and commitments in vast areas ranging from the free movement of labor, capital and services, to a common farm program and a common agricultural policy, the European Economic Community envisages the progressive establishment of a Common Market in three stages of four years each, the total transitional period not to exceed fifteen years. Its design to demolish the barriers which for hundreds of years guarded highly protected nationalistic economies and to substitute for historic rivalries a fusion of interests is momentous in its implications. It required a deep commitment to the European idea to bring the Economic Community into existence. It required even greater political courage to discipline the exercise of national power which has for so long served as a bulwark of economic privilege.

The change from a national to a European framework and the overcoming of the protectionist tradition in the Common Market countries are inconceivable in terms of purely economic interest. Without the idea of European unity in the background, it is difficult to imagine how the nations of Western Europe could have come to terms, for example, on a common agricultural policy. Indeed, the Common Market's supreme challenge was to arrive at a definition of a common agricultural policy and at an agreement on a single Common Market price, a single subsidy pattern and a uniform external tariff for all farm products. On July 24, 1966, the six Common Market nations brought to a successful conclusion negotiations on major agricultural prices and subsidy arrangements, and with them, the virtual completion of more than five years of strenuous effort to reach agreement on complex agricultural problems.[18] The success of July 24, has immeasurably enhanced the prospect of achieving the goal set for July 1, 1968, of free movement of all goods within the Common Market.

The significance of these agricultural agreements may be better understood if it is borne in mind that, as in the case of the United States, agriculture in Western Europe has been practically insulated from the production and price disciplines of the open market. European farmers, like their American counterparts, have come to be dependent on national agricultural policies and to look to their political leaders to protect their privileged status. The incomes of the French and German farmers, in particular, have been determined not by the free interplay of supply and demand, but by government decisions in the respective capitals. The agricultural agreements among the Common Market countries meant the abandonment of time-honored measures which have for so long served to protect the inefficient farmer against his more efficient competitor from abroad.[19]

The European Communities and the prospect of European political integration stand out majestically in civilized grandeur. But until the governments and the peoples concerned come to terms, finally and irrevocably, with their new roles as members of an evolving supra-national community, the true European reality will remain the nation-state committed to the primacy of the national interest. Grave issues still lurk unsolved in the background to challenge the sense of solidarity and common purpose of the member nations and to threaten to reverse the process of social inevitability. One of the fundamental issues is whether the members of the Communities will ultimately agree to establish an indisoluble union with supra-national executive, legislative and judicial institutions acting on the federal principle and deciding by majority vote in all matters which affect their common fate; or whether they will settle on a loose confederation of sovereign states, whose government and parliaments retain the power of final decision. The insistence on national sovereignty automatically sets severe limits to the potentialities of the Communities already in existence and affects the course of development of others. Without a political superstructure, superior to the sum of its parts, even the most omnipotent sense of higher purpose cannot unravel the many threads of conflict in which relations among sovereign states are normally enmeshed. Without a central authority capable of acting effectively on all, for all, and on behalf of all, the danger will be forever present lest the national interests of the confederation's members burst into conflict with one another and with the confederation itself.

There have been many warnings that economic integration is unlikely to endure without surrender of political sovereignty. "I am forced to the conclusion," writes Lord Robbins,

> that integration on a thoroughgoing scale is not likely to have permanent viability without much more surrender of political sovereignty than is implied by my minimum conditions. The pure logic of The Federalist has never been refuted, and I think it is supported by the verdict of history. Neither in the economic nor in the military sphere are we likely to succeed in adapting the political structure of the West to the requirements of modern conditions without much more far-reaching political integration than at present many of us are willing to contemplate...[20]

Similarly Jaques Maritain, anticipating the European experiment, wrote:

> An essentially economic interdependence, without any corresponding fundamental recasting of the moral and political structures of human existence, can but impose by material necessity a partial and fragmentary, growing bit by bit, political interdependence which is reluctantly and hatefully accepted, because it runs against the grain of

nature as long as nations live on the assumption of their full political autonomy. In the framework and against the background of that assumed full political autonomy of nations, an essentially economic interdependence can but exasperate the rival needs and prides of nations; and industrial progress only accelerates the process.[21]

There is no doubt that the member States of the European Communities still maintain their monopoly of power. Not only are powers ceded to the institutions of the Communities small in amount, but what powers they do possess are dependent upon the willingness of the states members to enforce their decisions. There is no instance where the vital interests of any of the Communities' members have been overridden in favor of the general interest of the Community. The rule of unanimity, against which the protagonists of European unity have inveighed for many years, is as strong as ever. Although the Rome Treaty which brought the Common Market into existence provides that the third and final transitional stage, which opened as the clocks of Europe struck midnight on December 31, 1965, should see the successive extension of majority voting in the Executive Commission on all matters coming within the purview of the Economic Community, the independence of the present and future Community authorities and institutions has been reduced. On April 8, 1965, the Common Market countries agreed to a treaty providing for the merger of the executive bodies of the Coal and Steel, Atomic Energy, and Economic Communities into a fourteen-member Commission appointed by the Member Governments "acting in common agreement" and for leaving the final decision on all important matters in the hands of the States Parties.[22]

There is no certainty yet that all the members of the European Communities have at last awakened from their dreams of grandeur. Attention has centered on President Charles de Gaulle, who has repeatedly stressed that "at the present time there is not and cannot be any other Europe than a Europe of States."[23] The French President has consistently opposed handing over any fraction of national sovereignty to any international organization, including the European Communities. He spoke out from his retirement against the Coal and Steel Community because of the supranational character of the High Authority which had been set up to guide the integration of the two powerful sectors of the

French and German economies and opposed the principle of supranational powers implied in the European Economic Community and the European Atomic Energy Community. Although he accepted the three Communities that had taken shape in the treaties negotiated by his predecessor administrations, his aversion to the supranational principle on which these Communities theoretically operate has never abated.[24]

However, as in the case of the North Atlantic Treaty Organization, it is difficult to say whether General de Gaulle's insistence upon cooperation, as opposed to integration, is closer to reality, or whether the voices of those who contest his idea that a "Europe of fatherlands" is consistent with the idea of European unity is the more authentic. The test is yet to come. Belgium's Paul Henri Spaak and one of the prime movers in the European integration movement has long maintained that the Western European nations cannot unite and keep their sovereignty too. In an address in New York on January 25, 1962, the then Foreign Minister of Belgium declared:

> The more I see, the more I travel and the greater my political experience, the more I grow hostile to international organizations in which the rule of unanimity reigns. I am against the veto power in the United Nations. I am against the rule of unanimity in NATO. I cannot conceive of a normally and efficiently functioning Europe unless all parties accept the rule of majority.[25]

Yet, it has been "integrationists" like Mr. Spaak who have fought for the admission of Great Britain into the Common Market and of broadening the membership of the European Economic Community, even though England's membership, at least at the time of her first application in 1962, would have made the achievement of European political unity even more difficult. When on October 11, 1962, the Conservative Party Conference at Llandudno, Wales, overwhelmingly endorsed the Government's decision to seek membership in the European Economic Community, the then Deputy Prime Minister, R. A. Butler, gave a solemn assurance that the British Government would "agree to nothing which undermines the position of the Crown, the essential powers of Parliament, or the domestic authority of our law courts in criminal and civil cases."[26]

Nor is there any guarantee that Germany, conscious of her weight and power, will not again strive to regain the necessary scope for the pursuit of what she may regard to be as her historic mission.[27] There is no doubt that France is seeking to carve out for herself a new destiny and perhaps to preside over a Europe strong enough politically, economically and militarily to constitute a third force in the affairs of the world. Until both Germany and France are part of an irrevocable United States of Europe, the deep-seated mutual fears of a renascent Germany and a proud France are bound to linger in the conscious and unconscious minds of their peoples and to burden their relations with the weight of suspicion. Germany knows the source of her power and is alive to her industrial, commercial and military might. France understands the forces that sustain the balance of strength and seeks to secure what she believes to be her rightful place in the council of nations. Thus Franco-German relations are heir to strains and stresses which cannot be diluted in a grouping of nations which leaves room for disagreement on long-term objectives and for clashes of immediate national interests.[28]

Also, not all propositions of European unity are dictated by the will and conscience of the member states concerned. Many of them spring from the inexorable imperatives of external challenges. The uncertainties, for example, raised by the division of Germany remain a dangerous focus of involvement and commitment for friend and foe alike. As long as Germany remains divided, her commitments will always be qualified by the requirements of reunification. A divided Germany can never be wholly immune to the blandishments from without, or to the siren calls of extremists from within. Reunited under Russian pressure, Germany might turn the tide of European history in the direction of deeper damnation than ever. Frustrated in her efforts at reunification, Germany might strike out in all directions to seek a satisfying framework for her national energies and ambitions.[29] In these circumstances, it is little wonder that not all the Common Market countries are ready to take the irrevocable step of surrendering their freedom of action to a European Community in which Germany's military, industrial and commercial power might eventually prevail.

Like the division of Germany, the division of Europe between the inner six Common Market countries and the outer seven of the European Free Trade Association[30] and between Eastern and Western Europe,[31] is another factor which has a profound bearing on the course of European integration. To the extent that the Western European experiment may bring to a final end the thousand-year old pattern of history in that part of the world of enmity and hatred etched deeply in the hearts of generations, its elimination as a source of international conflict is in itself an immensely important contribution to the cause of world peace. To the extent that a strong and prosperous Western Europe may be indispensible to the balancing of the hostile forces which face one another across the globe, its unity has vast and far-reaching implications for the stability of the world.[32] And to the extent that the consummation of Western European integration may release new creative forces to enrich old and new civilizations, it will devolve to the benefit of the whole human family. But insofar as a united Europe confined to the six Common Market nations may tend to grow inward, it carries with it the grave risk of putting the seal on the division of Europe, within the West and between East and West. An integrated Europe which might sharpen the differences which divide nations and regions, including the European continent itself, is bound to weave new threads of conflict and add to the strains and stresses of international relations.

There is no reason to assume that the Common Market carries with it a moral commitment to pursue policies and practices which would not only benefit the members of the Community, but take full cognizance of the needs and interests of non-members. The Common Market is essentially an economic vehicle for a political purpose—to make Western Europe economically prosperous and politically strong and self-reliant. The six nations which are joined in the several European Communities have sought to escape from an inner weakness into an outer strength; from a fragmented Europe unable to compete with the great power blocs of the modern world, to a composite giant of continental proportions and a great power in its own right. There is nothing in the nature of the European integration movement to compel it to enforce precepts which are widely different from those of any other power system. To expect a greater measure of altruism from the Common Market than from the states which compose it would be to fly in the face of fact and experience.

General de Gaulle's decision early in 1963 to deny to the
British entry into the European Economic Community, only confirmed the rigidity of the Common Market's constitutional frame
and its intolerance of anything suggestive of less than total commitment to the European point of view. On January 14, 1963,
President de Gaulle declared:

> The Treaty of Rome was concluded between six continental
> states ... of the same nature ... Moreover, they are adja-
> cent, they interpenetrate, they prolong each other through
> their communications.

> To link them in such a way that what they have to produce,
> to buy, to sell, to consume, they do produce, buy, sell, con-
> sume by preference among themselves is to conform to
> realities.

> How can we incorporate England, with her way of life,
> the nature of her production and her trade, into the Com-
> mon Market?

> The question is to know whether Great Britain can at
> present place herself ... within a tariff that is truly com-
> mon, give up all preferences with regard to the Common-
> wealth, cease to claim her agriculture be privileged and,
> moreover, to consider as null and void the commitment
> she has made (to her partners in the European Free Trade
> Association) ... Obviously Britain alone can answer.

> It must be agreed that the entry, first of Great Britain and
> then of other nations would completely change the whole
> system ... What would result is a very different Common
> Market ... one of Eleven, and then of Thirteen and maybe
> of Eighteen.

> In the end, it would appear as a colossal Atlantic Commu-
> nity, dependent upon and under the direction of America,
> which would make short work of absorbing the European
> Community.

> This is a hypothesis that can very well be justified in some
> eyes, but it is not at all what France wants ... which is a
> truly European structure ...[33]

In defense of the French position on Great Britain's membership in the Common Market, Foreign Minister Maurice Couve de Murville told the National Assembly on January 24, 1963:

> I have already had occasion, on June 12, 1962, to explain at this rostrum that the candidacy of Great Britain to the Common Market and, through that, all the future developments of European construction, posed a fundamental problem, that of knowing what character the European union being created was finally going to take.

> According to whether Europe remains a Europe of Six or whether it includes among its members Britain, then certain countries of the North, and finally still others, its character will be quite different in all respects. In the one case, the system remains regional, even if it is very powerful; it is relatively easy to manage effectively in the technical domain; there are numerous chances for it to be coherent and to possess a feeling of solidarity in the political domain. In the other case, becoming to a large part extra-continental, it necessarily joins in with a world system; it can only be much less homogeneous, much more loosely knit and consequently quite another thing. It will perhaps still appear to be Europe, but a Europe quite different from that which we imagined and desired...

> We welcomed, of course, with satisfaction a display of intention that marked, on the part of our British friends, a profound evolution in their state of mind and, undoubtedly, in their judgement of the future. We clearly indicated at the same time that it could not be a matter for them of simply being juxtaposed to the Europeans of the continent, that it was necessary for them to become an integral part of a single Community...

> Was this great country already prepared to contemplate all the consequences implied by the political gesture accomplished by farsighted leaders and which was, using the picturesque and significant expression of our neighbors across the Channel, to lead Britain to enter Europe? There indeed is the whole question that was raised and to which it was truly difficult to give an affirmative answer. Therein also lies the origin and the significance of the crisis in

which we find ourselves now. It appeared preferable to us to pose the question frankly, as it in fact exists, rather than pursue ad infinitum, and in reality hopelessly, a discussion that could only grow more bitter and lead finally to an even greater crissis...

Already in December, 1958, we had experienced similar vicissitudes. It was then necessary for France, in opposing the formation of a large free trade area, in which the nascent Common Market would have risked being dissolved, to preserve the chances of building Europe. Today, now that the Common Market is affirming itself, it is necessary to conserve its European character and, in consequence, all its political potential. I am sure that, all things considered, the door is not closed to Great Britain. An evolution is taking place across the Channel which is not likely to stop. If it has not yet reached the stage when the inevitable transformations appear acceptable, that time will come...[34]

The day has long since passed when groupings and alliances which do not take the whole world as a platform for their operations can long prevail. Any lasting political purpose today must have a far broader base than subregional or regional alignments. Such a purpose cannot be circumscribed by geography, nor restricted by historical affinities or political preferences. It must take the whole world for its arena and all mankind as its concern. The interdependence of the world is an inexorable fact, even though it manifests itself more by its tragic consequences than by its positive affirmations. The fundamental problems of the human condition know no national, political or ideological frontiers. In an instant of savage misfortune anywhere all local, national and regional advantages can vanish into oblivion. The basic facts of this mid-century repudiate any tenet and any doctrine which disavows the interdependence of the fate and fortune of all parts of the human family.

The merits of regional and subregional groupings which nations may create for the advancement of their common interests cannot, therefore, be determined solely by the rightness of their internal relationship without reference to external considerations. The expansion of regional interests, no more than the expansion of national interests, does not necessarily add up to universal gain. The great problems of war and peace, of equality and opportunity, of want and plenty, do not always yield to solutions at different stages and at different levels of international organization. Regional and subregional blocs and groupings, whatever their purpose, are by their very nature inward-looking and designed to serve specific ends. Like the states of which they are composed, these blocs and groupings are more concerned with the exploitation of immediate advantages than with long-range world plans which may benefit the peoples of all continents.

To recognize the limitations of regionalism is not to spurn it, nor to forego any fair chance of its serving its legitimate purposes. But we cannot remain sublimely indifferent to the traces of discord it invariably leaves on the horizon. The European Common Market was not designed to injure the economic interests of any country not within its embrace. Yet it has not brought closer the open world in which men and commerce move freely between nations in pursuit of a common ideal of freedom and well-being. On the contrary, it may have had the effect of impairing the future commercial interests of friends and allies. It is an inevitable consequence of a policy which seeks to preserve the interests of the Community's members by tearing down tariffs and other restrictions on trade and commerce within and erecting a common wall of restriction to trade and commerce without.[35] From the United States to Brazil, from Japan to Egypt, and from Australia to Finland, those outside the European Community ponder with increasing urgency the question of how to cope with the new trading conditions being erected by the Common Market.[36] The Common Market is potentially the greatest single trading unit in the world and as such, its external tariff is a matter of the most vital concern to all the nations on the outside. The Common Market has introduced a new power factor into international relations, with all its attendant consequences and implications. Just as the individual state which posseses a distinct preponderance of power in any area is likely to exploit it for the purpose of extending the range of its influence or domination, so a group of states, united for the achievement of common ends, is more prone to drift into the habit of self-aggrandizement than to gain in breadth and humanity.

What gives the utterances of General de Gaulle their special significance is that they express a general desire for recognition of Western Europe's place in international affairs which would more accurately represent the changed power relationship between the Common Market countries and the United States and between them and the rest of the world. The drama of Western Europe is being acted out on a broad economic, political and military stage. Its claim to parity with the United States in the Western Alliance, for example, is but a manifestation of its self-confidence and consciousness of its growing might. Once the Common Market reaches the stage of a common economic policy and the industries and agriculture of the member countries secure the advantage of a huge, unfettered internal market, the expanding power of Europe is bound to bring in its train an ever greater assertiveness in international councils. It cannot be taken for granted that the European grouping can or will long remain within the bounds set by the specific interests which brought it into existence. Sooner or later the Common Market is bound to compete in the world power market, in an encounter between national interests of giant proportions.

Aside from the question whether regionalism is capable of inspiring a vision of a better future for all of mankind, the areas in which the necessary conditions obtain for successful regional groupings are so far and few between, as to render the whole concept of regional organizations as stepping stones towards greater international unity nugatory. Thus, although the countries of the Western Hemisphere are bound to each other by geographical and historical ties and by many commonly-held ideals and aspirations and have since 1890 been associated politically, juridically and economically in one form of organization or another, the community of American States remains largely a concretion in discourse. The striking inequality between the "Colossus of the North" and struggling nations to the South has been the greatest single obstacle to the development of such a community. The enormous gap between the wealth and power of the United States and the poverty and weakness of the countries of Latin America cannot be bridged by pious incantations and appeals to abstractions. The fact is that the dialogue between the United States and the peoples below the Rio Grande has through the years remained narrow in scope and artificial in approach, just as their official relationship has been on the whole one-sided and non-reciprocating. Besides, the fortunes of the inter-American regional system have revolved too much around the policies of the United States to promote the unity and solidarity of the continent.

Beginning with the Monroe Doctrine, which was formulated in 1823 when the United States was a small power at the periphery of world affairs, through the fateful days in April, 1962, when the United States confronted the Soviet Union on the soil of Cuba, to the American occupation of Santo Domingo three years later, the nations of Latin America have never ceased to resent the special role the United States had assumed as protectress of the Western Hemisphere. Toward the end of the nineteenth century, when the United States was emerging as a major world power, Secretary of State Richard Olney, who won praise for his action in settling the Venezuela boundary dispute with England, interpreted the Monroe Doctrine in a manner which had in it a substantial element of truth and goes far to explain the evolution of United States—Latin American relations. In his instructions of July 20, 1895, to the American Ambassador to England, the Secretary of State wrote:

> ...To-day the United States is practically sovereign on this continent, and its fiat is law upon the subjects to which it confines its interposition. Why? It is not because of the pure friendship or good will felt for it. It is not simply by reason of its high character as a civilized state, nor because wisdom and justice and equity are the invariable characteristics of the dealings of the United States. It is because, in addition to all other grounds, its infinite resources combined with its isolated position render it master of the situation and practically invulnerable as against any or all other powers.[37]

Latin America's traditional fears and suspicions of the giant among the regional partners, generated by United States practices and emphasis on the unilateral character of the Monroe Doctrine, have been little allayed by the efforts over the past thirty years to make the protection of the hemisphere against threats and incursions from outside a collective hemispheric responsibility, which culminated in the signing of the Rio Treaty of Reciprocal Assistance in 1947[38] and the anti-Communist Caracas Declaration of 1954.[39] These steps have neither rescinded nor superseded the

Monroe Doctrine, which to all intents and purposes, remains a statement of policy of the United States and which, in the words of Elihu Root, "cannot be transmuted into a point or common declaration by American states or any number of them."[40] That its definition, interpretation and application is reserved exclusively to the United States, has been newly reaffirmed by President Kennedy on April 20, 1962.[41] It was restated three years later by President Lyndon B. Johnson in connection with the landing on April 28, 1965, of American marines in Santo Domingo. The action was justified in the beginning as a measure to protect the lives and property of American citizens caught in the midst of a revolution which had broken out in the Dominican Republic, but this soon gave way to an assertion that American intervention was necessary to avert the danger of the emergence of another Cuba-like regime in the Western Hemisphere. Addressing the nation in the evening of May 2, 1965, the President declared:

> The American nations cannot, must not and will not permit the establishment of another Communist government in the Western Hemisphere. This was the unanimous view of all the American nations when in January, 1962, they declared, and I quote, the principles of Communism are incompatible with the principles of the inter-American system. This is what our beloved President John F. Kennedy meant when less than a week before his death he told us, we in this hemisphere must also use every resource at our command to prevent the establishment of another Cuba in this hemisphere...[42]

Not all American nations, however, agreed that the unilateral action of the United States was justified and virtually all of them took exception to the assertion by Washington that time was of the essence and that circumstances did not permit prior consultation with, and approval of, the Organization of American States. Chile, Ecuador, Mexico, Peru and Uruguay refused to recognize not only the legality of the United States intervention, but the right of the Organization of American States to contravene Article 17 of its Charter,* by approving the formation

---

* The territory of a state is inviolable; it may not be the object, even temporarily, of military occupation or of other measures of force taken by another state, directly or indirectly, under any grounds whatsoever.

on May 6, 1965, by the Tenth Meeting of Consultation of Ministers of Foreign Affairs of an inter-American Force, to take over the duties and responsibilities the United States armed forces in the Dominican Republic had exercised since April 28, 1965.[43] Although order and constitutional government had ultimately been restored in the land, the assertion by the United States of the right to intervene against the threat of a Communist take-over, as it were, in any Latin American country struck at the heart of the Charter of the Organization of American States, which is Article 17. Whether the action of the United States was a carefully calculated step or an *ad hoc* response to events, the Monroe Doctrine emerged anew to all intents and purposes as a unilateral instrument of American policy.

Thus, is spite of the imposing structure of the inter-American regional system, which rests on the triple pillar of the Inter-American Treaty on Pacific Settlement, or the Pact of Bogota of 1948; the Charter of the Organization of American States of the same year, which restates and broadens commitments, formalizes institutional relationships and registers processes and procedures dating back to the beginnings of the Pan American Union more than sixty years ago; and the Inter-American Treaty of Reciprocal Assistance, or the Rio Pact of 1947, the unity and solidarity of the Western Hemisphere are as far away as ever. As in the case of the Atlantic Alliance, true partnership is possible only between equals—between equally strong, or equally rich, or equally influential in the council of world affairs.

But it is also true that just as the inter-American system has lacked the strength to overcome the problems which stem from the disproportion in size, wealth and power between the United States on one hand and the nations of Latin America on the other, so the regional idea has not availed to overcome the factors which have kept these nations apart for more than a century and a half. The centrifugal forces that were responsible for the fragmentation of the Latin American continent after the Wars of Liberation have lost little of their potency to frustrate the closer union among the nations below the Rio Grande.[44] Thus the Common Market, which the Presidents of the American Republics blueprinted at their meetings in April, 1967, at Punta del Este and which is to be created progressively beginning in 1970, envisages neither the supra-national features nor the political objectives of the European Common Market which inspired it.[45] Even in Central America, where the Treaty of San Salvador created a Central American Common Market more akin to the European experiment and aiming at ultimate political union,[46] the depth of feeling for political integration fluctuates with the changing and shifting national interests and policies. This is the third attempt in the history of Central America at political union of the five nations in the area.[47] Whether all those efforts at economic and political integration will succeed in altering the basic patterns of Latin American life, only time will tell. Overwhelming the dream are the many fundamental problems of interregional communications and transport, unstable currencies, political uncertainties, the size and diversity of the region and the traditional trading patterns and immediate economic interests, which militated against the success of the Latin American Free Trade Association[48] upon which the Common Market is to be erected.

Unlike Western Europe, where the Common Market countries have done most of their trade with each other, which are on a roughly equal economic footing, and whose economies are complementary rather than in competition, most of Latin America's trade is with the United States and countries overseas, their economies are highly competitive with each other, they look to protection to promote their economic development, and there is a strong tendency for the small and medium-sized countries to group together against the larger ones. Each Latin American country is a distinct entity and has its distinct problems. They have achieved contrasting levels of development, founded on contrasting societies, composition of population, rates of literacy and economic growth. Also, as former President Goulart of Brazil put it in a statement on November 11, 1963, welcoming the delegates to the second annual review conference in São Paulo of the Alliance for Progress, Latin America remains "an archipelago of nations, implacably separated by the sea of frustration of our own difficulties."[49]

The union of African States in the twentieth century is theoretically desirable, for the same reason that the union of American states was desirable in the eighteenth. The Balkanization of Africa is lamented by many of its leaders, who fear for its future as an assortment of independent states. "Africa must unite or perish," warned Kwame Nkrumah. "From Tangier or Cairo in the north to Capetown in the south, from Cape Guardafui in the east to Cape Verde islands in the west, Africa is one and indivisible," the former Ghanian President proclaimed.[50] "The African personality" has become a catchword throughout the continent, and the idea of "Mother Africa," or the "African soul" is invoked everywhere where Africans have grasped the march of events. The sense of a common destiny and a common purpose; the desire for cultural self-assertion and the conscious, urgent cultivation of things African; and the idea of uniting Africans of all kinds under the banner of freedom were given concrete shape and form on May 26, 1963, when the heads of state and government, assembled in Addis Ababa, affixed their signatures to a charter for continental solidarity and created the Organization of African Unity.[51]

In reality, however, Pan Africanism is but the evocation of a handful of people in search of their roots, who entertain a nostalgic, idealized notion of their continent. Africa, one and indivisible, has little foundation in fact or in history. There are many Africas and there are many African peoples. No part of Africa is like unto any other part in terrain, language, custom and civilization. No Holy Roman Empire has ever bound the continent together. More than the Sahara Desert divides the Moslem-Mediterranean littoral north of it from the tropical plateau south of it, and more than lines drawn on maps separate East from West Africa and both East and West from Central Africa. The bulk of the peoples on plain and hill and swamp and desert is too embedded in its tribal settings to create a common sense of African identity and purpose. The geographic, tribal, linguistic, religious, historic and economic differences which characterize Africa cannot be readily bridged, even though the more than thirty independent and emerging states are united in their common hatred of Western colonialism, their common determination to be free, and their common striving to span centuries of human development in moments of time.[52]

Africans have been harking to the song of unity for more than a decade. But while their leaders proudly pledge African unity and dream of a new brave continent, they are too much preoccupied with solidifying their newly-founded nations and establishing internal unity to divert their attention and energies to promoting solidarity abroad. The advent of independence has perhaps been the single most important reason for the limited appeal of Pan Africanism and its minor role as a political factor among the African nations. There is no evidence of a strong impulse toward unity at the expense of national sovereignty. None of the peoples who have won independence has shown any disposition to submerge itself in a wider whole, for its own salvation and the salvation of all of Africa. Dunduza K. Chisiza, one of the theoreticians of the African Malawi Congress party in former Nyasaland, put the matter in these terms:

> Nationals of various countries will not be favorably disposed toward the idea of surrendering national sovereignty to a Pan African political body unless and until the novelty of self-government and independence have been given sufficient time to wear off...[53]

In fact, if nationalism is to retain its dynamic and unifying force within each of the African States, it cannot be weakened or diverted by appeals to Pan Africanism. Until nationalism has been able to sweep away tribal barriers and unite the people under the banner of national freedom and sovereignty, no African country can look beyond its own frontiers to greater unity abroad.

All major efforts at cooperation over the past several years in Africa have been cast in the traditional mold of international relations. This was true of the principles the nations of the so-called Monrovia Group had accepted in Lagos in January 1962,[54] when they contemplated the creation of a permanent organization for mutual cooperation. It was true of the cooperative efforts of the more radical Casablanca Group, which included former President Kwame Nkrumah and other protagonists of African union,[55] of the Africa-Malagasy Union[56] and of the short-lived Union of African States (Ghana, Guinea and Mali). The same holds true for the Charter of Addis Ababa,[57] which has brought into existence the first continent-wide Organization of African Unity to reconcile, and ultimately to supersede, all the blocs and groupings into which the African nations had divided. And it was precisely at Addis Ababa that Pan Africanism, with its concept of a central political organization speaking with one voice for Africa at home and abroad, suffered its greatest rebuff. The unadventurous course of unhasty functional cooperation charted by the overwhelming majority of those who made up the Summit

Conference of Independent African States vanquished the ambitious dream of a United States of Africa, fostered by former Ghanian President Nkrumah.

Africa is far removed from anything approaching formal political unity. It lacks an industrial and operational center; economically and politically it points in all directions; and it is badly disunited linguistically and ethnically. On top of the original tribal differences have been superimposed the new differences of Africa's invaders. A United States of Africa would mean adjustment to an intra-continental thinking and alignment which the states with varying emotional, cultural, economic and political backgrounds and alliances are not ready to make. This is what emerges from a careful reading of the addresses of the heads of state and government at Addis Ababa.[58] The tone was set by Emperor Haile Selassie, who said:

> ...We are determined to create a union of Africans. In a very real sense, our continent is unmade, it still awaits its creation and its creators. It is our duty and privilege to rouse the slumbering giant of Africa, not to the nationalism of Europe of the Nineteenth-Century, not to regional consciousness, but to the vision of a single African brotherhood bending its united efforts toward the achievement of a greater and nobler goal...

> But while we agree that the ultimate destiny of this continent lies in political union, we must at the same time recognize that the obstacles to be overcome in its achievement are at once numerous and formidable. Africa's peoples did not emerge into liberty in uniform conditions. Africans maintain different political systems; our economies are diverse; our social orders are rooted in differing cultures and traditions. Further, no clear consensus exists on the "how" and the "what" of this union. Is it to be in form federal, confederal, or unitary? Is the sovereignty of individual states to be reduced, and if so, by how much and in what areas? On these and other questions there is no agreement, and if we wait for agreed answers, generations hence matters will be little advanced, while the debate still rages.

> We should, therefore, not be concerned that complete
> union is not attained from one day to the next. The union
> which we seek can only come gradually, as the day-to-day
> progress which we achieve carries us slowly but inexorably
> along this course. We have before us the examples of the
> USA and the USSR. We must remember how long these
> required to achieve their union. When a solid foundation
> is laid, if the mason is able and his materials good, a strong
> house can be built...[59]

If Pan Africanism and the posture of Pan African leadership
have some pragmatic basis in the desire to reshape the Balkanized
continent and to enable it to better support the burden and exercise of the responsibilities of independence, Pan Asianism is historically spurious and geographically, ethnically, culturally and
politically untenable. The things that unite Asians also unite
Africans and Latin Americans and all other peoples who are
in revolt against themselves, straining against the established
social order and reaching out for a new life. The things which
divide them are deeply rooted in race, culture, politics, religion
and history. The Near East, Iran, Arabia and Afghanistan have
been completely isolated from the historical currents of the rest
of Asia; the towering Himalayas and Pamirs have long effectively
sealed off the sub-continent of India from China and Japan and
other East Asian countries; while all of Southeast Asia and the
islands of the Southwest Pacific remained age-long strangers one
to another. No sense of common destiny or purpose, no feeling
of Asian solidarity lingered in the subconsciousness of the peoples
of this vast continent to inspire the thought of regional or continental unity. Life and loyalty have revolved too much around
family, village, clan, caste or tribe to tolerate more than provincial
cohesion. Besides, great centers of traditions, cultures and power
in which Asia abounds can be brought together only in intensified
conflict. Each of these centers, rich in history and experience, and
carrying the weight of ancient prides, aspires to regional hegemony, and each is being rebuffed by people who are assertive of
their own values and eager to evolve a civilization bearing the
stamp of their own genius. And all of Asia's nations, like all other
nations which have only recently thrown off the grip of impe-

rialism or foreign domination, are too jealous of their sovereignty and independence to share them with others even for their mutual advantage.[60]

The search for a United Arabia, stretching from the Atlantic to the Indian Ocean, is consonant with the corporate aspect of Islam, which regards Muslims all over the world as brothers, regardless of wealth, rank or nationality. A common heritage of language, culture, history and experience unites the Arab world with deep and abiding bonds, which in recent years have been elevated to a doctrinal commitment to Arab unity. The belief in their unity has become an axiom of Arab politics everywhere and is enshrined in the Constitutions of the several Arab States. Yet, while the vision of Arab unity has not dimmed and often serves as a rallying point for the achievement of political ends at home and abroad, its practical realization has invariably foundered on local interests.

Arabs have never been united in a single state or federation, although early Islam carried them along the same tide of dynamism. Neither the mystique drawn from the religious conquests of Islam in the seventh century and the defeat of the Crusaders in the twelfth, nor common memories of dispersion among foreign empires and humiliation at the hands of the conqueror, have been strong enough to counteract the centrifugal forces which would seem to impel the Arabs to divide. However strong the Arabs' yearning may be for identity and dignity as an Arab nation, it is not stronger than their deep bent for identity as Egyptians, or Syrians, or Iraquis or Algerians. The will to retain their separate identities goes far to explain the ill-starred union between Egypt and Syria in 1958-1961, and the still-born union of Egypt, Iraq and Syria proclaimed in a ringing manifesto issued in Cairo on April 17, 1963. However compelling the desire for unity may be, many violent cross currents rend the Arab world. They have their origin in the propensity of the Arab masses, innocent of political principles, to split into personal followings of rival political leaders, no less than in the juxtaposition of states at different stages of social, economic and political development.[61]

CHAPTER IV

The United Nations and Beyond

Regionalism was never conceived as the growing edge of an evolutionary process of international coalescence. It took a great deal of argument and debate at San Francisco, for example, before Articles 52-54 of the United Nations Charter, recognizing regional arrangements for purposes of defense and keeping the peace, were adopted.[1] The long march of history lent little encouragement to the notion that geographical propinquity, common racial, linguistic and ethnic origins, common cultural loyalties and traditions, or greater social affinity necessarily made for greater homogeneity of interest and for greater organized cooperation. On the contrary, where, as in the case of Pan-Slavism or Pan-Germanism or Pan Arabism, this notion was deliberately fostered, it only revealed its true colors as an instrument of imperialist expansion. Besides, the antecedents and consequences of World War I and II confirmed that, just as the most serious threats to the peace arose from tensions and conflicts which cut across sectional, regional and continental boundaries, so only institutions which transcended the confines of space and geography and were embedded in a universal ideal of an all-inclusive world community could avert disaster in the future. All important problems which affect the human condition are universal in character and global in scope.

The idea of regionalism, either as an alternative to international organization or as a necessary concomitant, emerged as an important political problem in 1948, when the hope that the United Nations could be relied upon to keep the peace had ebbed.[2] It was then that Ernest Bevin, speaking for the West, issued the following warning from the rostrum of the General Assembly:

> After San Francisco our hopes were high and we felt that
> at last, with all the mistakes of the League of Nations
> behind us, a new instrument had been created which would
> avoid those same mistakes. We felt that the terrible ex-
> periences which the world had suffered would lead all
> statesmen to cooperate...But, if we find in the end that
> we cannot proceed on a world basis as we had hoped, we
> must proceed on a regional basis...[3]

Great Britain's Foreign Secretary spoke at a time when the
then developing cold war had already shattered the foundations
upon which the power and prestige of the United Nations were
erected. Clearly, the United Nations was unable to close the
widening gap between the purposes to which it had been dedicated only three years before and its ability to carry them out.
Even the staunchest friends of the new world organization could
not in good conscience reprove the efforts of those who sought to
build new ramparts of peace, in the form of military alliances
outside the United Nations and regional organizations. But there
can be no doubt that the trauma the United Nations experienced
in its relative infancy affected the whole course of its future
development. It was never permitted to become the undisputed
institutional embodiment of the international interest and instrument of international policy, and it was cut down to size before
it had an opportunity to rise above its own limitations.[4]

Our perspective is too limited and our vision too blurred for a
real audit of the achievements of the United Nations. It is very
difficult to deduce from its varied activities general principles
which would illumine the workings of this organization. It is
even more difficult to generalize about it on the basis of the
relatively few instances in which the world body was committed
in the great conflicts which divide the world. For all its flaws
and inadequacies, the United Nations remains the closest the
world has yet moved toward some form of viable international
authority. With all its gross and palpable imperfections, the
United Nations remains far and away the most important potential force for international peace and justice. It is the major international platform for the assertion of the corporate will of the
community of nations and for the defense of the international
interest against all challenges.

The United Nations is at once a forum for debate, a place for negotiation, and an arena for action. Public debate has provided it with some of its greatest moments. It is a forum where not only all nations can freely present their cause and air their differences, but where the great dialogue of humanity is carried on. It is a place where governments have an opportunity of conducting, in the words of the late Secretary-General Dag Hammarskjöld,

> ...the quiet work of preparing the ground, of accommodation of interest and viewpoint, of conciliation and mediation, all that goes into the winning of consent to agreed solutions and common programmes...[5]

And as an arena for action, the United Nations can boast of many operations in the political, military, economic and social fields which could hardly have been envisaged at San Francisco. Since 1945, the United Nations has vastly expanded its area of concern and involvement and has assumed jurisdiction in many fields of international life which have plunged it ever deeper into the mainstream of the history of our times.[6]

A providential flexibility enables the United Nations to meet unforeseen stresses and is its greatest source of strength. The Uniting for Peace resolution which the General Assembly adopted on November 3, 1950,[7] is perhaps the most outstanding single example of its ready adaptability to changed circumstances. A broad interpretation of the Charter was needed for the United Nations to deal, for example, with such questions as *apartheid* in South Africa[8] or Angola, and it could never have played its vital role in the Congo[9] if it had viewed the Charter as being no more than a statement of broad rules of state conduct. Because it saw in the Charter more than anything else a constitution for the political organs it had created, by which those broad rules were to be interpreted and applied, the United Nations has been able even under extreme pressure of events, such as the Cuban crisis,[10] to become the bulwark of the community of nations. It has sometimes softened the asperities of the cold war; at others, it has managed to interpose itself successfully between the power blocs. It has assisted in the largely peaceful liquidation of the Western colonial empires. It has provided a link between nations old and new, large and small, rich and poor. It has stood sentinel on national borders,[11] mediated in time of tension and arbitrated international disputes, and it has become the international constellation for peaceful economic and social change.

"As long as there is still work to be done, we have achieved nothing," said the great liberator, Simon Bolivar. It is not the patient constructive work, nor success won in the face of many difficulties that are ultimately decisive. Great as the achievements may stand to the credit of the United Nations, its fate will be determined by its ability to rise above its source.[12] Until the United Nations becomes more than the sum of its parts, it will remain a brittle instrument of international policy, forever at the mercy of the embattling great powers and the impenitent nationalism of all its members. Like all other intergovernmental bodies, the United Nations, too, cannot escape the consequences stemming from the inherent contradiction between national sovereignty and effective international organization. The framers of the Charter envisaged the world organization as a community of independent nations, each free to work out its own destiny as it saw fit but cooperating effectively and loyally with other nations in matters of common interest and common concern. However, events have made it quite clear that common interests are no guarantee of loyal cooperation, and common concern is no bar to the assertion of the primacy of national interests. The veto in the Security Council and the voluntary character of United Nations recommendations still represent reality.

On January 11, 1946, Paul Henri Spaak told the General Assembly, upon his election as its first President, that the League of Nations was a noble ideal and that the men who sought to achieve it were men of good will. But, he went on to say,

> the fact is that, during the period that intervened between the two wars, we did not succeed in forming a real international spirit and it is that which is essential if the work we begin today is to succeed. ...Naturally, we must all watch over the interests of our respective countries, but we shall not succeed unless we are convinced that those interests must take their place in the wider setting of the general interest, and unless we are conscious, over and above the interests of our own country, of the interests

of the world and of mankind. We must not be here, 51 different delegations from 51 different countries whose only purpose is to add up 51 national interests. If we do this nothing good for the world will come out of our work. We must, on the contrary, have the feeling that we are 51 delegations to the same Assembly, which collectively represents the interests of the world. If we create that kind of spirit, and if we can practice what I regard as the two cardinal virtues of international meetings, that is to say good faith and good will, if we are to apply certain simple but important rules of procedure, we shall succeed...[13]

Almost two years later, Torres Bodet of Mexico, addressing the eighty-second plenary meeting of the General Assembly on September 17, 1947, said:

Our diplomatic language is to some extent the language of our era, but our actions are still very similar to those which strewed the path of history with millions of corpses...We speak of the welfare of man at a time when man is torn between the two opposing forces of juridical and cultural internationalism on the one hand, and political and economic nationalism on the other...In the opinion of my country, that is the cause of all our difficulties and the root of all our problems...Unless we consolidate the United Nations, all our efforts will again come to naught and, by losing the peace, we shall also have lost the war...But if we hope to consolidate our organization, we shall have to correct many mistakes, overcome much pride, and relinquish many of our advantages. That means that we shall have to adopt a policy of sincere international equality, making our liberties real, abolishing exclusive politics and confessing unreservedly that we would be deceiving the peoples of the world if, after having raised the banner of universality, we continue to destroy that universality by sophistries born out of the most sterile nationalism...The United Nations will be saved only if it is determined to be the true expression of the solidarity of mankind, of all the men of the earth...[14]

Fifteen years later, Secretary-General Dag Hammarskjöld told a meeting of the Security Council on February 15, 1961, that.

> Very many nations have not yet accepted the limits put on their national ambition by the very existence of the United Nations and by the membership of that Organization.[15]

The United Nations is an organization of sovereign states and neither in structure, nor in content has it compromised its character as a league of sovereign states. Only in few cases can the United Nations make binding decisions and under conditions which today are not likely to be honored. In an address on June 10, 1963, former President Sarvepalli Radhakrishnan of India told the General Assembly:

> ...We are are still believing in the nation-state and in the right to use force to have our aims realized. These are the things which have us by the throat. Though we are members of this international community, though we call ourselves Members of the United Nations, our loyalties are to our own nation-States; they are not to the world as a whole, not to humanity as a whole. We must break away from the past, we must get out of the rut in which we have lived...[16]

Secretary-General U Thant has similarly noted on a number of occasions that:

> The United Nations is not a world government, nor is its General Assembly a world legislature. It is, in a sense, of course, the parliament of mankind, as it gives opportunities for the large and the small countries equally to have their say on major issues, and this is the original meaning of parliament. But it is not a world legislature with the authority to pass laws binding on all Member Governments; its resolutions are more in the nature of recommendations than of statutes...[17]

The United Nations has been as much an arena for struggle as a forum of cooperation. Nations large and small have more often exploited it for national gain than used it for purposive international action. The springtime hopefulness which prevailed in 1945 for a peaceful and reconciled humanity was bound to be short lived, when the framers of the Charter vested the hopes for the future in a league of sovereign states. Not that they were expected to contrive an exemplary organization to set against the real world. It is one of the glories of the United Nations that as clearly as any mirror, it reflects the passions and conflicts of the world of which it is part and that it does not shrink from coming down into the dust of battle and sharing all its attendant dangers. But only a quarter of a century separated San Francisco from Versailles, where the first attempt to entrust the common affairs of man to the hands of a league of sovereign nation states was ratified. The League of Nations proved a frail shield against the rule of brute force, but its lessons were largely lost on the statesmen who twenty-five years later assembled to consecrate a new world order. From the point of view of the restraint it imposes upon Member States, the Charter leaves too much scope for independent action by governments to be able to enforce the judgment of the world community. Each nation remains free to decide for itself the domestic and international issues of concern to it and is the sole arbiter of its national interests. The jurisdiction of the United Nations is limited by the good will of all its Members, but even more by the forbearance of the more powerful nations.

All Member States resist United Nations incursion into their spheres of interest. The greater their power, the greater is their care not to allow their vital interests to become entangled in the proceedings of the organization. The efforts of the United States in 1954, for example, to block Guatemala's complaint to the Security Council of aggression by Honduras and Nicaragua by invoking Article 52 (2) of the Charter, which enjoins Member States parties to regional arrangements to try to achieve pacific settlement of local disputes on the regional level before referring them to the Security Council,[18] could not disguise America's vital national interests which were at stake in the dispute. The Soviet Union has never made any secret of her intolerance of any United Nations attempt to intrude into her sphere of interest, embracing first of all the countries of the Soviet bloc.[19] The forceful wave of internationalism invariably seems to stop at the national frontier or the frontier of interest.

In the United Nations, perhaps more than anywhere else, one sees at close quarters the divisive forces which keep nations apart. They are all firmly anchored in the nationalist creed. Nationalism in its exuberance is impatient of the idea of restraint for the benefit of the international community as a whole. Nobody will register dissent to what Ambassador Adlai Stevenson said on this subject, albeit in a different context. In a statement made on December 4, 1961, in the Political Committee of the General Assembly, on international cooperation in the peaceful uses of outer space, the United States representative said:

> We are conditioned to think in terms of nations. Our lives and concepts are predicated upon states whose boundaries are fixed by oceans and rivers and mountain-ranges, or by man-made lines drawn sharply across the two-dimensional and finite surface of planet Earth. We are conditioned to think in terms of nations defined by finite areas expressed in finite measurements—nations with more or less known resources and more or less counted populations. And especially we are conditioned to think in terms of national sovereignties.[20]

By the very nature of its task among the nations and peoples of the world, the United Nations' writ must run inside the frontiers of states. Until this comes to pass, the United Nations will not be a reliable shield for the weak to protect them against the strong and the strong from each other. Nations refuse to be controlled by laws which are no protection and to entrust their destiny into hands that are not steady. The United Nations cannot hope to move the world decisively from anarchy to ordered peace until it has the right of ultimate decision. It cannot hope to become an effective instrument of collective security, preserve the peace, ensure freedom and justice, and act as an agent for peaceful change, as long as its fate is decreed by those over whom it has no control, and as long as its very existence hangs on the outcome of Great Power confrontation. The United Nations cannot be expected to yield up its great and untried potentialities and to attain its unlimited goals, until the last threat to its independence is removed. As the conscience of mankind and the home where people meet in a community of equals, the United Nations can have no frontiers, bow to no ideology, and yield to no pressure of majority or minority. The United Nations can have room for no other but the highest standards of justice, morality and integrity.

The complex of institutions, ideas and activities that today constitute the United Nations is only the seedbed of the future. It is not the future itself. Its task is to maintain peace until all impediments to a just and peaceful order are no more and to hold the ring until law and order emerge from chaos.

CHAPTER V

Human Rights and World Order

Ordered progress toward an international regime capable of inhibiting the excesses of the nationalist creed and setting natural limits to the exercise of national power is neither beyond the imagination of modern man nor outside the limits of possibility. While we may not readily change the idol that is the nation-state, we may change the spirit in which it is worshipped. Man is capable of cherishing, at one and the same time, loyalty to nation and country implanted by the culture and reinforced by a complex of emotions and material interests, and loyalty to the whole of the human family, which springs from the logic of historical development and which conforms to the need of preserving the race from self-destruction.[1]

To break through the massive prejudices and irreconcilable interests that block the road to a lasting peace and just world order, we must look to a scheme of international relations which would operate outside the web of national histories, traditions and interests. The first step in that direction is the emancipation of the human individual from the shackles of nationality. Without international recognition of man's distinctly personal character, it is impossible to alter the pattern of the nation-state, which for so long has remained a fixed and static feature in international life. Second, to render concrete the concept of international community and to reduce the idea of a common humanity to the daily experience of the ordinary citizen, the fate of the human person, whoever and wherever he may be, must become the direct concern of the international community and its immediate responsibility. Nothing short of the internationalization of

man can bring about the great compromise between the prerogatives of national sovereignty and the requirements of international solidarity, and the reconciliation between the nationalist
creed and the idea of the community of man.

An international community centered on man and capable of
meeting his material goals and social ideals is far and away the
most compelling force that can successfully oppose the state's
quest for power and its claim to the absolute and undivided
allegiance of its citizen. Whether its claim to unfettered freedom
of action within its own frontiers flows from the principle of national sovereignty, or is justified pragmatically on the ground
of its responsibility for the safety of the state and the welfare
of the population, a government's undisputed sway over its citizens is the ultimate source of all state power. Until this power
is curbed at its source, the world will never know true and lasting
peace. For the monopoly the state holds over the loyalty of the
citizen is singularly susceptible to manipulation and perversion
as an instrument of oppression at home and aggression abroad.
National sentiments and love of home and native land have been
cunningly exploited for aggressive ends, and thoughtless emotions have been misdirected to threaten the peace of the world.[2]
History abounds in all too many examples where whole peoples
have been mesmerized by issues of no practical benefit to them,
and where the assertion of the immediate national interest as
the highest good, turned local quarrels into tragic international
disputes. There are many instances of states girding themselves
to battle for the peace and security of their citizens, only to
become locked in unceasing struggles with other states, which
undermine and destroy the welfare of the very people in whose
name and for whose benefit the battle is waged. The lawlessness
bequeathed by the nationalist creed will not abate until the state
can no longer marshal the forces let loose by it for aggressive
purposes and commit its citizens to policies and actions born
out of self-centered interest and nurtured by distorted pride in
nationality.

An international community, centered on man and recognizing
the supreme status of the human person and his significance as
the bearer of all values, will not only strike at the source of
international conflict but deprive the state of its ultimate rationale for the pursuit of power and its insistence on the absolute and
unqualified allegiance of its citizens. This rationale rests on the

fact that an international community which cannot safeguard the peace and enforce law and justice among nations is no protection. When force remains the supreme arbiter in the conflict among states, nations will rely for their safety and the defense of their vital interests on the strength of arms and military alliances. Only when the wide gulf which today separates man from the international community is bridged, will that community be able to perform its task among the nations. Nothing but international concern with the fate of the man whose life unfolds in the anonymity of the mass, can give corporeality to the idea of a common humanity. Nothing but an international community firmly anchored in the interests of the human personality can evoke the consciousness of the universal in man and the image of man in terms of the universal. And only an international community girded to respond to the aspirations of man can elicit the loyalty of the peoples and provide the emotional drive behind the logic of the international ideal.

The form of internationalism which recognizes only the community we know as the society of nations, of sovereign states pursuing different and clashing policies and interests, is as barren as it is unimaginative. The international community can no more endure without the allegiance of the peoples of the world, than the state can survive without the allegiance of its citizens. As people come to recognize that their destiny is bound up with the destiny of the international community, the hold of the state over its citizens will inevitably be loosened. As people become alive to their dependence upon an international community which can bring order and justice into the chaos of events, it will command their allegiance and derive its strength from it. Just as the centralization of royal justice and victory over competing communal, franchise and feudal jurisdictions contributed decisively to the creation of the modern state,[3] so international concern with the fate of the human person holds the key to the development of a society of citizens in an all-inclusive society of nations, existing side by side with the state and vis-a-vis the state. Ultimately, the state will find fulfillment in functioning as the administrative arm of international law and justice, to preserve the liberty of man, to free him to cultivate his traditions and to secure his full participation in the distribution of political, economic, social and cultural rights and privileges.

Moreover, no other formula better serves the need of a universal postulated framework within which to resolve the problems of the human condition than international concern with the fate of the human individual in the flesh, To focus on man is to focus on the matrix of all the world's problems and to attack them in their cradle and in their nurturing environs. Before the immeasurable resources of science and learning, of generosity and humanity can be harnessed in the service of all men, international discussion of the critical problems that bestride the world must be held in a setting of true human perspective. The problems of war and peace, population pressure and environmental change, racial, national, religious, linguistic and cultural diversity and mutual accommodation, economic development and social progress, and the myriad other problems which involve the destiny of man can never be understood, let alone resolved, when torn from their human context and thrown into the ambit of national interest and ambition. These invariably intervene to distort the true character and perspective of human problems and to falsify the enlightened interests of nations.

As long as international cooperation is unable to isolate the great problems of the day from the currents and pressures of national interest and ambitions, it cannot marshal the material, intellectual and spiritual resources of the nations in a massive and purposeful undertaking for the good of all and for the lasting benefit of the nations themselves. As long as international cooperation is not freed from the rigors of the nationalist creed, it will lack a firm moral footing from which to arbitrate between the opposing claims that bedevil international relations and to resolve the tensions and conflicts between universal values and the strategic interests of the state. International cooperation is at its highest when the human person, his existential self, is the immediate object and subject of its concern. It brings a new vision into international relations, which is capable of sweeping aside all the ancient and modern fallacies which have ordered the life of men for so many centuries. In its concern for the purely human dimensions of life, international cooperation can never be inhibited by considerations of national policies, nor fettered by refinements of particular doctrines or strategies. International concern with the welfare of the human person knows, for example, no agricultural surplus until the last person on earth has been fed, and no deficiency as long as the earth can be made to yield a harvest to spare every man, woman and child the pangs of hunger. Being in the service of no other interest than the interest of the individual human being, such cooperation can freely plan for the rationalization of agriculture and for the equitable distribution of its fruits. Above all, international cooperation for the sake of the human person can bring into play all the actual and potential creative forces in the world now held in check by the division of national frontiers and liberate others which may lie hidden under the crust of nationalism to provide freedom and abundance for people everywhere.

Two hundred years ago Immanuel Kant argued that it was illusory to expect an international association to enforce peace among nations without a common morality of democratic values and a consensus on human rights. He asserted the rights and liberties of the individual as a condition for all true morality and constitutionalism at home and abroad.[4] Almost two centuries later, "international cooperation in promoting and encouraging respect for human rights and for fundamental freedoms for all without distinction as to race, sex, language or religion" was affirmed as one of the principal purposes of the United Nations Organization.[5] To the Council of Europe, "the maintenance and further realization of human rights and fundamental freedoms" has been basic to the achievement of greater unity between its members, as well as the foundation of justice and peace in the world.[6] The same holds true of the Organization of American States[7] and the Organization of African Unity[8] and it reaches out to other regional organizations.[9] More and more, the world has come to recognize the validity of the claim of the human personality to be heard in every decision affecting the fate of man and to cast its decisive vote in the council of nations. Pope John XXIII spoke for all when he postulated a set of international rules of conduct and conscience, which rests on a conception of the universe in which the recognition of the moral personality of man and his dignity and rights stand in the center. In his celebrated encyclical *Pacem in Terris* of April 10, 1963, Pope John declared:

Like the common good of individual political communities,
so too the universal common good cannot be determined
except by having regard to the human person. Therefore
the public authority of the world community, too, must
have as its fundamental objective the recognition, respect,
safeguarding and promotion of the rights of the human
person...[10]

Above all the clamor of differences which divide people, men
and women of all continents and of all latitudes and longitudes,
regardless of the diversity in their background and outlook, are
united in their quest for personal dignity and for the satisfaction
of their human rights and fundamental freedoms. Just as the
cult of nationalism has cast its spell across the face of the earth,
so the rising aspirations of people for human dignity and their
rights and freedoms as men have spread far and wide throughout the world. The stirrings of untold millions for economic
betterment, their agitation for social advancement, and their
striving for human fulfillment have been the inevitable concom-
itants of the awakening of national consciousness and the
irresistible march toward freedom and self-determination. Those
whose forefathers endured patiently misery and want and all
manner of indignity are resolved to win their just inheritance.
Men and women everywhere are no longer content to flit about
the outskirts of life, while others take the fullness of it. "There
is throughout the world," Secretary-General U Thant declared
in his Human Rights Day Message on the occasion of the thirteenth anniversary of the Universal Declaration of Human Rights,
in 1961,

an increasing demand for the recognition of these rights
and freedoms. People everywhere have awakened to the
realization that the enjoyment of these rights is no longer
the privilege of the few but must and can be shared by
all. They expect the United Nations to secure the recognition of the inherent dignity of all human beings, and of
the equal rights of the human family, as the foundation
on which the defense of peace all over the world can be
built.[11]

In fact, human dignity and the rights of man are among the few points of concurrence of individual, national and international interests. The uncompromising acceptance of the principle that "all men are born free and equal in dignity and rights," has emerged pragmatically from the crucible of experience as the most valid of all working hypotheses of human relations. The whole world, practically, has a vital stake in preserving the integrity of this principle, however at variance its construction may often be with the philosophical foundations of democratic tolerance, equality of opportunity and free self-development. It is woven into the fabric of great civilizations, cultures and religions; it is the pillar which supports the whole modern movement for self-determination and national freedom and independence; it underlies the universal striving for equality among races, nations and peoples; and it is indispensible to the survival of the multi-racial, multi-lingual and multi-religious communities with which the world abounds.

In a very true sense, the dignity of the human person and his rights and freedoms provide a background of certainties for international cooperation which transcend all national considerations. These certainties are vibrant with a special sensibility that is capable of revolutionizing attitudes and positions even within the framework of largely conventional and inherited forms and ideas. Their potential capacity to integrate the vast diversity of the world is unlimited, as is their power to bring under control the blind and impersonal political, economic, social and cultural forces which have ordered the course of international relations for such a long span of time. And so is their challenge in exposing persuasively the gross fallacies which are forever distorting international life, including the belief that the state is the limit and measure of every advantage and of all good and justice.

For human rights and fundamental freedoms encompass so much of the totality of national and international life, that their deliberate promotion and defense constitute an ideal regulative principle of international relations. There is no doubt that the most signal and unmistakable advance in the conception of human rights registered in recent times is the addition of economic, social and cultural rights to the civil and political rights which appeared all-important to the revolutionaries of the eighteenth century. The twentieth century has rejected the notion that prevailed in the preceding hundred years, that the classic issue

of the rights of man has been settled for all time in the sense of
the American Declaration of Independence and the French Declaration of the Rights of Man.[12] Economic growth as an over-
riding objective and function of government, for example, has
been universally accepted by all political systems, whether Capitalist, Socialist, Communist, or any of their many variants. The
Charter of the United Nations has recognized the anxieties of
modern man and has laid great stress on the importance of international cooperation for the promotion of the economic and social
welfare of the peoples of the world. Economic, social and technical assistance on a bilateral, multilateral, regional and international basis has become an integral part of international relations. Being coextensive with all important aspects of human
endeavor, human rights provide a practical setting for international cooperation in the service of man. Each and every right and
freedom defined in the Universal Declaration of Human Rights
dictates a national and international code of conduct and conscience that goes far toward erasing the barriers which stand in
the way of marshalling the abundant resources of courage, energy
and imagination among nations for the advancement of the good
of all.

Nothing but international concern with the dignity and worth
of the human person can provide the depth of inspiration to all
international effort, now and in the future, to elevate the material
and social condition of man. Many of these efforts are drifting
in isolated orbits for lack of specific human reference, while
others are being dissipated by the distortions and strains and
stresses of national interest. As in the political area of international relations, so in the economic and social fields, international
cooperation invariably founders on the contradictions inherent
in a world of sovereign nation-states bent upon achieving national
advantages. Lasting progress toward the alleviation of the world's
economic and social ills, let alone their complete eradication from
the face of the earth, is impossible without an international
release from the pressures of national interests and ambitions and
of the political and strategic requirements of the state. For international cooperation for the promotion of the economic and
social welfare of the peoples of the world implies not only a pooling of material resources and the mobilization of the creative
forces of man, but the acceptance of definite ideas for system-

atically realizing definite objectives and studied, conscious decisions and the taking of steady and consistent initiatives to move events in the desired direction. When the points of departure are the needs of the state and its economic viability and competitive ability, international cooperation for the promotion of the economic and social welfare of the peoples is twice removed from the target at which it is aimed. The state and its needs devour not only the profits which accrue from such cooperation, but the capital investment as well.

To free international cooperation in the economic and social fields from the fetters of national interest and ambition, and to enable the world to mount a massive assault on the whole range of social and economic ills, such cooperation must be informed by principles and objectives acting directly on the needs and aspirations of the human individual. When the concern of international cooperation is for the purely human dimensions of life, it cannot be suppressed by considerations of national economic interests and policies, nor held in check by refinements of narrow social theories and practices. Thus informed and thus concerned, international cooperation can bring within its orbit the cares and preoccupations of man everywhere and lift the peoples of the world from generations of degradation and submergence to the heights of dignity and freedom.

The logic of human rights as the instrument of international cohesion is incontestable. What makes international concern with the fate of man and rights and freedoms the ideal fixed point of reference in international relations is, precisely, its quality as a means to an end, as well as an end in itself. Unless man is regarded as greater than the social purposes to which he can be put, the highest human ideals cannot find forceful expression and consistent application, on the national plane or on the international level. The most noble goals of human effort, of abundance, equality, justice and freedom for all are all too frequently negated by the means employed to realize them. International concern with the human individual as a mere statistic, as producer, consumer or resource will not suffice to change the political pattern of centuries. To move the world toward new forms of cooperation and association, international relations must be activated and energized by the capabilities and aspirations of the human mind and spirit. The international community can project an ideal of human destiny only if it acts directly on and in behalf of the human person. In the uneven struggle of the individual against overwhelming and impersonal political, economic and social forces, which tend ever more to reduce him to a mere cog in a vast machine whose meaning and purpose he can neither understand nor translate into personal experiences, the international community must intervene on the side of man.

CHAPTER VI

International Concern
with Human Rights

In 1945, at the United Nations Conference at San Francisco, the organized international community decided to intervene on behalf of man, when it reaffirmed faith in fundamental human rights and in the dignity and worth of the human person and made the promotion and encouragement of respect for human rights and fundamental freedoms of all the responsibility of the newly-created world organization. Whatever may have been the reasons which motivated the framers of the Charter to establish this corporate responsibility and whatever the consequences that may flow from it, the concern of the United Nations with human rights and fundamental freedoms has broken the chain of national authority and tradition at its strongest link. These rights and freedoms, which have traditionally remained within the pre-empted province of the state and its exclusive responsibility, have now become matters of international concern and the subject of relations between states.

To what extent this development and similar developments at the regional levels in Western Europe and Latin America indicate that the idea of international concern with human rights has taken root in the international conscience deep enough to venture, for example, into the precarious field of peace-making eludes a clear answer. With almost half the world in the grip of Communism, with one-third in the throes of social and economic convulsion, and with the erosion of human individuality everywhere, international concern with human rights cannot be said to be in the mainstream of contemporary thought and action. International concern with human rights has not yet produced a definite body of doctrines and deeply rooted convictions to compete with success in the market place of ideas. It has not crystallized into concrete patterns of thought to appeal to men of action, nor formulated distinctly enough for the clamor of the politician. It is still awaiting its prophets to proclaim and champions to defend.[1]

In the exultant spirit of the San Francisco Conference and the early days of the United Nations, the notion that international concern with the fate of the human individual was a necessary condition for world peace figured high in the order of truth. Thus China's Foreign Minister, Wellington Koo, could assert with authority before the first session of the General Assembly that,

> If the world is to enjoy lasting peace, the dignity of man must be respected as the first principle of the new order; and the implementation of this principle will not only strenghten the basis of our civilization but remove suspicion between nations and thus contribute to the cause of peace.[2]

There was general agreement that the Charter commitment to the promotion of human rights and fundamental freedoms marked the most important advance of the United Nations over the League of Nations and was its greatest promise. As former Prime Minister Clement Attlee noted in his welcoming statement at the opening of the first General Assembly in London,

> the Charter of the United Nations does not deal only with Governments and States or with politics and war, but with the simple elemental needs of human beings whatever be their race, their colour or their creed. In the Charter we reaffirm faith in fundamental human rights. We see the freedom of the individual in the State as an essential complement to the freedom of the State in the world community of nations. We stress, too, that social justice and the best possible standards of life for all are essential factors in promoting and maintaining the peace of the world...[3]

Other representatives of Member States went even further and asserted that the whole aim and purpose of the United Nations was the defense of the dignity and rights of the human person. "Our most fervent wish," said the representative of Uruguay, is that the order of the law in all spheres, national and international, should have as its ultimate effective end the freedom and the rights of man; and that if we were to be asked one day why we are here and what we are doing, we may be able to answer, simply and modestly, with the very words of the great American poet, Henry George, "We are for man."[4]

And no one rose to challenge the statement made in the course of the general debate at the same first session of the General Assembly by the representative of Peru that,

> ...Man as the central figure of international law was a theoretical conception of philosophers and jurists, for all practical purposes obscured by the political interests of the moment. No one can deny that today it is man, his liberties, needs and guarantees who is the real hub of the life of the world...[5]

It was no Golden-age vision that inspired the statesmen who had assembled in San Francisco to write the United Nations Charter to burden the new and untried organization with the responsibility of promoting human rights in a world of independent states whose sovereign equality they had just reaffirmed. It was World War II and its immediate antecedents that provided the most persuasive argument why the organized international community should be concerned with the rights and freedoms of the individual. The facts were all too clear. On January 30, 1933, Adolf Hitler assumed the reins of power in Germany. Within a very short time millions of Germans were deprived of their elementary rights and liberties and hundreds of thousands of others were forced into exile. Barely seven years later World War II broke loose on earth. The inexorable chain of events was revealed in all its brutal and logical sequence. But what had taken place inside Germany was beyond international control. The lesson that the state could not be left to remain the sole arbiter in deciding the fate of its citizens could not be ignored.

If the lesson was not completely ignored, neither was it fully understood. While the facts were stated correctly, the truth behind them remained concealed. What happened in Germany brought home the fact that if there are areas beyond which

human conscience cannot permit silence in the face of governmental action, the right of every one to speak the truth of his
conscience must prevail against the national consensus; that if
we accept the moral duty of every citizen to protest and, if
necessary, to refuse participation in governmental actions which
he believes to be contrary to the laws of humanity, he must be
protected against all retaliation; and that if the survival of the
race ultimately lies in the conscience and responsibility of man
to speak the truth as he sees it, silence becomes an international
crime. But no man can be held responsible for acts of commission
or omission when the choice is not always his to make freely, and
no man can be held accountable to an international community
which affords no protection against national authority. The pressure for conformity constricts freedom of thought and action
even in the most democratic societies. In authoritarian countries,
individual liberty and diversity of opinion are often crimes
against the state. When a citizen can be intimidated into silence,
he will rarely resist the temptation of the comparative safety of
private opinion. When the course of prudence is to march in step,
prudence will dictate the virtue of silence.[6]

In brief, what happened in Germany raised the fundamental
question of the relationship between the citizen and the state
and between the state and the international community. It required a fundamental answer, whose ramifications and consequences extended far beyond the immediate problem of defining
international responsibility in the face of violation of the rights
and freedoms of man. This, however, was outside the range of
thought and competence of the United Nations Conference that
convened at San Francisco to write the Charter of the new world
organization. It was not the task of this Conference to seek the
ultimate truth. The framers of the Charter convened to make
political decisions, and they were more concerned with continuity
than with change. They did not propose to revolutionize the conduct of international relations, nor to establish new forms of
international organization. Their concern with human rights was
essentially a reaction to the Nazi enormities, whose full impact
had burst upon the world just as the United Nations Conference
opened its session on April 25, 1945. This was not enough to give
depth to the United Nations commitment to promote, in the
words of the Charter, universal respect for, and observance of,

human rights and fundamental freedoms for all, nor to arm the newly-created world body with the power of conviction to encounter and respond to the multiple aspects of this elemental question. As the memory of the Nazi crimes against humanity receded—and it receded rapidly—the emotional drive and political impulse which organized and sustained the efforts to commit the United Nations to the promotion and advancement of human rights began to dissipate. They were almost completely spent by the time the Universal Declaration of Human Rights was proclaimed in Paris on December 10, 1948.

Neither East nor West was interested in distilling the essence of the human rights provisions in the Charter and establishing their relevance to the total work of the United Nations. Dialectical materialism, with its emphasis on collectivity, its view of history as the work of faceless masses and impersonal social forces, as well as its deep hostility to any expression of individual nonconformity, could not countenance an international program that rejected *a priori* a philosophy of government which ruled that in any conflict between the individual and the state, the state must always prevail. From the very beginnings of the United Nations and until very recently, the Soviet Union opposed any suggestion which as much as questioned the absolute authority of the state to order its relations with its own citizens without the intervention of the international community.[7]

The West has, by and large, been no less concerned than the Soviet Union with the consequences of international concern with the rights and freedoms of man and no more prepared than the East to compromise its sovereign freedom of action by conceding the right of international intervention in the relations between state and citizen. By its emphasis on gradualism and by its counsel of prudence, the West lent support and respectability to all the weak and natural human inclinations toward irresolution and timidity. All the rationalizations could not conceal its fear lest international concern with human rights and fundamental freedoms might loosen the traditional bonds between the citizen and his state.[8]

For a time it appeared as if the concept of international concern with the rights of man might, in the tradition of the French Revolution, be carried forward on the tide of national emancipation. Just as the French Revolution had linked individual liberty

with national sovereignty, so the post-War movement for national liberation and independence has been identified with the
longing of people for human dignity and equality. The right of
self-determination as the basis of all human rights and national
freedom as an indispensible condition of their enjoyment have
been cardinal tenets of the anti-colonialist creed.[9] From the very
beginning of the United Nations, the right of a people to self-
determination has been represented as postulating respect for
human dignity, and the fight against colonialism as a struggle
for human rights. Thus, in 1950, the General Assembly decided
to incorporate the principle of self-determination of peoples into
the international covenants on human rights.[10] It constitutes the
first article of both, the Covenant on Civil and Political Rights
and the Covenant on Economic, Social and Cultural Rights. In
1955, the first meeting of Afro-Asian nations at Bandung, Indonesia, declared that

> the subjection of peoples to alien subjugation, domination
> and exploitation constitutes a denial of human rights, is
> contrary to the Charter of the United Nations and is an
> impediment to the promotion of world peace and coopera-
> tion.[11]

In 1960, this declaration was endorsed by all but two of the
Member States of the United Nations when, on December 14, the
General Assembly adopted the Declaration on the Granting of
Independence to Colonial Countries and Peoples.[12]

However, beyond providing a platform for resounding pronouncements, United Nations concern with human rights has
played a minor, if any, role in shaping and guiding the anti-
colonialist movement and the movement for national self-determination and freedom. The peoples most directly concerned have
been too anxious to convert the vision of independence into a
practical reality, or too intent upon securing their sovereign
prerogatives, to divert attention to the problems of human rights
and liberties. The principal focus among the Afro-Asian nations
has been upon national rights and national freedom, unencum-
bered by any servitudes even for the noblest of reasons. In an
address in New York on December 13, 1964, former Assistant
Secretary of State for International Organizations Affairs, Harlan
Cleveland, told the audience that:

The moment will come, I hope and believe, when the third great issue of the United Nations' next twenty years is how—and indeed whether—to bring to life the human rights provisions of the Charter... Part of the trouble, I suppose, is a confusion between nationhood and freedom. Self-determination, that noble goal which brought a billion people out from under foreign rule, was sometimes a racial as well as a national battlecry. Too often in the modern nationalist revolution—let us say it with all honesty—the promise of freedom was a promise of "separate but equal" status in the world.

Thus the leaders of most nations were perfectly clear that they wanted a United Nations to protect the achievement of nationhood by pressing for the self-determination of groups and peoples. But there is a good deal of uncertainty as to how far we—and our fellow-members—want the United Nations to go in criticizing and correcting the ethical delinquencies of peoples once they have declared their national independence.

It is this uncertainty, this confusion between nationhood and freedom, this feeling that national and racial and ethnic groups, not individual men, women and children, should be the beneficiaries of the continuing struggle for freedom—which in the longer run may prove to be the most divisive and troublesome threat to a viable world organization. Yet if the central question about freedom is man's humanity to man, the United Nations' relevance to our future will partly rest on what it does, or neglects to do, about individual human rights.[13]

Other countries have not hesitated to exploit the idea of international concern with human rights to pursue self-serving political objectives. The words spoken in exultation of the rights and freedoms of man by representatives of even the most authoritarian governments have very often risen to heights no less serene than those spoken by representatives of the most libertarian countries. Still others have been caught in the web of their own virtuous professions and have tended to overlook the disparity between the principles they propounded and the strategies and tactics they employed to serve them.

An air of embarassing unreality has been hanging over the
debates on human rights in the United Nations. All the drama of
words, all the moving eloquence, and all attempts to give these
debates a sense of higher purpose have proved a poor substitute
for clarity of policy, for decency of motives, and for strength of
commitment. Clearly, the United Nations had lost sight of the
appeal of human rights as the supreme testimony of human
solidarity and overlooked their potency as a mighty weapon in
the struggle for peace and justice, at home and abroad. The cause
of international concern with human rights and fundamental freedoms has never been represented as a total conception of the
good life and its practicability as a philosophy of means and
ends has never been put to the test. Very few Member States,
if any, have cared to look beyond the immediate present, to
discern in the organic link between international concern with
human rights and international organization a new design for
human destiny, to guide the evolution of the United Nations into
an all-embracing world community in which are institutionalized
the permanent interests of man.

In 1960, the Committee on Programme Appraisals, which the
Economic and Social Council had appointed two years earlier to
consolidate the reports of the United Nations and the specialized
agencies on the appraisals of the scope, trend and costs of their
respective programs in the economic, social and human rights
fields, warned:

> There is one aspect of this general problem that deserves
> special attention. One of the greatest dangers in develop-
> ment policy lies in the tendency to give to the more ma-
> terial aspects of growth an overriding and disproportionate
> emphasis. The end may be forgotten in preoccupation with
> the means. Human rights may be submerged and human
> beings seen only as instruments of production rather than
> as free entities for whose welfare and cultural advance the
> increased production is intended. The recognition of this
> issue has a profound bearing upon the formulation of the
> objectives of economic development and the methods em-
> ployed in attaining them. Even when there is recognition
> of the fact that the end of all economic development is a

social objective, i.e., the growth and well-being of the individual in larger freedom, methods of development may be used which are a denial of basic human rights.[14]

Instead, the notion of human rights has been shrunk to fit a particular situation. After the adoption by the General Assembly on December 10, 1948, of the Universal Declaration, United Nations concern with human rights came to be increasingly centered on the elimination of racial discrimination, more specifically, on the removal of the color bar in South Africa. By the end of 1966, there was hardly an area of United Nations activity which had not felt the impact of the concentrated attack on the racial policies of the South African Government. Every method available to the world organization, including certain forms of economic and diplomatic sanctions, had been employed to combat these policies. Many inhibitions of a juridical and political nature which had stood in the way had been swept aside. Under the pressure of the Afro-Asian countries, the United Nations took one unprecedented step after another to compel compliance of South Africa with its many resolutions.[15]

To be sure, but for the concerted drive against the policy of *apartheid,* the question of human rights would likely have long ago disappeared from the active agenda of the United Nations. Its preocupation with South Africa's racial policies gave a measure of concreteness to the rather abstract concern of the United Nations with human rights and particularized its human rights program, which had remained largely a generality. It provided the political motive force which all the efforts of United Nations bodies to promote respect for human rights and fundamental freedoms and to establish international standards of conscience and conduct governing such rights and freedoms could not even remotely command. It has served as a focus for the struggle against racial discrimination, and helped safeguard the basic programatic propositions in the field of human rights, such as the international covenants on human rights, against the attrition of time and deep-seated scepticism. The completion and adoption of the international covenants on human rights in 1966, including the provisions for their enforcement, were made possible by the unanimous approval the year before by the General Assembly of an international Convention on the Elimination of All Forms of Racial Discrimination. That Convention, whose provisions for their international enforcement embody certain radical features of a juridical and political nature, would have been unthinkable were it not for its symbolic significance in the rising campaign against South Africa's racial regime and for self-determination in South West Africa, Southern Rhodesia and the Portuguese possessions in Africa.

However, much as may be owed to the United Nations' preoccupation with racial discrimination in African white-dominated areas, its politicization and intimate association with the question of colonialism, which was perhaps unavoidable, robbed it of its immediate relevance to the ordering of a system of international relations oriented toward the enhancement of the human personality, in which the considerations that encourage and perpetuate divisions among men and nations become irrelevant. It deprived the relentless campaign against racial injustice and the color bar of those moral and doctrinal qualities which alone could have transformed it into a wellspring of ideas and innovation. It is questionable whether racial discrimination, any more than other forms of denial of human rights, would have become the international issue it is today, but for the fact that it has become so intimately identified with the issue of colonialism. The overwhelming majority of Afro-Asian countries has never doubted that *apartheid* was only an extreme manifestation of colonialist policy and that the struggle against South Africa's racial policies was but part of the struggle against colonialism. Ambassador Dosumo Johnson of Liberia spoke for that majority, when he classed South Africa among the remaining European colonial territories on the African continent and declared that as such, it was subject to the special Charter provisions which governed all other colonial territories. In 1963, he told the Special Political Committee of the eighteenth General Assembly that,

> A policy founded on racial discrimination and wanton brutality ... cannot be regarded as a domestic matter within the meaning of Article 2(7) of the Charter. That provision has never been regarded as applying to colonial territories which all the signatories of the Charter had undertaken to emancipate and liberate. When the Charter was signed, all the countries of Africa, except Liberia and Ethiopia, had been recognized as colonies of European countries ...[16]

Nor have the manifold other activities of the United Nations in the field of human rights,[17] whether of a hortatory, expository or educational character, reached down into the wellsprings of man's creative instincts to seed the imagination of people and to catapult the idea of international concern with human rights to a fundamental design for the regeneration of the world. These activities have never been energized and directed by firm and purposeful hands. Improvisation, rather than deliberate purpose, has characterized the efforts of the United Nations to further the cause of human rights.[18] These have been too amorphous to produce an impact on practical statesmanship and too leaderless to stand in the center of international debate and discussion. It is difficult to pick one's way through the myth, fancy and sentimentality which have come to surround the United Nations human rights program. Never the focus of United Nations vision, the fundamental questions of human rights and fundamental freedoms have been increasingly removed from the mainstream of United Nations and world interests.

No reliable standards, criteria and techniques exist to enable us to evaluate the broader aspects of the United Nations' concern with human rights and its impact on national and international thought and action. The facts do not speak for themselves. In the first place, not all the facts are available or accessible. But more importantly, there is no authoritative body of knowledge and analysis to guide us through the vast labyrinth of endlessly variable and complex factors that come into play.[19] After all, international concern with human rights is still new to the world of both politics and scholarship. Still, it is by no means a matter of mere interpretation, conjecture or belief to say that, except for its policies and actions in the case of *apartheid* which, because of the extraordinary and exceptional nature of the circumstances surrounding it cannot be invoked as an illustration, the concern of the United Nations with human rights has lacked a central idea and purpose capable of developing its own motive power and moving into the minds of men. It poses no implacable, relentless and inescapable challenge, nor does it chart principles of right public policy. In brief, it lacks that purposefulness and dynamism which only a doctrine or movement looking to the future can impart.

The voluminous records concerning the question of human rights in the United Nations yield no theory of such rights as a scheme of national and international reconstruction, or their conceptualization as potentially the most potent single instrument for combating the many evils which plague the world and for opposing a national and international order of things born out of injustice and inequity, of selfish abuse of power and wealth, of arbitrariness and indifference, and of all the deliberate and accidental restrictions on the natural progress of human society. Neither as a human obligation, nor as an act of far-seeing self-interest has international concern with human rights been conceived as an idea capable of grasping the hardest political nettles to overcome the massive obstacles to international cooperation which lie deeply embedded in the myths and realities of the nation-state. There is little in the records to indicate that a serious effort has been made to relate such concern to the basic political, military, economic, social and cultural issues of the time. Because of that, international concern with the rights and freedoms of man has not only failed to become the distinctive political creed of the century, but it has been reduced to a marginal interest tangential to the main purposes of the United Nations and outside the mainstream of international activity.

In the absence of a central and centralizing idea and purpose, irrelevant criteria have often been used to assess timeless themes, and principles of broad dimensions have been tied to matters of passing interest. A careful examination of the origin and development of the different projects in the field of human rights undertaken by the United Nations over the past twenty years shows that these were rarely initiated in response to pragmatic needs or as parts of a larger design for the advancement of human rights and basic liberties. For the most part, they originated in circumstances and conditions extraneous to the subject of human rights or were the products of pure chance and accident. With few exceptions, they all betray the tedium of organizational routine. Only on rare occasions has a project been inspired by a conception of human rights that has a reality of its own striving for existence. Such, for example, was the decision taken in 1947 by the Commission on Human Rights to write an international bill of human rights to include a declaration, a convention and measures of implementation or enforcement.

For an illustration, we may turn to the system of periodic reports, which was introduced more than a decade ago and has since become a major item in the United Nations human rights program. This system was established on August 1, 1956, and, as amended in 1962, calls for the submission by governments of reports on developments and progress achieved in the field of human rights and on measures taken to safeguard human liberties in their territories, within a continuing three-year cycle covering all the rights and freedoms enumerated in the Universal Declaration of Human Rights. The declared purpose of these reports is to enable the Commission on Human Rights to learn the "results obtained and the difficulties encountered in their work for the observance of, and respect for, human rights and fundamental freedoms throughout the world," and to provide a basis for making "such comments and recomendations of an objective and general character in accordance with the United Nations Charter" as the Commission may deem appropriate.[20]

Now, it was not the need to encounter and respond to the multiple aspects of human rights that gave birth to the system of periodic reports. The idea originated with the United States. It was part of a three-point program of education, persuasion and example the United States Delegation in 1953 proposed to the United Nations, to take the place of the latter's program of advancing human rights by means of treaties and other international binding instruments which, because of certain purely domestic political reasons, the United States found convenient to reject. The program was reluctantly adopted, with the understanding that it would, at best, be supplementary to the international covenants on human rights then in preparation. Nevertheless, it did not take long before the periodic reports system evolved into an institution beyond contest and became virtually an end in itself. Member States seized upon it as a breakthrough of the barrier of conventionality, without really touching the center of things. The periodic reports provided a convenient predicate to engage the moralism of nations in fashionable confrontation.

If the assumption was that the periodic reports system would give events a frame and that the information received would yield rich insights and conclusions, it has long since been con-

troverted by the facts. Not only have governments been unwilling
and unable to escape the bias of their own perspectives, but the
information they have been furnishing can hardly be said to
provide an expanding vision of reality. In the first place, there
are fixed national habits of thought that assign different values
to the same fact or set of facts. Secondly, the separate facts do
not add up to make a whole, if for no other reason than that
they are rarely representative samples of the total situation they
attempt to describe. The irrelevancies contained in the reports
are only exceeded by their omissions. Besides, the reports necessarily lag from one to three or more years behind the fast-changing shape of political, military and other events and are in a
constant race against time itself. Ten years of periodic reports
have not given us a settled vision of the world scene of human
rights.[21]

Often, private or public effort is important as much for what
it attempts as for what it achieves. All information may not
provide a solution to immediate problems, but it serves the purpose if it provides an intellectual and historical framework in
which the problems can be assigned their place and value. If the
information contained in the periodic reports does not provide the
insights needed to illuminate the human rights situation in the
world, it is also because of the fact that the United Nations
organs immediately concerned have neither the authority nor
the organizational and technical capacity to look behind the deceiving façade, to probe beneath the surface, and to concern
themselves with the sociology of the events as well as with
their politics. In their efforts to evade responsibility for critical
judgement these organs, in the first place the Commission on
Human Rights, have aimed at an objectivity which robs their
assessment of the facts of all meaning. In their concern not to
tresspass upon the domestic jurisdiction of States, they cannot
go beyond such broad generalizations as to deprive them of all
relevance. For example, the Commission's judgement on the state
of political and civil rights in the world in the two-and-a-half
years beginning January 1, 1963, and ending June 30, 1965, is
contained in the following paragraph in a rather lengthy resolution it adopted at its twenty-second session in the spring of 1966:

...the information received covering the period under review indicates limited but significant progress in some countries in the field of civil and political rights, especially in dealing with racial discrimination and religious intolerance, in the enjoyment of the rights to vote, in the administration of justice and in equal rights for men and women.[22]

At its twenty-third session in March, 1967, the Commission on Human Rights confirmed these trends and passed on to comment on the state of economic, social and cultural rights in the world during approximately the same period, as follows:

...the reports on economic, social and cultural rights reveal the following trends as of special importance and common interest:

(a) the concern of member States to implement human rights according to standards established in United Nations instruments;

(b) the constructive efforts in law and practice in States with varying systems of government and at different stages of development to promote the right of education, including the interest shown in the question of adult education, the right to social security, the rights of the child and the family, including the provision of special care and assistance for motherhood and childhood, the right to work and the right to an adequate standard of living;

(c) the attempts by various States to overcome difficulties with respect to the implementation of economic, social and cultural rights, and, notably, the concern to make available remedies for the violation of these rights.[23]

No one will dispute that the Commission's comments and observations are, indeed, of an objective and general character, although some may wonder how these conclusions were arrived at on the basis of the information received. Its judgement of March, 1966, on the state of political and civil rights was based on reports received from twenty-five governments, or about one fifth the United Nations membership, and varying in length and contents. The reporting States were Denmark, Finland,

France, Italy, Norway, Poland, San Marino and the United
Kingdom; Argentina, Canada, Costa Rica, Cuba, El Salvador,
Jamaica and the United States of America; China (Formosa),
Laos, Pakistan; Central African Republic, Liberia, Nigeria,
United Arab Republic, Upper Volta and Zambia, as well as the
Maldive Islands.[24] The reports on economic, social and cultural
rights came from twenty-six governments, as follows: Austria,
Byelorussian SSR, Denmark, Federal Republic of Germany,
Finland, Italy, Netherlands, Poland, Rumania, Ukrainian SSR;
Union of Socialist Soviet Republics, United Kingdom and Yugo-
slavia; Cambodia, India, Israel, Japan, Kuwait, Nepal; Central
African Republic, Republic of the Congo (Brazzaville), Ghana,
Malagasy Republic and United Arab Republic, and New Zealand
and the United States of America.[25] Reports were also received
from the International Labor Organization, UNESCO and the
World Health Organization and from a number of non-govern-
mental organizations in consultative status. Taken together, the
periodic reports are too fragmented, quantitatively as well as
qualitatively, to make for creative synthesis. When assembled,
they do not demonstrate a consistency of theme, and when
analyzed, they present a series of unrelated images. Like a writer
who attempts an historical synthesis, the Commission on Human
Rights has been unable to rise much above its sources.

What is true of the periodic reports system is largely true
also of the series of studies in discrimination begun in 1953 by
the Sub-Commission on Prevention of Discrimination and Protection of Minorities, except that these may have an existence of
their own. As in the case of the periodic reports, the idea of
such studies arose not in response to the exigencies of the day,
nor as part of a larger program for the achievement of specific
ends. It made little sense to engage in studies of discrimination,
when governments denied human rights indiscriminately; and
to analyze particular aspects of human rights for their own sake
before viewing them as a whole appeared highly illogical. The
study program was contrived to ensure the survival of the Sub-
Commission, whose continuance was widely questioned. When it
became clear that the United Nations was averse to dealing with
questions pertaining to minorities, there was little for the Sub-
Commission left to do. By separating prevention of discrimination
from protection of minorities and assigning them distinct func-

tions, it was possible, without probing the theory for error, to fit the Sub-Commission's work into the United Nations human rights program, which was beginning to emerge at the time and which aimed broadly at changing the minds and attitudes of men.[26]

Similarly, the choice of subject matter for the studies was determined not in the order of urgency, magnitude or importance, but by the degree in which it was susceptible to governmental objection and criticism. For example, the Sub-Commission's first study concerned discrimination in the field of education. Certainly, the real problem in education at the time was not discrimination, but illiteracy and the inability of governments, especially in the developing areas of the world, to cope with it unaided. This problem was foremost on the agenda of UNESCO, which cooperated in the preparation of the study, and has only grown more serious with the passage of time. Governments risked little in approving the study and cooperating with its author in supplying information. The same can be said of the second in the series of studies, that of discrimination in employment and occupation prepared by the International Labor Organization.

Perhaps the most telling comment was made by Arcot Khrishnaswami, the author of the Sub-Commission's study on discrimination in the matter of religious rights and practices completed in 1959, as follows:

> The need for exercising continuing vigilance with respect to enjoyment of the right to freedom of thought, conscience and religion may not be fully grasped if one considers only the present situation. Let it be stressed again that the most acute forms of discrimination in this field are seldom in evidence in our day. But if one recalls the long history of the struggle to achieve freedom of thought, conscience and religion in different parts of the world, it will be realized that the march toward progress has never been straight. Bearing this in mind, the framers of the Charter declared that one of the purposes of the United Nations is "to achieve international cooperation... in promoting and encouraging respect for human rights and fundamental freedoms for all." So the championship of human freedom must be continuous, and one should never consider that the struggle is over or that victory has been achieved.[27]

In sum, the root cause of the hollowness of much of the United Nations human rights program lies, in the first place, in its detachment from practically everything that is real, vital and relevant. Its encounter with reality is mute. The program gives hardly a sense of connection with the world of action or achievement, and it is incapable of creating credible situations infused with the power of movement and progress. Because it skirmishes neither with wind nor waves, the program is sadly in eclipse. Except for racial discrimination embodied in *apartheid*, which, because of the extraordinary circumstances surrounding it is *sui generis* and cannot, therefore, be regarded as representative, the work of the United Nations in the field of human rights has remained anchored to a text, rather than to the living world. It is not a program that compels the United Nations to use its greatest strength.

Second, there is no singular aim or purpose toward which the disparate activities ascend. Neither is there a central idea to give each successive effort a sense of renewal and growth. We look in vain for an inclusive perspective which might embrace the whole, and we miss the sequential patterns which might serve as a guide. The activities lack a sense of interrelatedness and it is difficult to fit them into a clear and rational pattern. There is no way of studying the whole and the functioning of its parts in relation to objectives.

Third, international human rights is still waiting for its theoritician to systematize the thoughts and speculations on the subject and to define desirable goals. Intelligent truisms do not necessarily add up to a theory. No one has yet arisen to draw together into a positive synthesis the facts and fancies which emerge daily from events of bewildering complexity and to carry on an authentic debate. International concern with human rights is still very much a theme begging for a writer. And the scholar has not yet appeared to redress the distortions through a calm and systematic application of facts, to ground abstractions in the specific, and to define the limits of discourse. In the absence of a definite body of doctrine, as well as of deeply rooted convictions, international human rights have been dealt with on the basis of the shifts and vagaries of daily affairs and of evocations of daily events. There is a great need for technical resources and ability to channel the facts to greater effect. Human rights as a matter of international concern is an untrodden area of systematic research. But still a greater need is for superlative virtuosity to deal with international human rights in their multiple human dimensions.

In fact, the subject of international human rights has almost from the very beginning been dominated by the politician, who has been the true midwife of virtually all innovation in this field. But as politicians, they have inevitably followed the political standards set in the political arena, where the national interest and national traditions are the limiting conditions of diplomatic flexibility. They have put a premium on prudence, gradualism, continuity and incremental improvement when only challenge, criticism, innovation and protest could instill conviction into the popular mind. No wonder that the ideals which were born out of the travail of World War II turned to derision. The United Nations human rights program has not succeeded in inspiring and implementing significant innovation.

Finally, the world cannot be expected to become transfixed by a program which is an uncertain and unpersuasive guide to action. The work of the United Nations in the field of human rights has been oriented toward education and persuasion, rather than toward effective change in all realms of life and society. The tenor and tone were set with unchallenged authority by the Universal Declaration of Human Rights, which laid great stress on the power of teaching and education to influence the course of events. Like the philosophers of the Enlightenment, the architects of the United Nations human rights program have sought to change men's attitudes of mind without touching the political, social and economic power structure of which they are a part. But, just as the failure of the philosophers of the eighteenth century to consider the consequences of their ideas in terms of fundamental aspects of society weakened their ultimate effectiveness, so the failure of the program of the United Nations to promote human rights and fundamental freedoms for all to strike out into the maelstrom of international politics has deprived it of the force and authority equal to the demands of the problem. This program cannot be energized with adventitious aids, nor substituted for the moral dimensions of action. Even the most compelling ideas and ideals cannot remain sublimely indifferent to the possibility of failure. They must be clothed with the substance of power lest they drift toward an inconclusive anti-climax. Unless the United Nations becomes sensitive to the very possibilities for which it is searching, it will be condemned to spin out the implications of its own misconceptions. The opportunity and occasion are at hand. They have been provided by the General Assembly in 1966, when it adopted the International Covenants on Human Rights and agreed on international machinery for their enforcement.

CHAPTER VII

International Protection
of Human Rights

The adoption by the General Assembly of the Covenant on Economic, Social and Cultural Rights, the Covenant on Political and Civil Rights, and the Optional Protocol to the Covenant on Political and Civil Rights,[1] marks the beginning of a long process of investiture of a great idea with the substance of power capable of producing effective change in all realms of personal, national and international life. These international treaties are binding commitments of states toward their own citizens, toward one another, and toward the community of nations to ensure, observe and safeguard the rights and freedoms which are today almost universally acknowledged as being emanations of the human personality. By these multilateral legal instruments, governments undertake to hold themselves accountable, at home and abroad, for the way they honor their commitments. And by the Optional Protocol, they affirm the right of the individual to petition the international community for redress of wrongs at the hand of governments in violation of these commitments. Together the three instruments, for all their serious failings and omissions, provide the foundation for transforming an international ethic into norms of political action of such vast dimensions that they can be cast only in the broad perspective of history.[2]

Virtually all efforts of the United Nations in the area of human rights have been largely in the nature of a catharsis. Rarely has the world organization dealt with human rights problems in the concrete or tried to intervene in specific situations to avert injustice and to right a wrong. Long ago the United Nations proclaimed its own helplessness to come to the defense of the rights and liberties of man when, in January, 1947, the Com-

101

mission on Human Rights ruled that it had no authority to take action in the face of violation of human rights, no matter how grave.[3] There is no way in which the United Nations can intervene constructively in defense of human rights. It cannot call governments to account for their policies and actions at home without giving offense to their deepest sensibilities, nor summon them to abide by their responsibilities under the Charter without inviting political disputes. It cannot suggest specific remedial measures to specific situations without trespassing upon the domestic jurisdictions of states, nor make proposals to fit particular circumstances without violating the principle of their sovereign equality. As a rule, the United Nations has avoided identifying human rights situations which might embarass Member States and has imparted to its studies, inquiries and proposals a universality which deprived them of all corporeality.[4]

The Universal Declaration of Human Rights, which since its adoption in December, 1948, has been the bedrock of all United Nations activities in the area of human rights, is geared more than anything else to exegesis and commentary. Its emphasis is on teaching and education as the primary means of advancing the cause of human rights, and it calls neither for profound conviction, nor for total commitment, let alone for consistent action. Without these, the Declaration could never go far beyond its own brief to become a rallying point for action. Moreover, unlike the great documents of human freedom of the past, which were born amid strife and revolution, the Universal Declaration emerged from the relative calm of the conference table in a spirit of compromise and mutual accommodation. It was thus deprived from the very beginning of the spiritual intensity and collectedness needed to command the deeds of man. Casual assent entails no risk and demands no sacrifice. Besides, like a generalized belief which kills every definite and concrete conviction, the Universal Declaration never acquired specific referents in time and space to become a concrete blueprint for social and political regeneration. This great and clear universal statement of the rights and liberties of man has been abused as a platform for periodic and ritual rehearsals of commonplaces.

What distinguishes the Covenants on Human Rights and the Optional Protocol is that they convey the idea of movement and affirmative action. They are indispensable as a framework for the organization of international effort in the field of human rights and for the implementation of agreed objectives. Collective action, especially in an area that involves the delicate balancing of national and international competence, cannot be achieved at this juncture of history without formal commitments by way of international treaties. There was no other way in which the United Nations could make the transition from promotion to protection of human rights, with all that it implies, except by reference to specific international legal obligations. For all the impressive growth during the last twenty years in the number of international, regional and sub-regional instruments, procedures and institutions for the safeguarding of human rights, the development of an international law of human rights still depends wholly on the broad acceptance of the international human rights covenants. It cannot be derived from precedent nor deduced from practice at the regional or international levels.[5]

By transforming international concern with human rights from a political principle into legally binding international obligations, the Covenants have laid the groundwork for the erection of international institutions and procedures to give concrete expression to these obligations. Without institutions functioning continuously in their service, even the most solemn obligations tend to sink to the level of pious benevolence. These institutions are barely indicated in the Covenants, but the principle is well established. The most important institution and procedure are without doubt those established in the Optional Protocol to the Covenant on Political and Civil Rights, pertaining to the right of the individual to appeal to the international community in case of violation of his covenanted rights and freedoms. It is this right that more than anything else will breathe life into the Covenants and help them evolve into instruments for the creation of a new international public order.[6] The Optional Protocol is the first important step toward the emancipation of the individual from the restraints of nationality and his entry into the international community in his own right as a human person, as an object and subject of international concern. Just as the freedom of the citizen is the best safeguard internally against the excesses of nationalism and the propensity of the state to achieve its ends by all means at its disposal, whether noble or ignoble, so the emancipation of the human person from the shackles of nationality is indispensable to the reconstruction of international relations on just and humane foundations.

What lends the Covenants their intrinsic importance is that
they compel a redefinition of traditional thinking. The signature
and ratification of international treaties are not benevolent acts
of states concerned with the welfare of others. They are internationally binding agreements which impinge upon the most delicate
and most sensitive aspects of national life. Indeed, they are the
very incarnation of the most revolutionary idea of social reconstruction that has universal application. Were, for example, the
rights and freedoms set forth in the Covenants fully secured and
honored the world over tomorrow, all mankind would at long last
walk triumphantly through the gates of hope and opportunity
into a freer, brighter and more blissful condition. Were the claims
of the individual on the international community to redress the
wrongs committed against him by his own or other governments
universally sustained, it would herald the dawn of a new form
of international relations. In these circumstances, governments
cannot be expected to enter into treaties of this kind without
a backward glance of appraisal and without a sense of history on
the march. They will ask questions and challenge hypotheses
before they cross the philosophical divide and seek not only
popular support, but overwhelming assent, before they decide to
cross the fateful watershed. In the process, comfortable old prejudices are bound to give way to a fresh sense of purpose and
dedication and traditional ideas yield to the demands of the times.
This is part of every process of constructive change and it cannot
be leaped over without inflicting great devastation on the objectives sought. The final outcome is assured, for what the Covenants and the Optional Protocol stand for is coming in on a tide
that cannot be stopped from reaching the shore.

It is a rare idea that responds to all the basic needs of the
age. It is a still rarer program that embodies in a workable
equation all the important political, economic, social, cultural, as
well as moral, forces involved. Such is the idea of international
concern with human rights and fundamental freedoms. It not
only responds profoundly to the needs of the times, but defines a
program for delivering on the abundant promises of science and
technology of a radical improvement in the material and moral
conditions of peoples everywhere. "As the Charter proclaims,"
said the President of the Twentieth General Assembly of the
United Nations, Amintore Fanfani of Italy, in his United Nations
Day Message in October, 1965,

One of the basic tenets of the Organization is the determination of the peoples of the United Nations to reaffirm faith 'in the dignity and worth of the human person.' This fundamental proposition is the corner-stone of all the other purposes and aims of the Organization. And the fact is that all the very diverse and useful efforts of the United Nations to promote the maintenance of international peace, disarmament, the control of nuclear energy, the respect of international treaties, the establishment of the rule of law, social progress and technical and economic development are only so many ways and means of affirming and defending 'the dignity and worth of the human person.' The technical advances of the twentieth century, the aspirations of the masses, the need for integration have linked the destiny of each nation to that of all others. Today mankind is witnessing the dawn of a unity, a unity which was inconceivable for it in the past because never before did it have either the desire or the means to attain it. Every people must strive to make this unity a unity in life; otherwise it may well become a unity in death. Faith in and defence of 'the dignity and worth of the human person'; that is the corner-stone of our Organization. These words in the Charter point the way to the international community, for they define everything that the United Nations hopes to achieve, everything it intends to fulfil...[7]

In the same vein, Secretary General U Thant, in his Human Rights Day Message on December 10, 1965, answering the rhetorical question why the Universal Declaration of Human Rights was singled out for attention second only to that given to the United Nations Charter, said:

The answer, I believe, is that we need constantly to remind ourselves that the United Nations is firmly committed to the proposition that the eventual objective of all its functions and activities is the well-being of individual men and women—the freedom and opportunity to find their worth as human beings, whatever their race, language, religion or political belief. This is part of the fundamental philosophy of the United Nations, and it is natural to find

it spelled out in the Declaration. The very objective of the
maintenance of international peace and security is directly
linked to the assurance of respect for human rights and
fundamental freedoms ... The Universal Declaration ... is,
like the Charter, the firm base from which specific action
by the United Nations, by Governments and by mankind
at large must proceed.[8]

The ultimate logic of this proposition is to make the fullfilment
of the Covenants on Human Rights the direct, immediate and all-
embracing aim of the United Nations and its principal preoccupation. This is by no means stretching future hopes at the expense
of present realities. These instruments of universal validity rise
above principles and address themselves to an expanding vision
of reality. The fundamental reality is that the tide of events flows
ever stronger against the probability within the traditional
framework of international relations and international institutions of social reform and innovation in a measure and on a scale
large enough and deep enough to thwart the consequences of the
sins of commission and omission of this and preceding generations. New patterns of international institutions and relations are
needed for a new symbiosis and great redemptive efforts to rescue
idealism lost in the corruption of power. There is no other idea
than international concern with human rights as set forth in
the Covenants that can bring forth a vision of cosmic sweep to
confront a world hungry for answers to its perplexing problems.

In an age, for example, when government can no longer guarantee the survival of the species, the right to life, the first of the
human rights and fundamental freedoms of man, must be anchored
in more solid foundations than the traditional trappings of national security. When the modern weapons of war can meet no
national obligation nor preserve the national interest, the power
of the state is no longer the ultimate shield. More than palliatives
and inconclusive measures, which characterize practically all
bilateral and multi-lateral assistance programs in the economic
and social fields, are required to overcome the accumulated and
intricately interrelated miseries and problems of the vast masses
of the world's peoples. To provide a richer material existence
and a spiritually and politically free society for the whole of the
human race, means to establish a new relationship between the

individual and international institutions and to transform the community of nations into an orderly society. No creative action toward universal peace and prosperity is possible without extracting the last ounce of idealism and humanitarianism from all international cooperative effort and without bringing to bear upon the urgent needs of the world the zeal, the dedication, the interest and the devotion which can be lavished only on authentic humanity. They cannot be brought to bear upon the impersonal state or government, nor can they spring from them. No state is capable of taking an enlightened view of its own society, let alone of the world, to reach out for goals which perceive the total and varied requirements of the whole of man. No government can transcend the historical arena for a more universal commitment, to form bonds between peoples that are not conditional on mere expediency, to keep pace with man's accelerating evolution and society's accelerating change, and to fashion the tools to cope with this change. For, however much states might try to take a long-range view even of their own national interests, they invariably end up by looking to the immediate political and strategic interests to which particular norms would apply and act accordingly. The instances are rare when those who represent their countries can set aside their national interests and rise above them to redress the distortions that burden international relations.

In his discourse at the opening of the second session of Ecumenical Council Vatican II on September 29, 1963, Pope Paul VI said:

> Take courage, rulers of nations, today you can give to your peoples many good things necessary for their life, bread, education, work, order, the dignity of free and peaceful citizens, provided only you know who man is ...[9]

It is precisely the need to provide a framework of international relations in terms of honest human values that make the Covenants so eminently relevant to our day and age. They not only provide the depth of inspiration to all contemporary international cooperative efforts to elevate the material condition of man and to promote his social and spiritual welfare. They are the vehicle through which the great social ideas and ideals can express themselves forcefully in international relations and become far and away the most potent instrument of peaceful change. International cooperation for the express purpose of redeeming the commitments of the Covenants brings such an unsurpassed vision and a boundless humaneness to international relations as to constitute a fundamental design for a renewed humanity. It brings within the orbit of international concern practically all the cares and preoccupations of men everywhere and provides firm guidance and an abiding state for all who may be summoned to the task of reconstruction of the traditional form of international relations. For, if internationalism is to become more than a stirring idea and international solidarity more than an instructed desire, it must have the background of a broad common denominator of aims and aspirations shared by all men and international institutions geared to give working life to their common intent. These are handsomely provided by the institutionalization of international concern with human rights into a system within which the realization of abundance, equality, justice and freedom for all will take place.

Inspired and informed by a philosophy of human rights that projects a multi-dimensional program for dealing with the great problems of the human condition, the Covenant on Economic, Social and Cultural Rights, for example, constitutes a chart for wise pioneering in an area where the discipline imposed by the magnitude of the task of meeting the essential needs of man has been almost wholly lacking. Thus Article 11 provides that:

1. The States Parties to the present Covenant recognize the right of everyone to an adequate standard of living for himself and his family, including adequate food, clothing and housing and to the continuous improvement of living conditions. The States Parties shall take appropriate steps to ensure the realization of this right, recognizing to this effect the essential importance of international cooperation based on free consent.

2. The States Parties to the present Covenant, recognizing the fundamental right of everyone to be free from hunger, shall take, individually and through international cooperation, the measures, including specific programmes, which are needed:

(a) To improve methods of production, conservation and distribution of food by making full use of technical and scientific knowledge, by disseminating knowledge of the principles of nutrition and by developing or reforming agrarian systems in such a way as to achieve the most efficient development and utilization of natural resources; and

(b) Take into account the problems of both food-importing and food-exporting countries, to ensure an equitable distribution of world food supplies in relation to need.

This Article sets a background for international cooperation so surely as to herald events by preparing them. It argues from the realities of the present in favor of common action across frontiers of special interest to provide optimum conditions for human existence without the intrusion of national diversions and conflicting aims and purposes. When the destiny of the human person, in the concrete is the deliberate concern of the international community, the dichotomy between national self-interest and the internationalist ideal becomes too much of an anachronism to fit into a situation where society is galvanized to harness the energy of nations for the benefit of all. International affairs, which often are a fabric without much of a pattern, fall in these circumstances into a logical design. And international cooperation itself, which so far has failed to resolve the tensions and conflicts between universal values and the solution of immediate problems, finds a firm moral and practical footing from which to arbitrate the divergent interests which plague the world.

Each of the rights and freedoms in the Covenant on Economic, Social and Cultural Rights, as well as in the Covenant on Political and Civil Rights, not only postulates cooperation among peoples and nations, but is capable of providing the emotional drive behind the logic of the international ideal. Each of these rights and freedoms expresses notions and ideas of eternal relevance and validity, and each of them dictates a definite code of national and international conduct and practice. We have already noted that the right to life, liberty and security of person, for example, will remain an unfulfilled promise so long as it is no guarantee against death and violence resulting from war and so long as it does not vouchsafe that freedom and security which only peace can make possible. No state is any longer in a position to guarantee to its citizens freedom from war, nor secure to them the blessings of permanent peace. Such a guarantee can come only from an international community capable of enforcing its will against a recalcitrant state. But on this point, virtually all powers in the world have made the most serious reservations and committed themselves to a line of intransigence that they are unable to make the smallest concession to common sense. Thus, all debate on the subject of war and peace held within the context of traditional international relations is bound to remain sterile, for the reason that it cannot proceed to a logical conclusion without prior agreement on a conception of international organization which would make such a debate irrelevant.

On the other hand, an international policy directed immediately toward enforcing the right of everyone to life, liberty and security of person is in itself a decisive factor in opposing a national and international order of things in which there is place for war. Such a policy substitutes for the blind political and strategic forces the capacity and demands of human intelligence as the determining factors and considerations of international relations. If this be so, the international community must establish the rights and freedoms of man as an obligatory pattern of thought and as the criterion for essaying the goals and policies of governments. It must decide finally and irrevocably to take the human person and his rights and freedoms under its direct protective shield, or the world cannot win the struggle between international cooperation and competitive anarchy.

This decision will be extorted from a reluctant world, to paraphrase John Quincy Adams' reference to the adoption of the Constitution of the United States, by the grinding necessity of the times and its problems. As we shall see in the pages that follow, there are certain fundamental and insistent problems that are intensely human and personal, and they cannot be grasped, let alone resolved, without a similarly intense feeling for the full range of human aspirations. They demand an all-humanitarian commitment and international solidarity, which the traditional arsenal of diplomacy cannot supply. Such a problem, for example, is the so-called "population explosion" and the reduction of society to an undifferentiated mass and the murderous assault on the human personality under the many pressures of a bleak and depersonalized world. In this world of shattered and shifting values, the concept of the dignity and worth of the human person, without which the striving to raise man from the servilities of the age and to aid the individual toward the fruition of his natural talents and creative abilities makes little sense, is in mortal danger of becoming lost in the wake of the unprecedented rise in the world's population. Unless a premium is placed on human life and on the unique role of the human individual on earth, man will lose all his options and all humanity will become a desperate mass struggling forever in a vast and timeless wasteland.

Such, too, is the problem of the hundreds of millions of people around the world who form minorities of one kind or another and whose values, qualities and aspirations are often in conflict with the values and aspirations of the majorities which surround them. Frequently, this conflict is exacerbated by divisions along race and color lines, with all their attendant consequences. Finally, there is the problem of the division of the world into rich and poor—a breach which nothing short of the creation of a welfare world can heal.

CHAPTER VIII

The Pressure of Numbers: Impact of the Population Growth

Along with the problem of war and peace, whose urgency is emphasized by the threat of modern arms to the very survival of the human race, the population explosion has emerged as the dominant issue today and in the years to come. The unprecedented proliferation of the human species is a fact which is central to the fate of man. Already its concentrated impact in many parts of the world is an inexorable factor that severely limits all efforts to remove the obviously corrupting features from the environment in which the human person grows to maturity. Its ultimate consequences cannot but be the corruption of the whole of the human race and the dissolution of civilized existence.

Like war and peace, the problem of population explosion, too, cannot wait for the dialectic process to work out its benevolent inevitabilities. The pressure of numbers outpaces the growth of resources essential to their existence. This is a fact which even the prodigious inventive genius of man may not be able to reverse. To rely upon scientific discovery to redress the balance, is to set no bounds to the utilization of the forces of nature. Such optimism may accord with the hopefulness about the eternal promise of tomorrow. It offers no sure dawning signs of a rising sun behind the distant horizon to light the path for the coming generations.[1] Science advances by the slow attrition of ignorance and by the constant recognition of its uncertainties. It moves unevenly over longer or shorter periods of time from puzzled observation, through inspired guesswork to established conclusions. Besides, the world of man—his goals and aspirations and his motivations and conflicts—may remain forever beyond the reach of the scientific methods applicable to the physical world. The conditions of man's existence are no less important than his existence itself.[2]

Overpopulation is a rapidly growing environmental problem which today is most acute in the areas of the lowest subsistence levels in Asia, Africa and Latin America. In these areas, the grim struggle between population and subsistence is a stark reality.[3] In other areas of the world, it is barely perceptible. This is especially the case in the West, where technological advances in agriculture have increased crop yields at a faster rate than the growth of population. But sooner or later, the ghost of Malthus and the dismal spectre of population outrunning the supply of food will stalk across the face of the earth.[4] At the present rate of increase, the global population is expected to reach six billion by the year 2000 and the staggering figure of twenty-five billion by 2070.[5] Experts estimate that world food supplies must treble by the turn of the century, or the world will go hungry.[6] What will happen afterwards, few venture to predict. There is a growing consensus that unless effective limits are set on the ratio of reproduction of the human species, civilization will perish in a savage battle for survival.

The population explosion is much more than a problem of Malthusian ratio. Even if science could guarantee victory in the battle against hunger, at least in the foreseeable future, it will in no way solve this most overwhelming of all human dilemmas. Human life has meaning when it is internally coherent and externally reasonable. The pressure of numbers is bound to destroy the authenticity of man and topple him from the commanding heights of biological existence. When the virtue of man's uniqueness is dissolved in the teeming multitude and the sacred precinct of human life is invaded by doubts and misgivings, there is no place for human dignity and worth. A rising population pressing against the resources and services that make for civilized existence is as perilous as hunger. The population growth, we are told, is out of proportion to present and prospective rates of increase in economic development and imposes a heavy burden on all efforts to improve human welfare. In practically all the developing countries the need to keep pace with the population growth stands like a granite rock in the way of increasing per capita productivity and income. The slow rate of growth of national incomes, inadequacy of food supplies, and pressure of population are the three critical vacuums in the economic life of these countries, which are being filled by swelling numbers of "superfluous" men, women and children. Thus, for example,

> One finds in all of the Latin American countries a large lower stratum in the population that has not benefited from economic progress up to the present and is suffering from multiple deficiencies; lack of employment at wages permitting a tolerable level of living; lack of education and of skills and working habits that might help it obtain such employment; levels of housing, sanitation, and diet that reduce working capacity; unstable family life contributing and fostered by the other deficiencies. The more rapid the population growth and the accompanying redistribution of population, the greater the probability that this stratum will persist and grow in numbers despite industrialization, rising *per capita* incomes, and improving conditions for the remainder of the people. Such groups, both urban and rural, have persisted even in countries at the highest levels of development, and the increasing efficiency of industry and agriculture, with a stationary or declining demand for unskilled labour, decreases their opportunities for steady employment.[7]

Much the same can be said of the underdeveloped countries in other regions of the world, where the problem of unemployment and under-employment is becoming ever more acute as a result of the fast increase in population and labor force as compared with the slow rate of industrial development. While each major region undoubtedly presents a bewildering variety of local situations and problems, they all share certain basic traits which give rise to generalized poverty—diminishing opportunities for larger numbers. Almost all participants at the first Asian Population Conference in New Delhi, India, in December, 1963, agreed on the magnitude of the Asian population problem and on the threat it presented to the aspirations of the Asian people for economic and social advance. In a series of recommendations unanimously adopted at the close of the Conference, the point was stressed

that while it was for each Government to decide upon the kind
of population policy it wished to pursue, the policies they adopted
and the actions they took to deal with population problems were
of common concern to all Asian countries and that they all had
a stake in the success of efforts to give all the peoples dwelling
in them an opportunity for a more wholesome and humane existence.[8]

In the developed countries, the Greek theory of tragic irony is
being daily confirmed as swaths of poverty cut through areas of
plenty. Here man is unequally pitted against his own ingenuity
and seems to be unable to meet the requirements of fast-changing
technology with adequate concern for human values. The increasing benefits of technological progress are accompanied by a
growing number of unemployed workers, whose displacement by
the machine is coming to be regarded as irrevocable. In his annual
Economic Message to Congress of January 20, 1964, President
Johnson stated that two million jobs were being wiped out every
year by the increasing productivity of American workers and
their equipment.[9] Even though the immediate impact of automation may not appear to differ radically from the impact of technological innovation in the past, its long-range consequences are
pregnant with grave peril to the future welfare of man. On
September 6, 1963, Professor Andrew Hacker of Cornell University, in a paper entitled *Towards a Corporate America* read at
the fifty-ninth annual meeting of the American Political Science
Association in New York, foresaw a revolutionary crisis arising
from the denial of a productive role to an ever-increasing portion of the population as a result of the steady progress of automation. In his summation, Professor Hacker said:

> It may well be that two Americas are emerging, one a
> society protected by the corporate umbrella and the other
> a society whose members have failed to affiliate themselves
> with the dominant institutions. What of the second Ameri-
> ca? In part it will consist of small-business men and other
> independent spirits who manage to do well without cor-
> porate attachments. But more importantly, it will be com-
> prised of the unemployed, the ill-educated and the entire
> residue of human beings who are not needed by the cor-
> porate machine . . .

Thus far corporate America has escaped open attack because the new technology is not yet at the point where its victims outnumber its beneficiaries. But technology advances according to rules of its own, and support for the machine will diminish as accelerated automation contracts the corporate constituency. In this event the other America, the society of losers, may grow in number and power with increasing rapidity. The revolution will not be a pleasant one...[10]

While the seriousness of the problem arising from automation seems for the present to be confined mainly to the United States, sooner or later it is bound to confront all industrialized countries. The combined effect of uninterrupted technological progress and human fecundity compels us to look through all the arguments to the realities beyond. These realities dim the bright hopes of science and technology which for so long have held undisputed sway. Everywhere ominous questions are raised whether man, like the hero in Greek tragedy, is not working his own doom. More than the euphoria of magnificent achievements wrought by the mind of man is necessary to redeem his future.

Unsatisfied needs, frustrated desires and disappointed hopes do not add up to a bright future of a world stirred to its depths by the revolution of rising expectations. Certainly it cannot be expected that exploding populations would be satisfied to remain within their own territorial confines and to rely solely upon their own meagre resources. The struggle for *Lebensraum* was not invented by the Germans, nor did it die with the defeat of the Nazis. The acquisitive drive for a better life may be enormously dynamic for expanding opportunities, but a frustrated urge for growth and development can be shattering in its consequences.

Those who are concerned with the quantity of life cannot but be also concerned with its quality. Even if science succeeded in creating a new abundance of material resources to sustain the ever-growing number of people in reasonable comfort, it could not halt the inevitable decline in the quality not only of man's environment, but of man himself. "Man is the only organism that lives by destroying the environment indispensable to his survival," ecologists tell us. They whose calling is to take all forms of organic life as their subject and to make the whole world their laboratory envision the collapse of all natural harmony. Others who are concerned with the totality of life on earth and who follow the cycle of the seasons fear for the future of the great, seething, turbulent mass of people lest they blight the land and still the song of the birds. Although human history is the story of man's divergence from the rest of nature and the ways in which he has increasingly modified his environment, great uncertainty hangs over the consequences of his interference with the natural order and over the chances of his survival in the synthetic world he is creating for himself. Man, individually, may rise above the limitations of his natural environment; as a species, he has still to learn how to live within the framework of nature. At the present exploding rate of population growth, little room will be left for any other environment on earth except the synthetic. Thus naturalist Joseph Wood Krutch observes:

> For a large part of the existing human race in the centers of civilization, contact with the natural world is tending to diminish almost to the vanishing point, while he has little experience with anything except bricks, steel and concrete on the one hand and mechanical contrivances on the other. As the cities spread and the country shrinks he is more and more imprisoned with his fellows in a world that has ceased to be even aware of many of the things of which he was once an intimate part...[11]

Man's assault on his physical environment under the pressure of rising numbers cannot long go unpunished. "We are beginning to destroy our resources of true enjoyment—spiritual, aesthetic, intellectual, emotional," laments Julian Huxley.[12] "An overpopulated earth will bring forth unintelligent generations because culture demands leisure and silence which have become lost qualities," concludes Andre Maurois.[13] It means an end to all exalted visions of the destiny of man and to all purposeful patterns of living. "When population presses severely upon existing sources or supply," we read,

> rigidities begin to develop in societal relations. Opportunities for alternative decisions regarding all kinds of activity become fewer, and persons of wealth and power are inclined to maintain their positions by various devices which impinge upon the freedom of others. More and more

persons of inferior status are required by the exigencies of existence to perform assigned tasks and to accept the notion that they were born to a specific station in life from which there is little chance of escape...[14]

Indeed, how is meaning and purpose to be given to the life of the individual lived in the midst of drab uniformity and unrelieved monotony that come with large numbers crowding each other? What is in store for man in a world increasingly more regulated, more regimented and more standardized in the interest of survival of society? The requirements of society's survival have rarely been co-extensive with the needs of the individual of which it is composed, even in the most favorable of human circumstances.[15] It will be infinitely less in an overpopulated world which offers little hope for self-fullfllment. "Fulfillment," says Julian Huxley,

is probably the embracing word; more fulfillment and less frustration for more human beings through greater realization of possibilities. We want more varied and fuller achievement in human societies. We want more variety and less drabness and monotony. We want more enjoyment and less suffering. We want more beauty and less ugliness. We want more adventure and disciplined freedom, as against routine and slavishness. We want more knowledge, more interest, more wonder, as against ignorance and apathy. We want more sense of participation in something enduring and in worthwhile projects, as against a series of rat races, whether with the Russians or our neighbors on the next street.

In the most general terms, we want more transcendence of self in the fruitful development of personality. We want a greater flowering of human dignity and significance, not only as against human degradation, but as against further self-imprisonment in the human ego, and against mere escapism.[16]

The crisis created by the enormous expansion of population and the resulting misery for uncounted millions of men, women and children has prompted a widespread reappraisal of traditional positions both as to methods of limiting birth and as to the formulation of public policy on the subject of birth control. The realization that mammoth populations and prodigious fecundity are not necessarily assets that assure national greatness, but rather formidable obstacles toward the achievement of that industrial status so crucial to twentieth century power, has compelled a number of governments in particularly acute areas of overpopulation to adopt policies designed either to protect existing living standards and ensure their continuous expansion, or to prevent their great masses of people from sinking deeper into hunger and want.[17] But thus far, only Japan has succeeded in making birth control a truly national goal, even though the problem of stabilizing the population at a level corresponding to actual and potential opportunities for economic and social development has yet to be solved.[18] Neither India, which since 1952 has had an official policy of family planning; nor Pakistan, which defied a great tradition that equated large families and high fertility with the ultimate good to stem the rise in numbers; nor China, which at last seems to have freed herself of the inhibitions of Marxist dogma to recognize the perils of uncontrolled birth; nor the several other countries which, like the United Arab Republic, have read the future in the signs of the present, have made any perceptible progress toward controlling their population explosion.[19] If there be any single explanation, it is that people refuse to confront a fundamentally dissenting evaluation of their own place in the world and that of their children and to take personal issue, as it were, with impersonal forces that shape man's destiny. It will be a totally new man who will be persuaded that the destiny of the world hangs on his own private decision. Besides, the question of population explosion has not yet had time to impress itself on the minds of the masses to make it their direct and personal concern.

These and the other factors that enter into the problem of population explosion, including the geometrically-increasing birth rate, the steady decline in the death rate and of infantile mortality, the age structure and age distribution, make the growth of the world's population an irreversible fact, at least for the rest of this century.[20] If the gloom of today is not to be followed by catastrophe tomorrow, provision must be made for the inevitable increase in the world's numbers for the next fifty years and for an optimum population in the generations beyond. The need for success is as compelling as the penalty of failure is immense.

Like war and peace, the problem of overpopulation cannot be solved within the present framework of international relations. Aside from the fact that standards of living vary with space and time, the advantages or disadvantages of size and growth of population are still governed by immediate strategic considerations rather than by long-range visions. Governments are not likely to be deterred by the consequences from encouraging population growth if the immediate national interests dictate the need for larger numbers. Thus in the years between the two World Wars, fertility was raised to a patriotic duty in Italy, where the people were starved for land and in Germany, where her rulers found her frontiers so confining for her numbers as to justify conquest of neighboring lands. In Asia, Japan broke with a long tradition of population control going back to the pre-industrial Tokugawa period to pursue a pro-natalist policy in her already overcrowded islands.[21] More recently, for a time between 1957 and 1961, China's vast human reservoir was regarded by Peiping as essential to the success of the "great leap forward," and birth control was declared political heresy. It continues to be denounced as contravening Marxist doctrine in the Soviet Union, perhaps not so much because an admission that poverty and economic ills can have other sources besides non-Communist social systems, but because of her vast stretches of uninhabited land in Asia close to the teeming millions of China.[22] There are many other countries in which population growth is still an actual and potential national asset, economically, politically and strategically.[23] As long as there are strategic, military and political advantages to large numbers anywhere, governments will not be bound by a policy which requires some nations to place restrictions on their rate of growth, while permitting others to give free play to their productive proclivities.

Population control of a kind that is purposeful and humane, as well as promising of results, is conceivable only in conditions in which strategic, military and political considerations are irrelevant and in a society whose glory is the measure in which it enhances the personal worth of the individuals within it. The solution of the problem of population explosion requires not only the transcendence of doctrinal prepossessions and national interests, but the deliberate pursuit of a policy which only a common acceptance of the dignity and worth of the human person can keep on its appointed course. The concept of limiting the human population negates so many fundamental beliefs and convictions and offends so many feelings, sentiments and aspirations that only a superior concept of the dignity and worth of the human person and his opportunities for self-fulfillment can save it from the wasteland of illusion and cruelty and betrayal.

Population control can never be elevated to a moral imperative in a society which denies man his spiritual and moral authenticity or which regards him as utterly superfluous except insofar as he contributes to the production and consumption of wealth and the promotion of the national interest. Either it becomes an instrument for enhancing the dignity of man and freeing him for the creative exercise of his higher powers, or few people will be seduced by the prospect of some future benefit into giving up what they cherish today. It is rarely that one hears sincere murmurs of misgivings behind the cheers which everywhere accompany the birth of a child. People are still unatuned to the echoes which emanate from the larger world beyond their immediate narrow confines and which tell a tale of woe and hunger and of misery and squalor without end. For birth control to become a quest for personal salvation or a discipline of rigorous thought, the international community must dedicate itself in thought and in deed to the advancement of human dignity, or it forfeits the right to prejudge the destiny of unborn millions.

CHAPTER IX

Pluralism and Diversity

Nothing short of a common acceptance of the human person as the measure of all things will bring peace within and calm without in a world of such vast variety or race, language, religion and ethnic and national origin crossing and recrossing frontiers of history, culture and nationality. Barriers of race, creed, color, language and national and ethnic differences rise everywhere to cast their ominous shadows over a wide range of human experience. Their causes and consequences, their dimensions and manifestations are as infinite as they are complex. Very often they are intensely personal and beyond rational account. But the root cause of much of the grief and violence in the modern world lies in the intolerance of the nationalist creed of diversity and the unceasing quest of the state for national synthesis. It cannot be removed from the face of the earth until the traditional framework of international relations gives way to a new form of cooperation among nations.

Internal ties of association have a durability which no force on earth can destroy. Ethnicity is a quality which resists time and tide and one in which individual choice plays a very limited role. Individuals in any society can change their religion, learn a new language and forget an old one, abandon old loyalties and acquire new ones, and become part of the larger group in spite of differences in race or color. On rare occasions have such changes occurred on a larger scale. By and large, children grow up in the faith of their parents, speak in the parental tongue, and cling to the vital ideas to which they were introduced in the formative years of their youth. The loyalties that emerge from the family circle and from the concentric circles which surround it have an insistent force which only grows in strength as efforts are made to weaken them from without. All attempts to create unitary states by ignoring or suppressing the ethnic aspirations of racial, religious, linguistic or cultural entities have almost invariably succeeded only in aggravating internal and external strife and discord.

Yet the notion of national homogeneity and uniformity has not ceased to be an ideal to strive for, nor have ethnic distinctions and racial and religious differences come to be taken for granted and pluralistic societies accepted as part of the natural order of things. This is true of nations old and new. Few nations have accepted diversity for its own sake and as a necessary part of establishing the unity of the world, even though many preach the virtues of a wider, supra-national unity on a regional, continental or universal scale. Still fewer nations have succeeded in contriving a constitution of government which could still the resentment of dissident minorities and satisfy the aspirations of ethnic groups. The spirit and purpose which animate the countries of Europe, Asia, Africa and America have been spawned in the matrix of nationalist faith and morals which, in the last analysis, have proved far stronger than the preachment of a common humanity and a common human destiny.

"In the struggle between nationalities," Prince Bernhardt von Bulow wrote in the years before the outbreak of World War I in defense of his efforts to Germanize the Prussian State,

> one nation is the hammer and the other the anvil; one is the victor and the other the vanquished ... If it were possible henceforth for members of different nationalities, with different languages and customs, and an intellectual life of a different kind, to live side by side in one and the same State, without succumbing to the temptation of each trying to force his own nationality on the other, things on earth would look a good deal more peaceful. But it is a law of life and development in history, that where two national civilizations meet they fight for ascendancy.[1]

Few are the countries where state and nation are so at one as to leave no uncertainty of boundary and of national sentiment. Where, as so frequently is the case, uncertainty persists as to the geographic definition of nationality, or where the sense of nationality is insecure; where races mingle and where appeal to ethnic emotions is strong and loyalty to caste, tribe or linguistic community is fierce, the struggle to weld a united nation goes on forever. Its attendant strife and conflict, at home and abroad, are writ large all over the world. Internal dissension, communal strife, religious conflict, tribal warfare, racial antagonism, frontier disputes, irredentism and secession keep large areas of the globe seething and restive.

The mood and temper of the times are toward assimilation and national uniformity. The significance of national life and of the nation as centers of political action and spiritual tradition; the need to equip the state for a successful role on the stage of international politics; and the urgency of building state power to promote the national interest in time of peace and in the emergencies of war combine to produce an intolerance of anything that might appear to imperil the unity of the nation, or cast doubt on the outward identification of the nation-state with the whole body of citizens, or render precarious the absolute hold of the state over the citizenry. Even the most enlightened governments, while tolerant of diversity of ethnic characteristics and manifestations and disavowing uniformity, rarely abandon hope of ultimately casting the variegated elements of their populations into a common mold of national culture and tradition.[2]

With few possible exceptions,[3] no country has yet evolved an internal order which stands for a true pluralism in which human values are subject only to the minimum restraint required by the public order. Everywhere where ethnic diversity clashes with the ideal of national homogeneity, only iron restraint and relentless probing from within and without can stay the hand of oppression which always reaches out to crush those of another race, another creed, or another language. More than a century and a half of effort to transfer the struggle of ethnic loyalties from the field of battle to the conscience of the citizen has had but little effect on the practices of governments. Intolerance, fear, suspicion and mistrust characterize at large majority-minority relations in all too many parts of the world. Where international boundaries cut across ties of family, race, language or religion, those ties remain a fundamental reality of international relations.

Two world wars and events during the intervening years and after have given us a devastating demonstration of where the intolerance of the nationalist creed can lead and of the tragic consequences of the assertion of reasons of state. The search for national synthesis and uniformity carried to extremes leads to the crime of genocide. On April 24, 1965, the Armenian nation, everywhere on earth, commemorated the fiftieth anniversary of the most tragic event in its long history. This was the massacre by the regime of the Turkish Sultan in 1915 of more than a third of the close to two million Armenians in the Ottoman Empire, who were regarded as a threat to the integrity of the Turkish State.[4] Barely twenty-five years later, those dreadful events were surpassed by far in number and inhumanity by the genocidal acts of Nazi Germany, which claimed the lives of six million Jews and millions of other men, women and children throughout occupied Europe.

Genocide, expulsions and population exchange have done their work to solve in large measure Europe's more acute ethnic and nationalities problems of pre World War II days. The extermination of the Jews in Nazi-occupied Europe destroyed the most dynamic centers of Jewish concentration on the continent. Nazi policy and the rigid application of the Protocol of the Berlin Conference of the summer of 1945 on the "Orderly Transfer to Germany of German Populations or Elements thereof Remaining in Poland, Czechoslovakia and Hungary" erased all teutonic traces in that part of Europe.[5] A series of agreements between and among Poland, the Ukraine, Byelorussia, the Soviet Union, Yugoslavia, Hungary and Czechoslovakia, designed to remove from among the fraternity of the socialist states all sources of discord which might arise from unsolved nationalities problems in which they were directly involved, resulted in the exchange of each other's nationals and kinsmen and to the redrawing of their territorial boundaries along ethnic lines.[6] Who can say whether a similar fate is not in store for many of the hundreds of millions of men, women and children throughout the major part of the world who, because of race, creed, language or national origin, are as the anvil to the hammer that is the majority?

Nations new and old, large and small have yet to escape the bias of their own perspectives. In the Soviet Union, for example, where the nationalities policy was ushered into life in the wake of the October Revolution amid high hopes and pure aspirations, it proved only a humane interlude in an otherwise grim and hopeless drama.[7] There is growing evidence that the days have long since passed when ethnicity was recognized as a permanent quality of Soviet society. The trend is toward the effacement of

national and ethnic distinctions. This is what we read in the
Draft Program presented by the Soviet Communist Party to its
Twenty-Second Congress in 1961:

> People of many nationalities live together and work in
> harmony in the Soviet republics. The boundaries between
> the constituent republics of the USSR are increasingly
> losing their former significance, since all the nations are
> equal, their life is based on a common Socialist foundation,
> the material and spiritual needs of every people are
> satisfied to the same extent, and they are all united in a
> single family by common vital interests and are advancing
> together to the common goal—communism...
>
> With the victory of communism in the USSR, the nations
> will draw still closer together, their economic and ideolog-
> ical unity will increase and the Communist traits common
> to their spiritual make-up will develop. However, the efface-
> ment of national distinctions, and especially of language
> distinctions, is a considerably longer process than the
> effacement of class distinctions...
>
> The ideological unity of the nations and nationalities is
> growing, and there is a rapprochement of their cultures.
> The historical experiences of the development of Socialist
> nations shows that national forms do not ossify; they
> change, advance and draw together, shedding all outdated
> traits that contradict the new living conditions. An inter-
> national culture common to all the Soviet nations is devel-
> oping. The cultural treasures of each nation are increas-
> ingly augmented by works of international import.
>
> Attaching decisive importance to the development of the
> Socialist content of the cultures of the peoples of the
> USSR, the party will promote their further mutual enrich-
> ment and rapprochement, the consolidation of their inter-
> national basis, and thereby the formation of the future
> single world-wide culture of Communist society. While
> supporting the progressive traditions of each people, and
> making them the property of all Soviet people, the party
> will in all ways further new revolutionary traditions of
> the builders of communism common to all nations.[8]

When all these abstractions are grounded in the specific and all the generalizations are particularized, the physical realities in the Soviet Union reveal the operation of a governmental policy which is growing ever more hostile to the idea of national diversity. The maximum centralized control and expansion of Soviet power require a unified national culture, which the numerically and historically predominant Russians and Russian culture are more than willing to supply. The process of assimilation is constantly being intensified, as the Russification of politics, culture and language is proceeding apace and as the nationalities and other ethnic minorities strive to enter the mainstream of Soviet life. "The voluntary study of Russian in addition to the native language," we read further in the Draft Program,

> is of positive significance, since it facilitates reciprocal exchanges of experience and access of every nation and nationality to the cultural gains of all the other peoples of the USSR and to world culture. The Russian language has, in effect, become the common medium of inter-course and cooperation between all the peoples of the USSR.

Where voluntarism is not forthcoming, or when reasons of state dictate the hastening of the process of effacement of all ethnic distinctions, the Government can always fall back on the Party's promise:

> To pursue consistently as heretofore the principles of internationalism in the field of national relations, to strengthen the friendship of peoples as one of the most important gains of socialism, to conduct a relentless struggle against manifestations and survivals of nationalism and chauvinism of all types, against trends of narrowmindedness and exclusiveness, idealization of the past and the veiling of social contradictions in the history of peoples, and against obsolete customs and habits ... The liquidation of manifestations of nationalism is in the interests of all nations and nationalities of the USSR....

It is this coercive power to enforce uniformity employed by the Soviet Government that is decisive. This power was arbitrarily used in the past and continues to be used to assault the ethnic, religious and cultural integrity of some nationalities, and to jeopardize the survival of others.[9] Since the end of World War II, the

Soviet Union has been variously accussed of systematically destroying the ethnic unity and identity of the Baltic and other peoples, by a step-by-step plan for their deportation to other parts of the country and the re-settlement of their lands by Russians and other minority groups.[10] This policy was in part confirmed by former Premier Khrushchev himself in his speech to the Twenty-Second Congress of the Communist Party in the Soviet Union, when he said:

> The population in the various republics is becoming more and more mixed in national composition. There is a lively exchange of qualified personnel between them. All this promotes stronger international bonds between the peoples of our country.[11]

It would appear that the brunt of the "effaccment" policy is being borne by the peoples strategically placed along the Soviet Union's frontiers in Europe and Asia, including the Ukrainians and Byelorussians, as a measure designed to ensure the integrity of the Soviet State and to safeguard against the possibilities of secession from within and irredentism from without.[12] Once the ideological unity in the Communist world, which for a time appeared to have submerged national rivalries and conflicts of interest, was shattered abroad, its vulnerability was bound to increase at home. The Polish and Hungarian uprisings in 1956 and the progressive deterioration in Chinese-Russian relations demonstrated the hollowness of propaganda boasts that Communist ideology had created "unbreakable solidarity" among different peoples and nations. The Soviet Union could not misread the deeper significance of the tendency of nationalist traditions to take precedence over international creed. Along with other great powers in the world, Russia, whether Czarist or Communist, has at one time or another grieviously offended against the rights of people to self-determination and has been guilty of colonial practices.[13]

To the Chinese, for example, the history of their relations with the Russians since they first came into permanent contact more than three centuries ago recalls repeated victimization, humiliation and territorial losses by China at the hands of Russia. Above all the ideological disputes between the two Communist

States, China has seen fit to remind the Soviet Union that it had
never forgotten and will always remember the vast areas of Central Asia and Siberia wrested by Imperial Russia from the weak
Manchu emperors through a series of "unequal" treaties dating
back to 1858[14] As the Chinese territorial claims grow louder, they
conjure up all kinds of spectral visions, including the eventual
partition of the Soviet Union between its Slavic components to
the west of the Urals and the Asian peoples in the vast stretches
of trans-Ural Russia.[15]

Looming large in the background is, of course, the massive
psychological advantage China would have if she seriously pursued
the idea that she alone had the power to lead the colored peoples
of the world in massive opposition to the white masters who
once oppressed them. For the frontier which divides the white and
colored races of the world coincides in very large measure with
the dividing line between the privileged and underprivileged.
Together, they constitute a formidable combination for the generation of racial tension. The Soviet Union has repeatedly warned
against Chinese efforts to split the Communist movement along
racial lines and has fought bitterly against various Chinese efforts
to exclude Soviet delegates from Afro-Asian meetings and conferences on the ground that they are Europeans. The inference
of these attempts at exclusion of the Soviet Union is no other
than that Russia in Asia is a colonial power and usurper of Asian
land belonging to Asian peoples.[16]

In brief, whatever reasons may impel the Soviet Union to
seek the amalgamation of her various nations and nationalities
into an undifferentiated mass of Soviet citizens, Communism's
universalist and messianic pretensions can no longer be one of
them. The myth that Communism could permanently unite people
of the most varied national, cultural and historic backgrounds and
diverse interests has long ago been exploded.[17] Whatever was
left of it, was shattered once and for all by the national rivalry
between the Soviet Union and China, which all the ideological
disputes over Marxist doctrine could not long disguise. The Soviet
Union, like so many other multi-racial, multi-lingual and multi-
national societies, is susceptible to erosion from within and without by the twin forces of nationalism and racialism. These forces
must either be accommodated in ever larger freedom and respect

for the dignity and rights of the human person or, as seems to be the case, its alternative is oppression and supression, with all its incalculable consequences at home and abroad.

The unfolding of the tragedy on the Island of Cyprus, where the Greek and Turkish communities are locked in mortal conflict, shows how little the forward thrust of mind and reason avails against the strength of passion and tradition. The site where Aphrodite rose from the sea of Paphos is enveloped in hatred, grief and violence. The problem on that scenic island of the Eastern Mediterranean is how two distinct ethnic communities, in a ratio of more than four to one, with different and conflicting political aspirations and tied by umbilical cords to their mother countries across the Sea can create a community of Cypriots independent of both Greece and Turkey and a nation in its own right. The immediate issue is the reconciliation of the principle of majority rule invoked by the Greek-speaking population of almost half-a-million, with the claim of the Turkish-speaking minority of more than one-hundred-thousand to the preservation of its status as a separate legal entity, under constitutional arrangements which guarantee a permanent equilibrium between the two autonomous national communities. The issue has been further aggravated by the intervention of Greece and Turkey as parties directly concerned in the affairs of Cyprus, which automatically transformed an internal constitutional crisis into a major threat to world peace.

In August, 1960, the Republic of Cyprus was handed, along with its independence, a Constitution whose every virtue for one community is a vice in the eyes of the other. The Constitution is patently weighted heavily in favor of the Turkish minority. It provides an elaborate system of checks, balances and divided powers between the two communities and vests in the Turkish minority a virtual veto power over all important acts of state in the field of foreign and domestic policy, defense and security. The independence, territorial integrity and security of Cyprus, as well as the basic articles of the Constitution are placed under the guarantee of Great Britain, Greece and Turkey, whose political and strategic interests in Cyprus have been confirmed in special treaties, which recognize the full sovereignty of the United Kingdom over strategically important base areas on the island and provide for the stationing of Greek and Turkish military forces. These treaties, together with the Treaty of Guar-

antee and the Constitution, constitute the so-called settlement
that made the independence of Cyprus possible.[18] It was in the
nature of a compromise between *enosis,* or union with Greece,
which fired the Greek Cypriots in their struggle for independence
from Great Britain, and *taksim,* or partition of the island between
Greece and Turkey, as desired by the Turkish-speaking population.

But independence only spawned greater mutual distrust and
suspicion among the inhabitants of Cyprus, who have long been
divided by a barrier of ethnic, religious and sociological differences. A constitution which institutionalized these differences, not
only could not facilitate a process of integration around a common
Cypriote nationality, but also checked the natural process of majority and minority accommodation. The legalization of the right
of intervention by Greece and Turkey could not but encourage
and inspire mutual threats and fears, biased claims and distorted
interpretations of facts and events. And an independence shackled
and limited from within and without could not but frustrate the
majority and lead to a paralysis of government. The impatience
of the majority to rule and the intransigence of the minority who
would not abandon its entrenched position slowly but surely
ground the Constitution to a standstill until it finally broke down
completely. The violence and the tensions which have gripped
the island since December 21, 1963, were touched off by the
proposal of the President of the Republic to amend the Constitution in a way which, in his judgement, would strike a more natural
balance between the Greek and Turkish populations and permit
the normal functioning of government. The thirteen constitutional
amendments proposed by Archbishop Makarios spread alarm even
to the remotest Turkish hamlet in Cyprus and unleashed strife
and passions among Greeks and Turks which were not brought
under control before they worked havoc in the cities and in the
countryside and caused widespread misery and political and economic disorganization whose full consequences have yet to be
assessed.[19]

There is no ideal solution in sight and not even a practical
one that will not be rejected with passion by either the Greek
or Turkish Cypriots. The alarm felt by the Turkish minority at
the prospective loss of its constitutionally entrenched rights and
privileges and the protective shield of Turkey's right to intervene

in the defense of the *status quo* is no less understandable than the impatience of the Greek majority to enjoy the fruits of independence and to govern the country in accordance with the accepted principle of majority rule so basic to all political democracy. As long as the Turkish minority has cause to fear the preponderance of the Greeks and lacks assurance of the free development of its ethnic predilections, it will not readily be persuaded to surrender its present privileged and guaranteed position for promises which can be breached and for rights which can be violated. At the same time, the Greek-speaking population cannot realistically be expected to compromise on a distribution of governmental powers which institutionalizes an unequal partnership between majority and minority and to subscribe to treaties which legalize foreign intervention to enforce it.[20]

Islands of ethnic discontent and ferment dot the countries of the world. What is happening in Cyprus is being repeated in different contexts, in different forms, and on different scales especially in many of the new countries of Asia, Africa, Oceania and the Caribbean Sea, where the boundaries of state and nation diverge so vastly.[21] The emergence into independence, since the end of World War II, of more than three score countries in these areas has shifted the center of gravity of the ethnic problem from the European continent to Asia and Africa and has added gravely to its dimensions. As the new countries grope their way toward a full realization of the significance of nationhood, the conflicts, contrasts, polarities and antitheses which divide their peoples come to the fore and are accentuated to the point of threatening the fragile structure of the newly-independent states.

Most of the countries which have won independence since 1945 have been overwhelmed by the task of hammering out a framework of cooperation within which diverse loyalties, disparate territories, and groupings of people in various stages of historical and political development may be brought together to create a modern nation-state. They have been in the throes of fierce struggles to forge nations out of people of different regions, tribes, languages, religions, cultures and civilizations, with little common patriotism to hold in check the normal human resentments and the day-to-day clashes of interest. Where blood ties, common worship or common ancestry are decisive; where the range of government is limited; and where life and loyalty are largely centered in family, village, caste or local leaders, the preponderant ethnic element has great difficulty in projecting a national vision with which all the elements of the population can identify themselves. Very often, the same aspirations for liberty and self-determination which hastened the dissolution of empires, now challenge the integrity of many of the new states. Dissident groups and resentful minorities within their borders add further to the social instability which characterizes these pluralistic societies in transition.

Truly, fierce as the struggle may be to weld a united people to fight for independence, it is even fiercer and more prolonged after independence has been achieved. "The nationalism so emphatically proclaimed from the rostrum is not always easily delimited on the map, or as deeply etched within the civic consciousness of the nationals."[22] The maintenance of national unity in many countries around the world, in the newly emerged and in many that are not so old is perhaps their most severe political problem. For example, after more than two decades of independence India, whose nationalist movement led by Mahatma Gandhi bore a mass character and moved together in community to set an example to all colonial peoples, is still battling for survival as a nation against the many centrifugal forces she inherited from the past.[23] The one recurring theme in the late Prime Minister Nehru's addresses to the people of India was his warning that the greatest threat that hung over the country arose from internal conflicts over language, caste, religion and province. It is perhaps best summed up in the two following sentences from his 1960 Independence Day speech in Old Delhi. Standing on the ramparts of historic Red Fort where he first hoisted the flag of independent India, the late Prime Minister warned:

> The time has come when every Indian will have to realize where he stands in relation to his country. Does he stand by his country, or his group, or religion, or state?[24]

India's national leader, having led his country to revolutionary independence, had since 1947 found it necessary to lead his people into revolution against themselves and their own divisions. With all their political maturity into which they had grown since attaining independence, as attested to by the four democratic national elections, the Indian people remained as susceptible as ever to the divisive forces which have plagued their country. In fact, one of the principal tasks of an Indian Prime Minister has been to balance the demands of state against state, of the states against the center, of language against language, and of community against community. While the reorganization of India in 1956 and the redrawing of the boundaries of the Indian states along esentially linguistic lines has weakened a major threat to national unity,[25] linguistic demands, communal predilections and regional interests of varying character and degree continue to erode the structure of the Indian Union.

The strains and stresses resulting from frustrated linguistic aspirations and regional and comunal preferences are enormous. Barely four years after the reorganization of India, which led to the creation of fourteen states and six centrally-administered territories along essentially linguistic lines, a fifteenth state was carved out of Bombay to satisfy the demands of thc Marathi-speaking population for a state of their own. In 1960, after much bloodshed and violence, bi-lingual Bombay was divided to form the new Maharashtra-and Gujerat-speaking states.[26] In 1963, a sixteenth state—Nagaland—was added to the Indian Union. It was carved out of Assam to add to the complexity of India's federal-state relations. The new state of little more than 400,000 tribal people from the hills overlooking Bramahputra Valley in northeastern India came into existence on December 1, 1963, after more than ten years of guerrilla warfare waged in the cause of complete independence. The settlement guaranteed to the Naga people that no act of the Indian Parliament affecting their relig-ious or social practices, their customary civil and criminal law and administration, or their traditions governing land ownership or its transfer would have effect in Nagaland unless approved by the state's legislative assembly.[27] And yet, at the time of writing, peace had not yet come to Nagaland, as the insurgents keep on pressing for a special status within the Indian Union, if not for complete independence.[28]

Far graver in its consequences and implications, because of its challenge to the constitutional order of India and the secular character of the Indian Union, has been the successful campaign of the close to ten-million Sikhs to convert the better part of the Punjab, where both Hindi and Punjabi are spoken, into a Punjabi-speaking state. On March 9, 1966, the leaders of the ruling Congress Party adopted a resolution calling for the carving out of the existing Punjab state in northern India a seventeenth state,[29] in which Punjabi would be the official language. On March 18, a committee of India's Parliament approved the Party's recommendation and the new states of Punjabi Subha and Hariana came into existence on November 19, 1966.[30]

For a number of years, the Sikhs, who constitute one of the major religious communities in India, have been demanding the creation of such a state to coincide not only with their linguistic, but also with their religious boundaries. They made no secret of the purport of their campaign for a state of their own, which was to safeguard their people, their religion and their culture against Hindu preponderance.[31] The Indian Government has consistently opposed the Sikh demands, even though Punjabi is one of the thirteen languages recognized in the Constitution, precisely because of their religious overtones and implications. In the view of the Indian Government, accession to the demands of the Sikhs was tantamount to giving official sanction to religious communalism—a persistent danger in India. The Sikhs constitute a 55% majority of the Punjabi-speaking population in the territory of the new state and its communal-religious character is almost unavoidable.

The reason why the issue of a linguistic Punjabi state was left undecided for so many years is quite understandable. The introduction of the religious factor in the determination of regional groupings and state frontiers not only summons forth unholy specters of the past, but conjures up new portents for the future. Although communalism has so far failed to make a bid for general public support, there are strong communal forces at work which, if let loose, could not long be held in check. The centrifugal tendencies in this gigantic multi-racial, multi-lingual, multi-religious and multi-ethnic mosaic that is India are formidable. Were communal affiliation or preference admitted as a basis for self-determination, even for limited purposes within the framework of the Indian Union, not only the subdivision of India, but the partition of the Indian subcontinent itself could never be regarded as finished.[32]

In a very true sense, India and Pakistan exist as separate nations only because of religious differences, even of religious intolerance. The partition of the subcontinent in 1947 was born in the religious hatreds and animosities between Hindus and Moslems and was sealed in bloodshed and the forcible migration of many millions across the frontiers of the two hostile states.[33] It left behind a legacy which is the root cause of some of the most grievious internal and external problems in this part of the world. The bone of contention between India and Pakistan is not alone the future of overwhelmingly Moslem Kashmir, but the fate of the more than fifty million Moslems in India and of the more then ten million Hindus in Pakistan. Kashmir itself is only the symbol of the trouble left behind by partition. The real issue which divides India and Pakistan is their definition as nation-states. India cannot concede Kashmir without inviting assault on the whole concept of the Indian Union and of the secularism used to hold its parts together. Secular democracy has assumed for India the significance of a political faith, which makes possible the achievement of a free society in a land of almost half-a-billion people belonging to diverse religious, linguistic and ethnic groups. If there is no room in the Indian Union for over-whelmingly Moslem Kashmir, there is no room for the more than fifty-million strong Moslem minority in the rest of India and, by the same token, for other minority groups and for Indian diversity. Neither can Pakistan relinguish her claim to Kashmir and its people without being unfaithful to the idea which brought the country into existence and which constitutes the *raison d'être* for its separation from the Indian subcontinent. In both cases it is the religion of the Kashmiri people which gives the territorial dispute over this area its special character that is unlike any other territorial dispute between states. For despite the sophisticated arguments over the rights and wrongs of the Kashmir dispute, the real dynamic of the conflict lies in the mutual distrust and historical animosity between Hindu and Moslem.[34]

The same ties which bind the Moslem majority in Kashmir to its co-religionists in Pakistan also bind the Moslem minority in all of India, as do the ties which bind the Hindu minority in Pakistan to its co-religionists in India. These ties ignore the artificial international boundaries which were drawn between the two states in 1947. They make, at best, for a sullen, uneasy and suspicious peace between majorities and minorities. At worst, they give rise to savage violence within and conflict abroad. Recurrent Hindu-Moslem clashes in the two countries have shattered the lives of millions of people and inflicted death on countless thousands across the Indo-Pakistani frontiers. In January

1964, the whole subcontinent reverberated to the rumbles of violence, as Moslems attacked Hindus in Pakistan and Hindus retaliated against Moslems in India. In August, 1965, the Kashmir dispute brought India and Pakistan to the verge of an all-out war, which only the decisive intervention of the Security Council of the United Nations, followed by Soviet mediation at Tashkent, prevented from taking a disastrous course.[35]

India's problem as a multi-racial, multi-lingual, multi-religious and multi-ethnic amalgam may be peculiarly her own. But along with her neighboring countries in Southeast Asia, India faces the formidable task of hammering out a nation-state out of a pluralistic society which has its matrix in a rich history of the past. Most of the countries of Southeast Asia are confronted with demands made by regional, linguistic, religious and ethnic groups for broader rights, greater autonomy or independence. Many of them have had to fight against open rebellion or secession. The difference lies in the manner in which the efforts to forge the bonds of common citizenship and national loyalty are made.

As we turn southward, we find the Ceylonese, for example, almost hopelessly divided by linguistic disputes between the Sinhalese, who constitute almost 70% of the population of over 10,000,000, and the more than one million Tamil-speaking Ceylonese nationals of Indian origin.[36] These disputes are aggravated by the division also along religious lines between the Buddhist Sinhalese and the largely Hindu Tamils and the movement for a Buddhist-oriented State,[37] as well as by the presence of one million or more Tamils from India, who provide the bulk of labor for Ceylon's tea industry. Civil disobedience, violence and open revolt have marred the peace of the country, especially since the legislation establishing Sinhalese as the sole official language came into force early in 1961.[38] The demands of the Tamil-speaking population range from full equality as Ceylonese citizens, through the formation of an autonomous Tamil state in the northern and eastern provinces, where they are in a majority, to freedom to unite with their Tamil brethern in the south of India.

In Burma, the never-ending struggle between the predominant Burmans and the other indigenous ethnic groups like the Karens, the Shans and the Kachins, which has kept the country at war with itself, has frustrated the many efforts which successive governments have made since independence to blend their people into a unified nation.[39] Ever since 1948, Burma has experienced waves of revolt and insurrection on the part of the various ethnic groups of more than seven million people, which have been fighting for greater autonomy from the more than thirteen million Burmans than the most liberal government was willing to grant them. In fact, the growing threat to the unity of Burma, and its survival as a state was given as the main reason for the military *coup d'etat* of March 1962, which brought into power General Ne Win's Revolutionary Government. It brought to the fore a new power elite dedicated to bringing all the people of Burma under a common authority, to breaking down the long-harbored feelings of fear and resentment among the various ethnic groups, and to replacing them with a sense of partnership in which all sections of the population may have a vital stake in the integrity of the Burmese Union. The federal structure has been changed in favor of stronger central control; a strong bid has been made to institute a uniform code of law for the whole of the country; and a national budget has been introduced designed to ensure that all ethnic groups share equally in the benefits of what is called "Burmese socialism."[40] But it is not certain whether these and the many other efforts to create a unitary state in Burma are sufficient to counteract historical animosities going back for centuries or to allay the fears and suspicions engendered by the encroachments of the dominant language, religion, dress and custom upon the lives of the several ethnic minorities. Nor is it certain that the so-called ethnic minorities, especially the more than one-million Indians and half-a-million Chinese, have been accepted as part of the total community.[41]

These half-a-million Chinese in Burma, are part of the estimated fifteen million Chinese among Southeast Asia's congeries of races, languages, creeds and cultures in the lands of former Indo-China, in Thailand, Indonesia, the Philippines and Malaysia. They constitute the most influential and yet insecure and also the most explosive minority in that part of the world and pose problems reminiscent of similar problems in pre-War Eastern Europe. Their traditional position as Southeast Asia's merchants and traders, financiers and entrepeneurs has combined with the fear of their powerful motherland and the inwardness of their lives, separate and apart from their neighbors, to make the ethnic and immigrant Chinese a resented, suspect and feared minority. And as the shadow of China lengthens across the continent of Asia, the conscious or involuntary choice of Chinese abroad between loyalty to their ancestral home, for which they show a marked affinity, and the challenge of local nationalisms to which they must bow in the interest of their survival, is being constantly narrowed. Their efforts to turn outward are frequently rebuffed, while the doors to their naturalization and assimilation are being shut to them ever so tightly.[42]

Indonesia's more than 3000 islands stretching from Malaya to Australia, with its sixteen major ethnic groups and ten major languages, were held together for many years under the strong hand of President Sukarno and his motto of "unity in diversity." The abolition in 1950 of the Indonesian Federation in favor of a unitary state and the establishment of the National Front Congress embracing members of all political parties and mass organizations and cutting across all regional, linguistic and ethnic boundaries have been purposely directed towards weakening group loyalties, factionalism and separatist tendencies of every kind in the land.[43] To what extent these centrifugal forces have been permanently neutralized, is difficult to say. However, next to the dissident groups in the South Moluccas, which since 1950 have been in open revolt, Indonesia's most serious encounter with the minorities problem has been with the Chinese population of three million.

These Chinese, many of whom descend from settlers who came to Indonesia a century ago or longer, have for generations served the Indonesian people as traders, middlemen and creditors. The long smoldering resentment of native sons against the prosperous aliens and successful outcasts has since independence found expression in a variety of hostile official and unofficial acts and measures. Sweeping regulations which entered into force on January 1, 1960,[44] banning aliens from trade and other occupations in rural areas, have affected virtually the entire Chinese population, if for no other reason than that documentary evidence of naturalization is not readily available. The Bandung Agreement of 1955 between Indonesia and China to end the dual nationality of the Chinese in Indonesia[45] and the protests of Peiping and Taiwan against their maltreatment by Jakarta have not deterred the Indonesian authorities, whether national, provincial or local, from pursuing a determined policy of dislodging the Chinese from their traditional economic positions in favor of the majority ethnic groups. In many cases this policy has been tantamount to expulsion and exile of Chinese who have lost all means of livelihood and have often been exposed to excesses in many parts of the country, such as the anti-Chinese riots in May, 1963, on the island of Java.

Indonesia's bloody persecution of its Communists, which began in March 1966, and which claimed an estimated one-hundred thousand lives or more from Sumatra to Timor, and the reorientation of its foreign policy from close association with Communist China in a Peking-Jakarta axis to outright hostility between the two countries, all in a matter of days, were undoubtedly made possible in part by the inherent anti-Chinese bias among the Indonesians, born out of their historic animosity towards the Chinese "sojourners" in their midst. They have become targets for all kinds of natural and induced hostility and easy prey to political bias and exploitation from the right and from the left, at home and abroad.[46]

Both the beginnings and the partial break-up of the Federation of Malaysia have their source in the peculiar position of the Chinese in Southeast Asia, whose pre-eminence in the economy and other private sectors of society, strong sense of ethnic identification and abiding attachment to their motherland, set them apart from the rest of the population among whom they live. Political expediency was largely responsible for the creation of the Malaysian Federation on September 16, 1963.[47] Ethnic rivalry between Malays and Chinese led to the Federation's partial break-up less than two years later. It was fear of a possible take-over of predominantly Chinese Singapore by the Communist Party there and the consequent extension of China's political frontiers that first gave stimulus to the idea of uniting the diverse states of Malaya, Singapore, Sabah and Sarawak and thus reducing the political weight of the ethnic Chinese in this vast and strategic area of Asia. It was the communal structure of Malaysian politics aimed at the containment of ethnic Chinese expansion that was immediately responsible for the separation of Singapore from the Federation. The Malaysian Constitution of 1963, which was designed to ensure political paramountcy to the four million-strong Malayan agricultural community and leave the more than four million Chinese in the possession of their economic positions in city and hamlet, failed to bridge the widening gap

between the two communities. The Chinese began to challenge
the basic power structure of Malaya, while the Malays became
increasingly dissatisfied with their lack of business and pro-
fessional opportunities. Communal rioting in the streets of Singapore in July, 1964, weakened the Federation's resistance to division almost at birth.[48] The clash of interests between Malays and
Chinese all along the political, economic and ethnic lines frustrated all efforts to establish a viable multi-racial state, strong enough
to withstand the moments of passion which threatened to upset
the balance among the Malays, Chinese and the two million
Indians and Pakistanis and tribes of different kinds. On August 9,
1965, Singapore broke with the federation and launched on an
independent existence.

As we turn westward we find, for example, Afghanistan and
Pakistan violently at odds over the fate of about ten million
people almost evenly divided by an international frontier which
cuts acros the land of the Pathans known as Pakthunistan. These
Pushtu-speaking people to the west of the Indus share a common
history, language, culture and traditions with the Afghans who,
ever since the partition of India in 1947, have championed the
right of the Pathans to freedom and independence from Pakistan
and have taken up the cudgels on their behalf to the point of
severing diplomatic and commercial relations with their Pakistani
neighbors. Thus for twenty-two months, between May, 1961, and
July, 1963, the two Moslem States had no diplomatic and commercial relations with each other. But even though these had
been restored, the basic issues which have kept the two nations
apart have not changed. The fate of the Pathans will long continue
to come between them.[49]

The rebellion of the approximately two million Kurds in Iraq,
which has continued almost uninterruptedly for five years since
March 1962, is only the latest chapter in a story more than one
thousand years old. This sturdy race of mountaineers, whose
numbers are variously estimated at from twelve to eighteen
million, spread over a sweeping plateau region extending across
modern Iraq, Iran, Turkey, Syria and the Armenian and Azer-
baidzhain sectors of the Soviet Caucasus, have always been in
revolt against the conquerors of their native lands which go
under the name of Kurdistan. Since the end of World War I,
when the abortive Treaty of Sèvres between the Allies and the

Ottoman Government envisaged the formation of an independent Kurdistan between Iraq and Armenia, the Kurdish question has caused upheavals throughout the Middle East. In 1946, the Kurds established the Mehabad Republic in Iran, only to be suppressed less than a year later at the cost of many lives and much bloodshed. Thereafter, the scene of revolt shifted to Iraq, where as the largest single ethnic group differing from the Arab majority in language, custom and origin, the Kurds have continually fought for autonomy and self-determination.[50]

As in Asia, the greatest political problem attending the young peoples of Africa in the formative years of their statehood is the welding of nations out of disparate territories and out of races which are often at the opposite poles of historical development. The barriers and obstacles to nationhood are many and deep-seated throughout Africa and the impediments to the growth of national cohesion are especially great in the countries south of the Sahara. A thousand tongues and more than three times that number of tribes and tribal groupings and a vast diversity of cultures, traditions and loyalties divide and subdivide the more than two-hundred million people from the Tropic of Cancer in the north to Capetown in the south, from the Atlantic in the west to the Red Sea and Indian Ocean in the east. The colonial partition of Africa, with its careless disregard of ethnic and linguistic frontiers, has only added to the problems of border disputes and irredentisms and created new ones where none existed before. The national boundaries of many of the African states are but lines the colonial powers had drawn on the map to divide their spheres of influence and cut across ethnic and linguistic communities and geographic units. Most of the new countries in Africa harbor a variety of racial and ethnic aggregations which have in common neither history, nor language, nor other traditional ties to bind them together. They all conspire to keep the African cauldron boiling.[51]

The traditional African groups are so many foci of separatism and dissidence throughout the continent, where the tribe is still the center around which all life and endeavor revolves and which shelters all, and where kinship, community, region and ethnic identification continue to stand supreme in the hierarchy of values of the common African. They are very often the foundations on which the constitutional and administrative structure of the state is erected and the basis for parties functioning in the territorial political arena. The new Constitution of Kenya,[52] for example, is a formidable instrument of government. More than anything else, however, it is a treaty or a tribal contract, which seeks to provide for virtually every contingency in which the tribal regions might clash with the federal government. It has been drawn up between the Kenya African National Union, which draws its strength from the Kikuyus, and the Kenya African Democratic Union, which embraces a number of smaller tribes united by a common fear of Kikuyu domination. Uganda's Republic includes four semi-autonomous kingdoms, as well as federal districts.[53] From six provinces into which it had been divided before it received its independence from Belgium, the Congo grew to twenty-one provinces in 1963. These have been drawn along largely tribal lines to satisfy tribal rivalries.[54] Much the same holds true throughout virtually all of Central Africa.

With the removal of the *pax colonia*, long-suppressed ancient and more recent tribal, regional, religious, cultural, linguistic and other divisions among Africa's heterogeneous population have risen to the surface to mar the peace of city and hamlet, while traditional grievances among tribal, regional and other elements have assumed modern forms to threaten the political stability and territorial integrity of the new states. "The pressures of change in Africa," the United Nations High Commissioner for Refugees, Prince Saddrudin Aga Khan, observed:

> are often of an extreme violence. The emergence of new nations may be an occasion for settling old scores that date back for centuries. New governments who see in unity a prerequisite for stability are not always inclined to welcome the existence of minority ethnic strains or religious groups, if they seem to be in any way seedbeds of dissidence...[55]

Prince Aga Khan was referring, in the first place, to the tragic fate of the Watusi tribe in Rwanda—the tall, proud and graceful warrior-aristorcrats who for more than four centuries were Rwanda's feudal lords and who are now at the mercy of their former vassals, the Bahutus. In November, 1959, while Rwanda was still part of Ruanda-Urundi and administered by Belgium as a United Nations trust territory, the Bahutus, who constitute a majority of Rwanda's population of approximately 2,750,000, rose in revolt against the traditional monarchy of the Watusi minority which then numbered about 400,000. At least ten thousand Watusis were estimated to have perished in the revolution and in its violent aftermath, while about one-hundred-fifty-thousand were forced to seek refuge in neighboring Tanzania, Burundi, Uganda and the Congo. Since then, many more Watusi men, women and children have perished at the hands of the hostile Bahutus. In December, 1963, ten thousand Watusi were reportedly massacred in reprisal against the raids and incursions of Watusi exiles from across the borders.[56]

As in Rwanda, so in Burundi—a sister republic carved out of the former Trust territory of Ruanda-Urundi—the Watusis constitute a minority of about 15% in a population of over two million which consists mostly of Bahutus. Although the Watusis in Burundi, unlike their fellow-tribesmen in Rwanda, have for some time been sharing power with the Bahutu majority, their inevitable fate has been decreed by events across the frontiers. The implacable hatred of the Bahutus in Rwanda against their former overlords to the point of genocide has spilled over into Burundi. The shame and humiliation the Watusis have suffered in Rwanda have been shared by their kin in Burundi.[57] The declaration of martial law toward the end of October, 1965, following an abortive coup against the Mwami of Burundi, saved the Watusis from a fate suffered by their fellow tribesmen only two years before in Rwanda.

Stretching across the whole width of the African continent, from Sudan through Chad, Nigeria and westward and through Ethiopia to the east is, of course, the great ethnic dividing line between the Islamic-Arab north and pagan-Christian south. This adds to the forces of disunity which are hard at work in almost every one of the newly independent countries. Thus political developments in Nigeria have from the beginning revealed deep-seated tribal and religious, as well as regional, divisions of dangerous proportions beneath the surface of what had once been regarded as the most stable and democratically most advanced of the African states. The national elections in December, 1964, the first since independence four years earlier and boycotted by the main opposition group from the southern regions in protest against the monopolization of power by the regions in the north, brought into sharp focus the fundamental division between the

Moslem North and the largely pagan-Christian South.[58] It was
this ever-present threat to the integrity of the Nigerian Federation that was in part, at least, responsible for the military *coup
d'état* of January 15, 1966,[59] that brought to power a generation
of men which was determined to remove the ancient and modern
obstacles to the unity of Nigeria, only to be defeated six months
later.

For no sooner did the leader of the military junta announce
on May 24, 1966, his plans for the creation of a unitary state of
Nigeria in place of the old tribal and regional power structure,[60]
when a new wave of tribal and regional strife brought the country one step closer to the brink of dissolution. A weekend of inter-
tribal violence in the Northern Region brought death to close to
one hundred persons and injury to more than five times that
number.[61] The unofficial figures for the dead and wounded were
much higher. The fact that General Ironsi, a member of the Ibo
tribe dominant in the Eastern Region, led the January, 1966,
coup against the Moslem Hausa-dominated central government
only nurtured the suspicion of the Northern Region that his
quest for Nigerian unity was no more than a disguise for Ibo
domination. On July 29, 1966,, General Ironsi's regime was overthrown by Hausa tribesmen and he himself was put to the
sword.[62] And so were many thousands of his fellow Ibo tribesmen,
more than 3000 in number, in the Northern Province.[63] Three
hundred thousand Ibos who remained in that Province, after close
to a million had returned home from the North, were evacuated
to their native province.[64] The passage of time only deepened the
division between the warring tribes. On May 30, 1967, the Eastern Province seceded from Nigeria and established itself as the
independent state of Biafra.[65]

In the Sudan, to cite another example, close to four million
pagan-Christian black Africans, in the three southern provinces
of Equatoria, Upper Nile and Bahr-al-Ghazal, have since independence in 1956 been in open revolt against the Moslem North
and its Arab majority of close to twelve million, until they were
reported to have been defeated in March, 1967. It was the accident
of British imperialism that tied the two areas across the tenth
parallel, so famous in the history of the slave trade, together. The
Sudanic and Nilotic tribes of the South and the Arabs of the
North are continents apart in culture, language, race and religion,

and the causes of their conflict date back to Lord Kitchener's era. A Sudanese Government report on the causes of the uprising in the South, frankly acknowledged that:

> There is very little in common between the Northern and Southern Sudanese. Racially the North is Arab, the South is Negroid. Religiously, the North is Moslem, the South is pagan. Linguistically, the North speaks Arabic, the South some 80 different languages...For historical reasons the Southerners regard the Northern Sudanese as their traditional enemies.[66]

To these tensions within may be added the tensions without generated by tribal loyalties which cut across national frontiers. The same tribes, for example, that populate Togo spread into Ghana on one side and seep through Dahomey into Nigeria on the other. The division of the Ewe tribe by the Togo-Ghana border has kept the two neighboring countries at sword's edge. The frontier dispute between Somalia and Ethiopia has its cause in similar tribal dismemberment. No sooner had Somalia won her independence from Italy in 1960, than she was engaged in heavy fighting with Ethiopia for the "redemption" of her kinsmen in the Ogaden region of that ancient empire. An uneasy truce was reached in February 1964,[67] between the two warring countries, but this did in no way diminish the enthusiasm of the two million Somali tribesmen in Ethiopia for union with their fellows in a Greater Somalia.[68] Kenya had been barely independent for two weeks when, on December 25, 1963, her army moved in defense of the territorial integrity of the state against 200,000 dissident Somali tribesmen in the Northeastern Frontier Province.[69] Like their kinsmen in Ethiopia, these Somali tribesmen clamored for union in a Greater Somalia. Early in 1966, Ethiopia and Kenya established a joint military liaison committee to coordinate action against Somali raiders who have been carrying on a guerilla war along their countries' frontiers with the two states. So vulnerable are the African nations on the question of colonial borders, that the Organization of African Unity, at its meeting in Cairo in 1964, resolved by an overwhelming majority to maintain the *status quo* of national frontiers as established at the time of each member's independence, in order to maintain the peace and to forestall the rise of irredentist movements in the various lands.[70]

Tribal animosities and irredentism also plague the countries north of the Sahara. Thus, territorial disputes have come between Morroco and Algeria and there seems to be no settlement in sight. An agreement reached between King Hassan II and the President of the Algerian Provisional Government in July, 1961, which called for the creation of a Commission to settle the border dispute between the two countries,[71] has brought only temporary relief. On March 3, 1967, King Hassan renewed his frequent plea to Algeria to stop preparations for "a violent showdown" and to accept a negotiated settlement of their territorial disputes.[72]

Rounding out the picture of ethnic and racial relations in Africa, and for that matter in Asia, too, is the uncertainty of the situation of the large number of immigrant groups of Asian and European origin which had established themselves in Africa in the wake of European colonization. The gulf that separates the immigrant from the autochtonous population is too wide to be readily bridged by professions of mutual tolerance, respect and good will and by appeals to reason and common interest. These immigrant communities, wrote Tom Mboya, constitute one of the greatest challenges of nation-building in Africa. And he placed the burden squarely on these communities when he stated:

> ...The challenge of acting in such a way that Africans can bury the past really faces the immigrant minorities. One test Africans will apply is that of how many Europeans and Asians apply for citizenship and prove they are serious about staying in Africa. The figures in Tanganyika, so often held up as a model of race relations, are not very cheering. After nearly a year of independence, only forty Europeans and twenty-five hundred Asians had applied for citizenship. This must lead Africans to doubt the sincerity of immigrants who continually talk about being Tanganyikans.

> For this reason, I do not think the offer of "dual citizenship" is a wise move. It does not help our kind of societies to integrate rapidly if some hold back from considering themselves as a part of a single nation. If a European insists that he must retain dual citizenship, Africans are bound to think: 'This man says he is Kenyan but wants to

keep an emergency exit which I as an African citizen do not have.' The test of sincerity is, has he given up everything else to become a Kenya citizen? Is he with us in the same melting pot?... The Asian community, which in Kenya is twice the size of the European and in Uganda and Tanganyika many times the size... their need to integrate swiftly and wipe out the memory of discrimination is probably greater than among Europeans, many of whom can leave East Africa if they cannot adapt to change. The majority of Asians here have no other home...[73]

In the years that followed, many Europeans and Asians left Africa to return to their respective countries of origin, either because of their reluctance to shed the protective umbrella of dual citizenship, or because of the rising competition of Africans, which deprived them of their livelihood. On May 5, 1966, Tom Mboya, speaking in Nairobi as Kenya's Minister for Economic Planning, warned European and Asian businessmen to get more Africans into Kenya's commerce or face the risk that their businesses might be taken over. Said Mr. Mboya:

The Government cannot accept that businesses in the main streets of our urban areas will continue to be owned exclusively by non-Africans. Nor would it be right for such a situation to prevail in a predominantly African country...[74]

The same holds true of many other African countries where, as in Sudan for example, the old-established Greek community is rapidly dwindling under the pressure of a rising Sudanese middle class eager to take over the functions of middlemen long performed by the immigrants from across the Mediterranean Sea.[75]

Across the Atlantic Ocean, in the New World, for example, differences in racial, religious, linguistic and cultural backgrounds have kept Canada divided into two main and uneasy parts, as the English-speaking and French-speaking populations clash over the future of the Federation created a century ago by the British North American Act of 1867. For the first time, the rise of a dissatisfied minority extended its shadow across the North American continent and threatened the integrity of a nation. On

February 25, 1965, the Royal Commission on Bilingualism and Biculturalism, appointed by Prime Minister Lester Pearson in 1962 in the wake of terrorist acts let loose by an insurgent separatist movement in Quebec, issued a preliminary report in which it warned that Canada was experiencing her greatest crisis and that "if it should persist and gather momentum it could destroy Canada." The Commission reported that:

> All that we have seen and heard has led us to the conviction that Canada is in the most critical period of its history since Confederation. We believe that there is a crisis, in the sense that Canada has come to a time when decisions must be taken and developments must occur leading either to its break-up, or to a new set of conditions for its future existence.[76]

The essence of the problem is the French Canadians' growing insistence on economic, cultural and linguistic equality with the rest of Canada. Since 1960, the close to six million people of French origin, language and culture, numbering one-third of Canada's population, have been in revolt not only against the political, economic and cultural predominance of their English-speaking fellow-citizens, but also against a century of drab quiescence of their own making. For almost a hundred years Quebec has lived within itself, an island, almost a nation, under siege. In 1960, the old regime toppled and French Canadians emerged from their shells to demand recognition of their true stature, their indigenous culture, their language and their equal place in the Canadian family.[77]

Perhaps these demands, whose legitimacy is not denied, can and will be satisfied within the framework of greater autonomy for the ten Provinces which compose the Canadian Federation. Quebec is not alone in seeking a more clearly defined division of rights and responsibilities between the Federal Government and the Provinces. Tension between Ottawa and the Provincial capitals has risen in proportion to the growth of federal powers and the consequent erosion of Provincial autonomy in such fields as taxation, education and welfare services.[78] The danger lies in the fact that separatism has become an accepted philosophy, as evidenced by the several studies in recent years under the auspices of the Quebec Legislature of the consequences of a politically independent Quebec.[79] It is nurtured by the fear that in the struggle against the predominance of the majority, the minority, no matter what concessions it may win over the political bargaining table, is ultimately bound to fail and that French culture cannot survive in the long run except in conditions of political independence. However temperate the so-called "quiet revolution" of the French Canadians may be, it is the radicals who normally write the score for the drama of national liberation movements.

In the northeast corner of South America, Guyana came into sovereign independence on May 26, 1966, burdened with a record of communal strife which dates back to 1953, when Great Britain granted to what was formerly known as British Guiana a transitional Constitution with virtually complete internal self-government. This land of about six-hundred thousand people, of whom about three-hundred thousand are East Indians, less than two-hundred thousand Negroes, and the rest Chinese of mixed origin, Amerindians, Portuguese, and others has been polarized to the extreme along racial and communal lines. Rigid racial and ethnic lines divide this small South American enclave, with the East Indian community entrenched in shop and on farm and the Negro community in the cities, professions and civil service, and each organized into distinct political parties competing for power. The prospect of independence only heightened the tension between the two major communities, as the East Indian majority won governmental control at the public polls and the Negro community became alarmed at the consequences of its minority status and sought the protection of the Colonial Power. The result was bloody violence, which claimed hundreds of lives, caused grievious dislocations in both communities, and left a legacy of hate and fear. Although the year preceding the coming of independence to Guyana was marked by relative calm, the East Indian community never forgot nor forgave the Colonial Power for having introduced in 1964 a system of proportional representation which broke its hold on the government and handed over authority to the Negro community.[80] The Declaration of Intent, which was agreed to by the British Guiana Independence Conference in London on November 19, 1965, carries the ominous warning,

> That there should be an end now to the communal divisions
> by which Guyana has for too long been plagued and that,
> with the coming of independence, all Guyanese should put
> aside forever all prejudice and bitterness, and should strive
> together as one nation for the peace and prosperity that
> are the right of all free men.[81]

The Negro is a conspicuous minority throughout most of the
Americas and a protesting one in several of their countries. "In
far too many ways," President Johnson told Howard University's
graduates in a commencement address in Washington on June 4,
1965,

> American Negroes have been another nation, deprived of
> freedom, crippled by hatred, the doors of opportunity closed
> to hope.[82]

Although tremendous progress has been made in the United
States since 1954 toward removing the disabilities long suffered
by the Negro population and redressing the historic wrongs committed against them, it in no way alters the fundamental reality
of the polarization of American society along the color line, with
all its attendant consequences. These lines cannot be easily
erased, neither by the courts, nor by the Congress, nor by the
President, not even by the citizenry at large. The truth is that
the most difficult problem in American life is the acceptance of
the Negro as an equal human being, rather than as a "separate but
equal" human person. In the celebrated decision of 1954, the
Supreme Court held that segregated schools, no matter how equal
technically, were inherently unequal because of the fact that
they were also "separate." Segregation itself, the Court implied,
enforced and perpetuated the role of inferiority assigned to the
Negro. If the absolute equality for the Negro depends on the
absolute end of his separation from the rest of the population, he
will for a long time remain a member of that "other nation"
to which President Johnson referred. Even if all the social afflic-
tions that hold the Negro population in thrall were cured, it would
not necessarily demolish all the barriers erected by that instinctive
consciousness of skin color that exists in nearly every adult
American, whether in the North or in the South. Besides, neither

the protection of the law, nor the decency and good sense of the majority population can guarantee against minorities turning inward in defense of their human dignity to draw inspiration for their daily struggle with themselves as well as with their environment.[83]

CHAPTER X

The Rights of Man and the Fate of Minorities

The limit of United Nations commitment to the protection of minorities may be gauged from Article 5 of the Convention Against Discrimination in Education adopted by the General Conference of the United Nations Educational, Scientific and Cultural Organization at its eleventh session on December 14, 1960, and from Article 27 of the International Covenant on Civil and Political Rights adopted by the General Assembly of the United Nations on December 16, 1966. Article 5 of the UNESCO Convention provides:

> It is essential to recognize the right of members of national minorities to carry on their own educational activities, including the maintenance of schools and, depending on the educational policy of each State, the use or the teaching of their own language, provided, however:
>
> (i) That this right is not exercised in a manner which prevents the members of these minorities from understanding the culture and language of the community as a whole and from participating in its activities, or which prejudice national sovereignty;
>
> (ii) That the standard of education is not lower than the general standard laid down or approved by the competent authorities; and
>
> (iii) That attendance at such schools is optional.[1]

Article 27 of the International Covenant on Civil and Political Rights reads:

> In those States in which ethnic, religious or linguistic minorities exist, persons belonging to such minorities shall not be denied the right, in community with the other members of their group, to enjoy their own culture, to profess and practice their own religion, or to use their own language.[2]

Yet even these severely circumscribed and highly qualified rights were only grudgingly conceded. When the Sub-Commission on Prevention of Discrimination and Protection of Minorities convened for the first time in 1947 to map out its program of work, it was almost unanimous in its conclusion that minority rights were more a concession of the largesse of the State, than an inherent right of a group that differed from the rest of a country's population in race, religion, language or ethnic origin. The Sub-Commission defined the protection of minorities as:

> The protection of non-dominant groups which, while wishing in general for equality of treatment with the majority, wish for a measure of differential treatment in order to preserve basic characteristics which they possess and which distinguish them from the majority of the population. The protection applies equally to individuals belonging to such groups and wishing the same protection. It follows that differential treatment of such groups, or of individuals belonging to such groups, is justified when it is exercised in the interest of their contentment and the welfare of the community as a whole. The characteristics meriting such protection are race, religion or language. In order to qualify for protection a minority must owe undivided allegiance to the Government of the State in which it lives. Its members must also be nationals of that State.[3]

This definition proved unacceptable to its parent body, the Commission on Human Rights, which returned it to the Sub-Commission for further study. The Commission, as well as the General Assembly, was concerned lest any imposition of a positive obligation on States, even by implication, to ensure the rights of minorities, might awaken or stimulate minority consciousness and obstruct the processes of assimilation. It proposed to restrict the application of the term minority to groups which were patently separate and distinct, well defined and long established on the territory of a state. And it sought to formulate United Nations concern with minorities in such a way as to discourage the creation of new minorities and encourage the natural processes of integration and assimilation.[4] This accounts for the negative wording in Article 27 of the International Covenant on Civil and Political Rights, which is in sharp contrast with the preceding Articles. The obligation of the state is limited to the negative duty of permitting the free exercise of the rights of minorities.[5] The Commission rejected the notion of national minorities because of its political connotations and was anxious to give the narrowest possible construction to the rights of minorities.

The note struck by the Commission on Human Rights in 1949-50, echoed a basic United Nations position which has changed little in the years that followed. The debate on Article 27 in the Third Committee of the General Assembly in 1961, was not much different from the debate more than ten years earlier in the Commission on Human Rights. Delegations representing countries of immigration sought to make it emphatically clear that the Article could under no circumstances be construed as implying that persons of similar background who entered their countries as immigrants could even remotely be categorized as minorities. While they conceded that immigrants were free to use their own language and to follow their own religion, the interests of national integrity required them to become part of the national fabric. Other delegations insisted that the provision of Article 27 could not be invoked to justify attempts to undermine the national unity of any state. Still other delegations stressed that, in voting for the adoption of the Article, they understood it to apply only to existing minorities which succeeded in maintaining their separate identities and hoped it would not encourage the rise of new minorities. The Article was adopted in the original text by a vote of 80 to none, with South Africa abstaining.[6]

These and other debates in the United Nations, bearing directly or indirectly on the question of minorities, have a significance beyond their immediate relevance. The overwhelming majority of Member States appears to be committed to a line of intransigence in the matter of majority-minority relations that

makes it extremely difficult for the United Nations to intervene
in this area to relieve the underlying stresses of the minorities
problem around the world.[7] For the new countries of Asia and
Africa especially, it is a compulsive act of self-preservation to
make common cause against any suggestion which might cast
doubt on their territorial integrity. One of the strongest arguments invoked by India against Pakistan's appeal to the principle
of self-determination in the dispute over Kashmir, for example,
has been that its application beyond the limits of the anti-colonialist campaign would disrupt the unity of many states and
prejudice their territorial integrity. Thus at a Security Council
meeting on Kashmir in February, 1964, the representative of
India warned that,

> Pakistan has made a great deal of play with the idea of self-
> determination ... It would lead to disastrous consequences
> if the expression were extended to apply to the integral
> part of any country or sections of its population, or to en-
> able such integrated part or section of the population to
> secede. The principle of self-determination cannot and must
> not be applied to bring about the fragmentation of a coun-
> try or its people ... In the world today we have innumerable
> countries in Africa and Asia with dissident minorities.
> Many of these minorities might like to set up governments
> of their own. We should have to repaint the map of the
> world and many States Members of the United Nations
> would be broken up. Many countries today have living in
> them people of different races, religions and cultures, and
> the future of the world depends upon the evolution of
> multiracial States and nations in different parts of the
> world ...[8]

No one has yet arisen to challenge publicly this thesis and no
country has dared to put it to the test. The notion of incom-
patability of the principle of self-determination with the requirements of national unity is widely shared. It was crystallized
during the long debates in the early nineteen-fifties in United
Nations bodies over the propriety and wisdom of including a clause
on self-determination of peoples in the International Covenants
on Human Rights.[9] The sponsors of this clause, which included
virtually all Member States but the Western Powers, exclusive

of the United States, obviously intended it as a dramatic assertion of the right of subject peoples to independence and national sovereignty. Its purely propaganda purposes as a weapon in the anti-colonialist campaign could not be disguised. Nor could its incongruity with the letter and spirit of the Covenants be denied. These international treaties were meant to safeguard the agreed-upon basic political, civil, economic, social and cultural rights of the individual. They did not purport to state the rights of peoples. There were thus valid reasons for opposing the insertion of the self-determination clause in the international human rights treaties. But when all other arguments proved unavailing, opponents of the clause conjured up visions of secession and revolt of minorities, fired by the assertion of the right of self-determination as a fundamental human right. Australia's Sir Percy Spender challenged the majority to heed the lessons of history, when he warned the Third Committee of the 1955 General Assembly, that,

> It is common knowledge, to give but one example, that before the Second World War the German people were not confined to the German Reich but were to be found in communities of varying sizes and importance within the borders of many nations, big and small, extending from the Atlantic to the Urals. Is this Committee prepared to endorse the thesis that these German minorities being a separate people within the State to which they owed allegiance had the right, either in isolation or in collusion with Hitler's Reich, to self-determination, and by exercising it, the right to disrupt and dismember France, Czechoslovakia, Roumania, Poland or the USSR, to mention only the larger pre-War States which possessed large German minorities, living in compact communities? And I would ask a further question. Do any of my distinguished colleagues in this Committee, whose countries possess distinct and compact ethnic minorities—and several of the leading spokesmen in favor of the right of self-determination fall into this group—suggest that their countries would permit, or should permit these minorities to exercise a right to set up their own self-government or should they so wish, to secede and perhaps even to link themselves with other States whose relations with that of which they are now a part may be strained?[10]

Canada's Paul Martin recalled that his country's historical experience was one of evolution tending to free and equal association. "Our nation," he said,

> encompasses peoples of many racial origins with varying religious beliefs and cultural heritages. We live freely together, and each citizen is free to think according to his own conscience and to act as he sees fit within the limitations imposed by the law. It would be a serious matter indeed, if, through a decision of the United Nations, member countries were placed in a position of being morally and even perhaps legally bound to grant to these minority groups the right to determine their own institutions without consideration for the wishes of the community as a whole...[11]

Great Britain's representative asked very bluntly whether those who were so anxious to include the self-determination clause in the human rights covenants were prepared to face the consequences of assuming a legal obligation to promote the right of self-determination within their borders. Self-determination, Sir Samuel Hoare declared,

> means in essence that any group which considers itself a people or a nation should be free to choose the government under which it wished to live.

> The right set forth in Article 1 would apply not only to colonial peoples, but to minorities, inhabitants of disputed border territories, and irredentist and dissident groups as well... The concept of self-determination cannot be whittled down to exclude minorities or groups wishing to secede. Its great force lies precisely in the fact that it is all-embracing...[12]

These warnings did not deter the majority of the States Members from pressing the self-determination clause to a successful conclusion. They only served to alert them to the importance of setting precise limits to the application of the principle which, in the opinion of the majority, coincided with the traditional frontiers of colonialism. The debates made it clear that the principle of self-determination could be invoked only for the liberation of colonial peoples and territories. It was not to be construed as implying the right of individuals within nations to express their special ethnic, cultural or religious characteristics or the exercise of the democratic method in internal affairs. If any lingering doubts remained, they were laid to rest by the famous Declaration on the Granting of Independence to Colonial Countries and Peoples, which the General Assembly adopted without a dissenting vote on December 14, 1960. Operative paragraph 6 of the Declaration warns that,

> Any attempt at the partial or total disruption of the national unity and the territorial integrity of a country is incompatible with the purposes and principles of the Charter of the United Nations.[13]

One can doubt the practical relevance of the debates on the inclusion or exclusion of a self-determination clause in the draft international covenants on human rights to the accession to freedom and independence of so many countries and peoples, which in less than a decade more than doubled the membership of the United Nations. But there can be no doubt that these debates have helped shape an attitude and conception which virtually excludes the question of minorities from the purview of legitimate international concern. Thus, the General Assembly decidedly refused to be drawn into the substance of the complaint made in 1960 by Austria against Italy for the latter's alleged infringement of the rights of the German-speaking population in the Province of Bolzano. It was the first time that a minorities question was officially raised in the United Nations and the reactions of governments were especially instructive. Because of its significance as a case study, a brief review of the proceedings in the General Assembly may be in place.

A first intimation that Austria proposed to seize the United Nations with the problem of the Austrian minority in Italy was given by her Foreign Minister in his statement to the General Assembly on September 21, 1959.[14] Although his announcement was received cooly, the Austrian Government decided to raise the question formally at the next, or fifteenth, session of the General Assembly in 1960. In a letter dated June 23, 1960,[15] Dr. Bruno Kreisky, Austria's Foreign Minister, requested the inclusion in the agenda of the 1960 General Assembly "The Problem of the Austrian Minority in Italy." Austria complained that the Paris

Agreement of 1946,[16] which provided for legislative and executive autonomy of the South Tyrolean population as a measure for the protection of the ethnic and cultural character of the Austrian minority in that area, was interpreted and applied by Italy in a manner that contradicted its purpose in many essential respects. She requested that the General Assembly consider her dispute with Italy in order to bring about a just settlement based on democratic principles by which the Austrian minority in Italy would be conceded a true autonomy, so as to enjoy the self-administration and self-government it needed for the protection of its existence as a minority.

When the Austrian request came up for consideration by the Bureau of the General Assembly, the immediate reaction was that the inclusion of the item on the agenda as formulated by Austria would compel the United Nations to enter into the substantive problem of the Austro-Italian dispute and pass judgement on a matter which was potentially explosive for many countries represented in the world body. The Bureau looked for a formulation which could in no wise establish a precedent for United Nations intervention in minorities questions. A solution was provided by the representative of Canada, who proposed that the title of the item to be included in the agenda at the request of Austria read: The Status of the German-speaking Element in the Province of Bolzano (Bozen) : Implementation of the Paris Agreement of September 5, 1946. This formulation reduced the question to a dispute between Austria and Italy over the implementation of an international agreement and obligated the United Nations to go no further than to urge the parties to the dispute to come to an amicable settlement.[17]

That the General Committee's acceptance of the Canadian formulation was far more than a procedural decision was made clear when the item reached the floor of the General Assembly's Special Political Committee. It was, as the representative of Uruguay noted, a definition of the substance of the question.[18] The debate in the Special Political Committee showed how sensitive the overwhelming majority of Member States were to the problem of minorities and how careful they were to emphasize that States bound by a specific international agreement alone had obligations under international law in regard to the treatment of minorities. Thus, the Argentinian representative stated that, the approach to minorities questions had changed radically since World War II; the idea of special regimes for the protection of racial, linguistic or religious minorities was intimately connected with the League of Nations and died with the death of the League; the concept of special protection of minorities was alien to the Charter of the United Nations and was not recognized at the present time; its place was taken by the obligation to ensure human rights and fundamental freedoms to all inhabitants of a country.[19]

The representative of Brazil declared that his Delegation

would have hesitated to give approval to Austria's raising the question of autonomy to a minority group in Italy, were it not for the existence of the Paris Agreement of 1946. He would have opposed it even if the status of that minority had been the result of boundary revisions or forced resettlement, for that did not as a rule entitle a minority to special political or economic rights and privileges.[20]

Bolivia's representative found it difficult to understand the importance being attached to the problem of minorities, which seemed to him

outmoded in the light of new trends in contemporary thought. Those new trends found expression in provisions which were supra-national in scope and had become rules of international law such as, for example, the provisions of the Universal Declaration of Human Rights and the Charter of the United Nations, which prohibited all discrimination based on class, color, religion or sex.[21]

The representative of Peru agreed with his Argentinian colleague that,

special protection of minorities was inspired by an outworn concept of international law. Today the United Nations protected human rights and sought to secure freedom from discrimination for all groups, including minorities. The principle that all citizens were equal before the law was the historical foundation of Latin American nations, including Bolivia.[22]

Yugoslavia's representative declared that,

> his country had always considered that the problem of
> national minorities could best be solved by the guarantee
> of democratic rights and opportunities for the free devel-
> opment of the ethnic groups concerned. The realistic and
> appropriate method of dealing with the problem at hand
> was by bilateral negotiations between Austria and Italy.[23]

The representative of Lebanon said that,

> the United Nations could not possibly support claims by
> any ethnic, linguistic or religious minority for complete or
> partial autonomy within an independent sovereign state.
> The principles of the Charter did not support the request
> for autonomy as stated in the Austrian draft resolution.
> At one time the protection of minorities had been an
> institution of international public law, but it had been
> made an excuse for interfering in the domestic affairs of
> States and was now obsolete. Today, under the Charter of
> the United Nations, relations between states were based on
> equal sovereignty, and any interference in their domestic
> affairs was prohibited. Individual members of minorities
> had the same status as other citizens and were protected
> by the Charter and the Universal Declaration of Human
> Rights.[24]

The representative of Libya declared that,

> it was indisputable that international law did not grant
> any special rights to minorities unless there was a treaty
> to that effect concluded between two or more sovereign
> states.[25]

Pakistan's representative stressed that,

> the competence of the United Nations in the matter under
> consideration derived exclusively from the fact that it was
> the subject of an international agreement between Austria
> and Italy. The political status of the German-speaking
> minority in the South Tyrol was not within the competence
> of the United Nations except insofar as that competence
> derived from the Paris Agreement of 1946. The human

rights and fundamental freedoms of minorities, on the other hand, were among the basic principles of the United Nations and unquestionably came within its jurisdiction. It was not Austria's contention, however, that the treatment accorded the German-speaking element in the South Tyrol violated the provisions of the Charter relating to such rights and freedoms.[26]

The representative of Turkey declared that,

if the problem was to be usefully dealt with, it was important to keep strictly to the title of the agenda item, which referred to the Paris Agreement. It was only from that point of view that the Committee could and should study both the extent and nature of the rights of the German-speaking population and Italy's obligations. To invoke any other principle, e.g. the principle of minorities or of human rights, in order to support the claims of the German-speaking population, would mean recognizing minority rights beyond those required by international law and custom. It would set up a dangerous precedent incompatible with the spirit of the Charter of the United Nations.[27]

The representative of Ghana noted that his country

was well acquainted with problems of the kind under consideration, for in nineteenth-century Africa no heed had been paid to the interests of ethnic groups. However, such problems could be solved only in a spirit of understanding between the countries directly concerned.[28]

India's representative suggested that

the question of autonomy for the area in which the German-speaking population was centered was one which came within the scope of the Italian Constitution and its inhabitants were right in bringing their grievances before the Italian Parliament. India felt that it would not be advisable for the United Nations to become involved in a thorough discussion of the subject. The Committee, in discussing the issue between Austria and Italy, should bear in mind the history of the area and the implications which the discussion might have with regard to problems affecting certain other states.[29]

The Western powers were generally agreed that the dispute between Austria and Italy concerned the application of the Agreement of 1946, not its substance, and that bilateral negotiations were therefore the best solution. They agreed with those who argued, like the representative of Greece, for example, that the sole basis for the rights the German-speaking element in the Province of Bolzano claimed was the Italo-Austrian Agreement and that it was precisely the Paris Agreement which gave the question an international status.[30] Of the few dissenting voices, that of Afghanistan was perhaps the most pronounced. The representative of Afghanistan declared that he recognized

> Austria's natural interest in the people of South Tyrol who had been separated from their kinsmen in Austria by political arrangements of the kind which produced tragic consequences in other parts of the world . . . If direct negotiations were resumed, due regard should be paid to the legitimate ethnic and cultural rights and the political aspirations of the peoples concerned. If no agreement could be achieved, the people themselves should be allowed to determine their own fate.

He hoped, however,

> that a settlement could be arrived at through the efforts of the United Nations, thus establishing a basis for the solution of other international problems of a similar nature.[31]

Of the so-called Communist bloc, the representative of Cuba was the only one to participate in the debate. He took issue with those who contended that the wording of the agenda item affected the substance of the problem before the Special Political Committee. He also contested the view of the majority that the dispute between Austria and Italy could be reduced to a mere legal controversy regarding the implementation of the Paris Agreement of 1946. The problem of the 250,000 Austrians of the South Tyrol, Ambassador Bisbe said,

continued to exist in the heart of Europe, with all the
risks which that involved; and it would be absurd for
the United Nations to make no effort to settle the Austro-
Italian dispute and seek a just and satisfactory solution
for the problem... The Cuban delegation therefore supported the Austrian request.[32]

In the end, however, the Italian point of view prevailed. From
the very beginning, Italy maintained that what Austria asked
amounted to a request for unilateral revision of a treaty in force
between the two countries and an invitation to the General Assembly to request Italy to grant the German-speaking inhabitants
of the Alto-Adige a new autonomy which would be foreign to the
system of protection of human rights laid down in the Universal
Declaration. In his statement on October 18, 1960, to the Special
Political Committee, Foreign Minister Antonio Segni warned:

You will readily appreciate the situation we would have
to face if, by admitting the Austrian claims, we should
create a precedent for a wider revisionistic movement
which might well endanger the very principle of the Charter to which we are bound. And I am sure that once these
things are made perfectly clear to you, you will not hesitate
to take a firm stand in defense of our Charter. In doing so
you will doubtless give assurances not only to European
countries, but also to the young States, newcomers to our
Organization, which having fought hard to gain their
independence are determined to defend it against all...[33]

The resolution which the Special Political Committee adopted
by acclamation, reflected faithfully the sentiments of the overwhelming majority. It limited itself to urging the two parties
to the dispute to resume negotiations and, in case these had
failed, to resort to one or another machinery envisaged in the
Charter of the United Nations for the settlement of international
disputes.

The counsels of caution have bequeathed an attitude toward
the question of minorities of such great weight and substance
that they tend to obscure a very real and increasingly critical
problem which in time will present an implacable, relentless and
in the end inescapable challenge to the United Nations and the

world. When in December, 1948, the General Assembly adopted
the Universal Declaration of Human Rights, it went out of its
way to explain why that historic document contained no specific
measures for the protection of minorities. In a formal resolution,
the General Assembly pointed out that

> it is difficult to adopt a uniform solution of this complex
> and delicate question, which has special aspects in each
> State in which it arises.

It requested the Sub-Commission on the Prevention of Discrimination and the Protection of Minorities

> to make a thorough study of the problem of minorities in
> order that the United Nations may be able to take effective
> measures for the protection of racial, national, religious or
> linguistic minorities.[34]

No such thorough study was ever made and effective measures
have yet to be taken for the protection of minorities. The Secretary General early came to the conclusion that the validity of
the claims of minorities to specific rights or protective measures
could be decided only on the basis of the conditions and arrangements under which the minority was included in the State and
of all other relevant circumstances and that each case, therefore,
had to be considered on its own merits.[35] His judgement only
confirmed the general knowledge of the difficulties in the way of
agreement on measures for the protection of minorities which
would meet the varying conditions and circumstances. But it
also had the effect of removing the question from active consideration by United Nations bodies, as a subject of an essentially
political nature which could better be dealt with and determined
on a political level. Accordingly, the Sub-Commission, in agreement with the Commission on Human Rights, the Economic and
Social Council and the General Assembly, decided to concentrate
on the prevention of discrimination as a practical measure for
the protection of minorities.[36]

It had been cogently argued that prevention of discrimination
and protection of minorities were overlapping categories. Since
race, color, creed, nationality and language were normally grounds
for discriminatory practices which denied to members of racial,
religious, linguistic and ethnic minorities human rights and fun-

damental freedoms, prevention of discrimination was a most potent measure for the protection of minorities. Indeed, freedom from discrimination and equality of treatment in law and in fact have been their most insistently defended rights. But beyond their aspirations for equality, racial, religious, linguistic and ethnic minorities are also concerned to safeguard their group rights, or they are doomed to extinction. Freedom of religion, communication and association, for example, must be translated into group rights, or their denial to groups severely circumscribes, if not completely destroys, their proper exercise by the individual belonging to such groups. Freedom of religion, to be fully exercised, must include not only the freedom of adherents to assemble to perform rites and practices or to receive religious instruction, but also to share in spiritual life. Embraced in such life are many imponderables, but it includes such practical matters as contact with correligionists abroad, participation in international religious congresses and associations, and attendance at religious schools in foreign countries. The same holds true of the other group rights.[37] Ethnic differences very often depend for their survival on language, schools and other cultural institutions which spring from the needs of such differences and which meet their purposes. Unless a member of an ethnic group has the right and opportunity to nurture the traditions and culture of his group, he is grieviously injured in the enjoyment of his human rights and fundamental freedoms. This is so, regardless of the rights and freedoms he may enjoy in all other respects. If the survival of his group is jeopardized, the survival of the individual as a member of his group is likewise jeopardized.[38]

In retrospect, the omission in the Universal Declaration of Human Rights of any reference to rights of minorities only served to encourage a comfortable illusion and to nurture a solemn complacency. By proclaiming individual human rights and freedoms as its principal concern and distinguishing them from the rights of the individual as a member of a racial, religious, linguistic or ethnic minority, the United Nations made concessions to an abstraction which not only ignores experience but fastens on obvious contradictions. The essence of equality is the refusal to recognize irrelevant distinctions, not the erasure of all distinctions. The individual whose human rights and fundamental freedoms the United Nations seeks to proclaim and defend is man in his national, cultural and spiritual environment. Stripped of

his environmental, national and cultural characteristics, spiritually adrift from his past and loosed from his traditional
moorings, man loses his essential humanity. Yet these are the
inevitable consequences of a doctrine or policy that carries the
distinction between the rights and freedoms of the individual as
a human person and his rights and freedoms as a member of a
racial, religious, linguistic or ethnic group to its logical conclusions.

If the United Nations is to address itself to realities and meet
the legitimate requirements of the many millions of people all
over the world who constitute minority groups of one kind or
another, it must redress the distortions of the past twenty years
which have tended to separate the human individual from his
immediate environment. The rights and freedoms of minority
groups that are of universal interest and application are those
which derive from the merits of the individuals who make up
those minorities and which are but an extension of their human
rights and fundamental freedoms. They are the rights and freedoms which are essential to the survival of the group and the
preservation of its cultural values and historic heritage. They
have been denied in some countries, circumscribed in others, and
reluctantly conceded elsewhere, on the general theory that diversity ultimately undermines the integrity of the state and that
uniformity is the surest guarantee of national cohesion. Fundamentally, however, it is a conception of intra-state relations which
is very often intolerant also of all other forms of human freedom
and liberty. Its root cause, as we have noted at the beginning, is
the promotion of the interests of the state as the supreme objective and as an end in itself.

An international concern with human rights and fundamental
freedoms, which reaches down into the wellsprings of all creative
instinct and imagination, can hold no brief for uniformity. An
international order whose purpose is the elevation of the human
personality has all the room for diversity. It is, therefore, within
the framework of international concern with the fate of man
that the world can best overcome the massive political and
psychological obstacles to the universal acceptance of diversity.
For such acceptance will not only satisfy the legitimate requirements of most of the world's minorities but reduce the pressures
and tensions which give rise to demands threatening the territo-

rial integrity of states and encumbering their international relations and put forward by minorities as indispensible to their survival or the maintenance of their identity. As the demands of minorities come knocking at the doors of the United Nations with increasing force, events will force the hand of the international organization and move it toward international protection of human rights as an urgent and practical necessity.

As the embodiment of the reasoning forces of the world, the idea of international concern with the fate of man moves unobstrusively forward to the rhythmic plod of history. As the need to encounter and respond to the gathering storms grows more urgent, it is bound to come forward as a fundamental design for the reconciliation and regeneration of humanity. A case in point is the critical situation in Cyprus. The peace of Cyprus depends upon the association of Greeks and Turks as loyal citizens of a common fatherland in which the right of the majority to govern is respected and the right of the minority to preserve its identity and the values it cherishes is safeguarded. Neither *enosis*, nor union with Greece, nor partition, nor a shift in population to draw the scattered Turkish communities into more easily defended concentrations, nor a federalist structure will bring peace to the Island. If the two communities cannot learn to live with each other, they will not learn to get along next to each other either. There is, of course, the possibility of an exchange of population, but this is an extreme solution which depends upon the Greeks in Greece and the Turks in Turkey, not upon the Greeks and Turks of Cyprus.

The core of the Cyprus problem remains the protection of the Cypriot Turks in their individual and group rights, so that they may be assured of their free development in accordance with their ethnic predilections. The alarm felt by the Turkish minority at the prospective loss of their constitutional guarantees, including the protective shield of the right of Turkey to intervene in defense of the *status quo*, is as understandable as the impatience shown by the majority, especially in the light of the treatment accorded their minorities by other newly independent countries. It is too much to expect that the Turks would lightly agree to changes in a Constitution heavily weighted in their favor by an elaborate system of checks and balances and divided powers, without receiving in exchange even more reliable guar-

antees. Their mistrust of the Greek majority is too deep to be
exorcised by promises which can be breached and guarantees
which cannot be enforced.

Who is there who can secure the Turkish minority entrench-
ments the Greek majority cannot touch? Not until the United
Nations can intervene effectively in defense of the human rights
and fundamental freedoms of all of Cyprus' citizens can the
world organization intervene successfully in the role of umpire on
constitutional reform involving the relationship between majority
and minority.[39] Not until international concern with the rights
and freedoms of man becomes an operating principle of international relations will the people of Cyprus, and people everywhere,
rest their lives, security and liberty on the strength of the United
Nations. But there is no alternative, and sooner or later the
United Nations will have to follow the course indicated by its
former Mediator on Cyprus, Dr. Galo Plaza, in his report of
March 26, 1965, to Secretary-General U Thant, as follows:

> One of the principles of the Charter which I regard as
> having the highest relevance to any settlement of the
> Cyprus problem is that of respect for human rights and
> fundamental freedoms, without discrimination. The fact
> that the population of the island continues to consist of
> two principal ethnic communities, the further fact that
> they are unequal in numbers and finally the gravity of
> the conflict which has developed between them—all these
> elements have given and must continue to give rise to
> serious difficulties in applying this principle, and must be
> made the subject of special attention.
>
> From the moment a settlement is in sight, the Charter's
> insistence on respect for human rights and for fundamental
> freedoms for all, without distinction as to race, sex, lan-
> guage or religion, will assume a capital importance in
> Cyprus. It will be an indispensable condition for the pro-
> gressive rebirth of confidence and the re-establishment of
> social peace. The obstacles against the full application of
> the principle cannot be over-estimated; and they are no
> less psychological than political . . .

For all these reasons there is no doubt in my mind—and on this point all parties are in agreement—that there must be established in Cyprus the most rigorous possible guarantees of human rights and safeguards against discrimination. For some time, in order to help the two communities to find their way out of the vicious circle of deep distrust between them, I am convinced, indeed, that certain international guarantees must be provided...

In any progress made toward a settlement, the question of the means of guaranteeing its provisions will inevitably arise... On the one hand, the conception of treaty arrangements which would affect the internal affairs of the Republic is anathema to many Greek-Cypriots... On the other hand, the Turkish-Cypriots feel also that they have had a painful experience in placing excessive faith in treaties, having seen many of their treaty rights forcibly suspended and the Guarantor Powers fail to act in the crisis as the Turkish-Cypriots expected them to do.

It may be that a different form of guarantee will have to be devised. In this regard I see an opportunity for the United Nations to play an invaluable part, if it so agreed. The possibility could be explored, I believe, of the United Nations itself acting as the guarantor of the terms of the settlement. It might prove feasible, for example, for the parties to agree to lay before the United Nations the precise terms of the settlement and ask it not only to take note of them but also to spell them out in a resolution, formally accept them as the agreed basis of the settlement, and request that any complaint of violation or difficulty in implementation be brought immediately before it. Such a role for the United Nations would, I believe, be in full accordance with the letter and the spirit of the Charter.[40]

CHAPTER XI

The International Color Bar

Not until the notion of national homogeneity and uniformity ceases to be an ideal to strive for will ethnic distinctions and racial, religious and linguistic differences be taken for granted and pluralistic societies accepted as part of the natural order of things. But great compassion and a deep commitment to the idea of a common humanity are necessary to overcome the deep-seated prejudices which stem from differences in the color of man's skin.

Cutting across national, racial, religious and linguistic divisions is the color bar, which separates White men from Brown and Yellow men and both from Black men. The differentiation of the human race according to hue and shade of skin is an inexorable reality. It cannot be disavowed by professions of mutual respect and tolerance, nor minimized by appeals to reason, science and logic. Color consciousness in man runs swift and deep, and its waters are fed by many streams rising from many sources. At home, the tolerance of unintegrated and unassimilable minorities of any color, anywhere, is undergoing severe trials. The antagonism, for example, between the Africans and the expatriate Asian communities in their midst has often burst into open violence.[1] The gap between the expectations of the American Negroes and the adaptability of their white fellow-citizens only confirms that the habits of generations die slowly. There is general agreement that the large-scale transformation of basic attitudes which would make real for all Negroes the promise of equal opportunity has yet to occur. The protests in 1963-1964 of African students against the bias and prejudice of their Chinese, Russian, German, Czech and Bulgarian hosts have shown that the color line stretches far and wide in all directions, without regard to political, social and economic systems or ideological convictions.[2] The emergence in England of a race problem in the wake of the influx, since the end of World War II, of almost a million brown-skinned and black-skinned immigrants from the Commonwealth countries in Asia, Africa and the West Indies has shown anew that the meeting of peoples of different colors and different cultures can only too easily lead to friction whether in Peiping or Moscow, London or New York.[3]

Abroad, the color bar forever awaits the casual spark to ignite age-old prejudices, mistrusts and resentments. The intrusion of racism into contemporary ideological conflicts has only increased the susceptibility of color to exploitation for political ends and the promotion of national interests. Massive psychological and political advantages are in store for the power that emerges as the leader of the downtrodden, Colored races against the White masters who once oppressed them. For the echo of debates among the races of man is still the discontent of those whose skins are black, brown or yellow at the domination by those whose complexion is white. History, science and technology have conspired to draw the color line to cincide with the affluence of the White man's northern part of the world and the poverty of the Colored man's southern end of the globe. This in large measure compensates for the division within and among the Colored races by political and ideological conflicts, ethnic and cultural differences, power rivalries and fears of domination and unites them in a fellowship of the disadvantaged and dispossessed. For example, in their bid for leadership of the Communist world and in the interest of their Great Power status, the Chinese are not likely to abandon the advantage affinity of color gives them among the darker-complexioned races of Asia, Africa and Latin America to try to lead them in revolt against the White race. As Chinese imperialism probes for vassals in Asia, Africa and Latin America, it can employ racism just as readily as it uses Marxist-Leninist doctrines in its struggle with the Soviet Union.[4] Even though the underprivileged nations cannot be blind to the possibility or probability of China seeking to enlist their aspirations in the service of her own national ambitions, they are too vengeful over the injustices of the past and too resentful of the lingering privileges and advantages of the former colonialists to look beyond the immediate present.

Immediately at issue is the status of the Black man in the southern triangle of Africa. The arena of battle over this issue has for the largest part been the United Nations. United Nations concern with racial discrimination is, of course, an absolute interest. It is not conditional on whether such discrimination has international repercussions or not. Nor is it dependent on whether a majority discriminates against a minority, or a minority against a majority. If the equality of man is a desirable end anywhere, the accident of race or color must be neither a burden nor a privilege everywhere. What distinguishes the situation in South Africa from racial discrimination elsewhere is that *apartheid*, or racial segregation, is an official and uncompromising governmental policy. South Africa's is the only government today that makes racial discrimination the foundation of its philosophy and the separation of races the basis of its conduct. What makes South Africa's racial policies a matter of such urgent concern to the international community is the identification of the non-White world with the cause of the Black man there. To the overwhelming majority of the Afro-Asian nations, there is no conceivable crime greater than *apartheid*.[5]

The struggle against *apartheid* has been a cause of no doubtful purpose ever since it was raised for the first time in 1952 in the General Assembly of the United Nations. It has served as a focus of resistance against all forms of racism and racial discrimination in the world which, along with decolonization and economic development of underdeveloped areas, has figured on the United Nations agenda among the most crucial problems of the age. The insistence of the Colored races and peoples everywhere on a full measure of social respect has made racial discrimination and the drawing of the color line one of the most explosive problems of our time. The Asian and African peoples and those of the islands of the oceans and the seas have been intent upon reclaiming not only their right to nationhood, but to dignity and equality. For them, as for the underdeveloped countries in general, it has become a compulsive common act of self-assertion to unite against any and all forms of racial inequality and to rescue the dignity of man from beneath the heels of those who would trample on it.

As long as the stronghold of White supremacy in South Africa, the disfranchisement of Africans in Southern Rhodesia, and the frustrations of Black nationalists in South West Africa and in the Portuguese colonies of Angola and Mozambique remain to challenge the whole idea of African maturity and independence and to perpetuate the notion of the Africans' inferiority, racial passion and bias will continue to sweep the world and the Colored races will move to dreams of violent change. "South Africa's race rule," we have been warned,

> is an ever present incitement to the rest of Africa where oppression of the African people on the grounds of race is a cause of the most intense provocation. South Africa is seen by independent Africa to be not only an extreme manifestation of colonialism, but also as a center of aggression and counter-revolution that menaces the principles and practices of the new independent Africa. In the view of the African nations, the continuance of colonialism and racialism in this form, constitutes a menace to the peace of the continent and the world; and this is a vital factor in the foreign policies of all the independent States, cementing all-African unity and inspiring their determination to act against a force which challenges the very basis of independence in Africa.[6]

Diallo Telli, one-time Guinea's Ambassador to the United Nations and present Secretary-General of the Organization of African Unity, warned repeatedly that,

> The African States are determined to rid themselves at any price, but preferably by peaceful means, of the humiliating and degrading practices of racial discrimination, which has been raised to the rank of State doctrine and official policy by a Government in the south of our continent. We for our part think that in the face of such a situation, which degrades the colored man in South Africa, to such an extent, which flouts the United Nations Charter and tramples under foot the dignity of the African people and the very dignity of man, neither the international community nor any people in the world can remain indifferent, for they are directly concerned ...
>
> United Africa is determined, come what may, to ensure respect for the principles of equality, justice and democracy in South Africa.[7]

To the overwhelming majority of nations represented in the United Nations, *apartheid* is not only a crime against the Black man, but an insult to the non-White races around the world. "The African and Asian countries," the representative of India on the Special Political Committee of the General Assembly in 1963 declared,

> might be plagued by scarcities of such material require-
> ments as educational facilities, employment opportunities,
> proper nutrition and health services. However, when it
> comes to self-respect and the personal pride of their citi-
> zens, they are no poorer than any European country. The
> world should realize that they regard *apartheid* in South
> Africa as an affront to that pride and self-respect and so
> long as South Africa remains racist, Africans and Asians
> everywhere would feel that their own freedom is not com-
> plete...[3]

Clearly, *apartheid* is far, far more than an issue between the White minority and the Black majority in South Africa. South Africa's racial policy involves the broader problem of relations between the White and Colored races everywhere. The determina-tion of the emancipated peoples of Africa to demolish the color bar in that unhappy land is an earnest of their absolute and intense solidarity on an issue which leaves little margin for error. Al-ready, they compelled aquiescence in an interpretation of the United Nations Charter, which in straining its procedures has offended the sensibilities of jurists and parliamentarians alike. The racial policies of South Africa have been one of the intract-able problems which have faced the United Nations since its very inception, when India first denounced what was then the Union of South Africa for discriminating against persons of Indian origin. Not only has the tone of the statements against South Africa grown sharper and increasingly more emotional, but each of the thirty-odd resolutions on the subject through the middle of 1966 adopted by the General Assembly and the Security Council has become successively stronger and more demanding and received ever-greater support. Thus in 1952, fifteen out of fifty-eight Member States either voted for, or abstained on, a South African motion to declare the General Assembly incom-petent to deal with the question of *apartheid* on the ground that it constituted a matter within the exclusive jurisdiction of the Union.[9] Simultaneously, seventeen Member States voted against, while seven others abstained on, the principal clause in Resolution 616 (VII) adopted by the General Assembly, which established a three-member commission to study the racial situation in South Africa.[30] On December 16, 1963, all but Portugal and South Africa of the one-hundred two Member States present and voting approved a General Assembly resolution which, *inter alia*, appealed to all States Members of the United Nations or the specialized agencies,

> to take appropriate measures and intensify their efforts, separately and collectively, with a view to dissuading the Government of the Republic of South Africa from pursuing its policies of *apartheid* and requests them, in particular, to implement fully the Security Council resolution of December 4, 1963.[11]

The measures referred to are those the General Assembly approved on November 6, 1962, in resolution 1761 (XVII), adopted by 67 votes in favor, 16 against, with 23 abstentions, as follows:

> (a) Breaking off diplomatic relations with the Government of the Republic of South Africa or refraining from establishing such relations;
>
> (b) Closing their ports to all vessels flying the South African flag;
>
> (c) Enacting legislation prohibiting their ships from entering South African ports;
>
> (d) Boycotting all South African goods and refraining from exporting goods, including all arms and ammunition, to South Africa;
>
> (e) Refusing landing and passage facilities to all aircraft belonging to the Government and companies registered under the laws of South Africa.[12]

The Security Council resolution of December 4, 1963, solemnly called upon all States

> to cease forthwich the sale and shipment of equipment and materials for the manufacture and maintenance of arms and ammunition in South Africa;[13]

reinforcing its resolution of August 7, 1963, which called upon all States,

> to cease forthwith the sale and shipment of equipment and munition of all types and military vehicles to South Africa.[14]

To emphasize the gravity with which it viewed the situation, the General Assembly decided on November 6, 1962, to establish a special committee of representatives nominated by the President of the General Assembly, for the purpose of keeping South Africa's racial policies under review and to report to the General Assembly and the Security Council as appropriate.[15] Since it began functioning on April 2, 1963, the committee, known as the Special Committee on the Policies of *Apartheid* of the Government of the Republic of South Africa, has held a number of public and private hearings, amassed voluminous documentation bearing on most recent developments in and about South Africa, and submitted a series of reports and recommendations to the General Assembly and the Security Council. It was largely on the Committee's recommendation that the Security Council, for example, called on August 7, 1963, upon the South African Government,

> to liberate all persons imprisoned, interned or subjected to other restrictions for having opposed the policy of *apartheid*.[16]

A similar resolution was urgently adopted by the General Assembly on October 11, 1963,[17] against the lone dissent of South Africa and repeated by the Security Council on June 18, 1964.[18] On December 15, 1965, the General Assembly, acting on the Committee's initiative, approved the establishment of a United Nations Trust Fund, for the purpose of providing legal assistance to South Africans who pit themselves against the Government and of assisting their dependents, as well as of relieving refugees from South Africa and other victims of the Government's racial policies.[19]

Last, but not least, in what appeared to be a final attempt to resolve the problem of *apartheid* by conciliatory means prior to acting upon the General Assembly's recommendations of November 6, 1963, that the Security Council,

take appropriate measures, including sanctions, to secure
South Africa's compliance with the resolutions of the
General Assembly and of the Security Council on this
subject and, if necessary, to consider action under Article
6 of the Charter,

the Council, in it resolution of December 4, 1963, requested the
Secretary-General

to establish under his direction and reporting to him, a
small group of recognized experts to examine methods of
resolving the present situation in South Africa through
full, peaceful and orderly application of human rights and
fundamental freedoms to all inhabitants of the territory
as a whole, regardless of race, colour, or creed, and to
consider what part the United Nations might play in the
achievement of that end;

and invited the Government of South Africa

to avail itself of the assistance of this group in order to
bring about such peaceful and orderly transformation.

In their report to the Secretary-General dated April 20, 1964,
the group of experts, which was headed by Mrs. Alva Myrdal of
Sweden and included Sir Hugh Foot, now Lord Caradon, of England, Mr. Dey Ould Sidi Baba of Morocco and Sir Edward Asafu-
Adjaye of Ghana, stated that it regarded the primary principle
as of first importance to be the following:

The future of South Africa should be settled by the people
of South Africa—all the people of South Africa—in free
discussion. There can be no settlement and no peace while
the great majority of the people are denied the fundamental freedom to participate in decisions on the future
of their country. We are convinced that a continuation of
the present position, including a denial of just representation, must lead to violent conflict and tragedy for all the
people of South Africa. We wish, therefore, to emphasize
the first and basic principle that all the people of South
Africa should be brought into consultation and should
thus be enabled to decide the future of their country at
the national level.[20]

The four experts recommended, among other things, that the Security Council endorse the idea of a National Convention and work for its realization and that it seek to ascertain the views of the Government of South Africa, even though it had refused to cooperate with them and barred their proposed visit to the country. They also recommended that, pending receipt of the South African Government's reply, by a given date, the Council should examine the logistics of economic sanctions which, in their view, were the only means of a peaceful yet effective nature at the disposal of the Council to resolve the South African situation should the Government persist in its *apartheid* policy.

On June 18, 1964, the Security Council endorsed the main conclusions of the four experts and after reiterating its admonitions and appeals to the Government of South Africa and giving it until November 30, 1964, to present its views on the main conclusions of the expert group, decided to establish

> an Expert Committee, composed of representatives of each present member of the Security Council, to undertake a technical and practical study, and report to the Security Council as to the feasibility, effectiveness, and implications of measures which could, as appropriate, be taken by the Security Council under the Charter of the United Nations.[21]

Meanwhile, other organs of the United Nations and other members of the United Nations family of organizations have also been concerned with the *apartheid* question. Thus on July 30, 1963, the Economic and Social Council decided by six votes in favor to two against, with ten abstentions,

> that the Republic of South Africa shall not take part in the work of the Economic Commission for Africa until the Council, on the recommendation of Economic Commission for Africa, shall find that conditions for constructive cooperation have been restored by a change in its racial policy.[22]

In June, 1961, the 45th International Labor Conference voted 163 to none, with 89 abstentions, for the withdrawal by South Africa from membership in the International Labor Organization, until such time as it abandoned its *apartheid* policy. The Government of South Africa challenged the constitutionality of the Con-

ference's resolution and returned to the 1962 Conference, where
an unsuccessful attempt was made to invalidate the credentials
of South Africa's Employers' and Workers' delegates. In 1963,
objections to the presence of South Africa at the 47th session of
the Conference, in the form of a walk-out by the African and
Arab Delegations, broke up the Conference and led to the resignation of its President. The Conference adjourned before it barely
got down to business, but not before the Credentials Committee
invalidated the credentials of South Africa's Workers' delegates.[23]
These events, together with actions and decisions taken by the
Governing Body of the International Labor Organization in June
1963 and in February 1964, finally prevailed upon South Africa
to withdraw, as of March 11, 1964, from the intergovernmental
organization. Among the decisions taken by the Organization's
Governing Body, were:

> To exclude the Republic of South Africa from meetings
> of the International Labor Organization the membership of
> which is determined by the Governing Body;

> To consider as an urgent matter such amendments to the
> Constitution and/or Standing Orders and any other action
> within the competence of the International Labor Or-
> ganization as might be necessary in order to achieve the
> objectives of the 1961 resolution on *apartheid*.[24]

Mounting pressure for decisive action by the United Nations
against the Government of South Africa came also from official,
semi-official and private groups outside the world organization.
In May, 1963, the Conference of Heads of African States and
Governments, held in Addis Ababa, appealed to all States, "particularly to those which have traditional relations and cooperate
with the Government of South Africa," to strictly apply the General Assembly's resolution of November 6, 1963, which called for
a series of punitive measures against the South African Government.[25] On June 21, 1964, the second Conference of Heads of
States and Governments, which met in Cairo, went a step further
when it agreed to urge all the oil-producing countries in North
Africa and the Middle East to refuse petroleum shipments to
South Africa.[26] At the initiative of the Anti-*Apartheid* Movement,
a private grouping, an International Conference on Economic

Sanctions against South Africa was convened in London during April, 1964, under the patronage of the Chiefs of State of Algeria, Ethiopia, Ghana, Guinea, Liberia, Senegal, Tanganyika and Tunisia, and the Heads of Government of India, Kenya and Malaysia. The sponsors included notables from Argentina, Belgium, Canada, Colombia, Denmark, France, Iceland, Ireland, Italy, Japan, Norway, Poland, Sweden, Tanganyika, the Soviet Union, the United Kingdom and the United States. Attending the Conference were official delegations representing Governments or ruling parties of twenty-nine countries, as well as the Chairman and three members of the Special Committee on the Policies of *Apartheid* of the Government of the Republic of South Africa. The tone of the Conference was set by the Chairman, Tunisian Foreign Minister Mongi Slim, who emphasized the importance of arriving

> at decisive and concrete conclusions which would clearly show that sanctions against the South African Government are an obvious and efficient measure in order to make it give up, definitely, its racist policies.[27]

When, at the end of 1965, it became clear that the effectiveness of economic sanctions demanded the mandatory compliance of all States Members of the United Nations, but especially of South Africa's major trading partners, the General Assembly began to prepare the ground for Security Council action under Chapter VII of the Charter. On December 15, 1965, the General Assembly adopted a resolution which urgently appealed to South Africa's major trading partners to cease their "increasing economic collaboration" with the Government of South Africa, and drew the attention of the Security Council

> to the fact that the situation in South Africa constitutes a threat to international peace and security, that action under Chapter VII of the Charter is essential in order to solve the problem of apartheid and that universally applied economic sanctions are the only means of achieving a peaceful solution;[28]

Whether or not there is much reality to the initiatives and actions of the United Nations bodies is immaterial. What is real is that the forces which have taken the Africans in so much of the continent across the line that separates White supremacy from African self-government will not stop at the borders of South Africa. Also real is the identification of the non-White peoples everywhere with the cause of South Africa's Black man. The revolt of the Afro-Asian world against the myth of White superiority and its resentment of any and all forms of racial segregation have exploded with a torrential force which will not be contained until it has spent itself. The dignity and self-respect of the African States dictate that they shall not rest until they have achieved majority rule in South Africa.

It is difficult to visualize the mechanism of change in South Africa without disaster. It is equally difficult to imagine it remaining unchanged. Almost two decades of *apartheid* legislation have reduced to acquiescence those who would protest against it if South Africa had not become the efficient police state it is now. There is no indication that the White minority, including those who register conscientious objections to the racialism that defines the whole context of South African life, will voluntarily surrender the reins of power to the Black majority almost five times its present strength and constantly increasing in number. Among other things, this minority of four million is too much aware of the implications of the disabilities the White man has placed on his Colored subjects for so many generations to forget that there is a morality in history, if no happy ending, that visits upon the children the sins of the fathers. A heavy legacy of injustice and inequity bestrides its path to the future. In its quest for security and stability, the White population seeks, consciously or unconsciously, to ignore the indissoluble problem which surrounds it and to close ranks against the future.

The longer the way to an integrated society and government is barred, the more bitterly anti-White become the sentiments of the Blacks. Their psychological reaction to White domination is deeply personal. It derives from their sense of inferiority, of deprivation and of loss of land at the hands of the acquisitive settler from across the seas, and this is far more potent than their physical oppression and harried existence. The sense of humiliation of their race only increases as they watch their fellow Africans to the north make their patterns on world events, while they are forced to accept a life of degradation and subservience. The frustrations this breeds can only erupt into violence. There is no way of quickly eliminating either the sentiments or the basic conditions and historical heritage from which they derive. The time required to erase the scars of generations cannot serve to arrest the explosive force in the Black community. The South African situation is too much dominated by the violent and irrational, and the pressure for change from within and without is too great to ignore the portents of a calamitous future for White and Black alike.

We do not know all that will be relevant to the outcome of the final struggle between Black and White in South Africa. Will the dream of *apartheid,* with all its inequities, in time be buried under a tidal wave of hate as immense as the African continent? Or will South Africa's policy of racial segregation, because it is so at odds with reality, collapse under its own weight? Will economic necessities and the rising demand for skilled and unskilled African labor undermine the foundations of *apartheid,* or will the economic might of the White community sustain it? Above all, will the White community, in the interests of its very survival, make the necessary adjustment in time to ensure it? Whatever the answer to these and other questions of the White man's future in Africa, the African's tenure in Africa is secure. Africa is his continent. The Black man, by sheer weight of numbers, will sooner or later take control of Africa on his own terms.

The African States have accepted a collective responsibility for the liberation of the last White-dominated parts of their continent and have served notice that either the White man yields control to the Black majority gracefully or suffers the consequences. African nationalism's waves pound steadily at the remaining strongholds of White supremacy not only in the Republic of South Africa, but in neighboring Rhodesia and in Portuguese Angola and Mozambique. The issue in Rhodesia,[29] which since November 19, 1965, has been in rebellion against the British crown, is not whether it should or will be independent. The issue is independence for whom? The Africans are determined that Southern Rhodesia shall not become another South Africa, where in 1910, England, they maintain, had made the fatal mistake of handing over twelve million indigenous inhabitants to two million White settlers. They are determined to use force, if necessary, to prevent the 220,000 White minority from usurping the rights of four-million Blacks and their quest for freedom and independence. The United Kingdom, the British Commonwealth

of Nations, the Organization of African Unity and the United
Nations have made common cause against the rebellious Rhode-
sian regime and sealed its fate.

In fact, the fate of every minority White regime in Africa was
sealed from the moment when, on December 14, 1960, the General Assembly of the United Nations adopted the momentous
Declaration on the Granting of Independence to Colonial Countries and Peoples which, *inter alia*, called for:

> Immediate steps shall be taken, in Trust and Non-Self-
> Governing Territories or all other territories which have
> not yet attained independence, to transfer all powers to
> the peoples of those territories, without any conditions or
> reservations, in accordance with their freely expressed will
> and desire, without any distinction as to race, creed or
> colour, in order to enable them to enjoy complete independ-
> ence and freedom.[30]

It was on the basis of this Declaration that United Nations
organs have been calling on Portugal to give immediate recognition to the right of the peoples of the Territories under its administration to self determination and independence and to enter
into immediate negotiations with the authorized representatives
of the political parties within and outside the Territories for the
purposes of transfer of power and the granting of independence
in accordance with the aspirations of the people. It availed Portugal little that in 1951 the colonies became "Overseas Portugal"
and an integral part of a multi-racial and pluralistic society at
home and abroad. Neither the organic change in the constitutional
status of the Territories, nor the many reforms Portugal introduced especially since the rebellion in Angola in 1961, in any
way redeemed Lisbon from the sins of colonialism. Along with
South Africa, Portugal has been under United Nations interdic-
tion and subjected to partial sanctions.[31]

Within the framework of political developments in Africa and
of world policy, *apartheid* undeniably constitutes a source of
grave international tensions. The revolt of the Afro-Asian world
against anything reminiscent of the myth of racial superiority or
sanctioning racial segregation and the maintenance of the color
bar cannot be tamed by whatever restrictions the United Nations
Charter may have imposed upon the Member States. All doubts

as to the propriety and justification of singling out the racial injustices in South Africa for United Nations intervention have been swept aside by the mounting impatience of the Afro-Asian nations for racial justice and equality. Its authority has been thrown into the scales against the South African Republic and its actions have been supported by world public opinion. The majority of the Member States sees the issue of *apartheid* in unambiguous terms as the one unforgivable sin in the world today,[32], which justifies the use of the United Nations as an instrument to force from without fundamental changes in the internal structure of a sovereign state.

In a matter charged with such deep emotions as *apartheid*, it is very difficult to sort out the discrepancies in the arguments for and against the position taken by the United Nations. But the validity, fairness and virtue of United Nations policies and actions cannot be judged solely by the target at which they are aimed. They demand a background of certainty and consistency of both principle and practice to avoid exaggeration and false emphasis and to guard against miscast hopes and deceptions. Above all, they must look beyond the passions, sorrows and angers of the moment to their long-range consequences, or reckless confrontation at the United Nations might only bring disaster. Not that the United Nations is to be cut down to size because some of its ideals may threaten vested interests or the *status quo*. It is because the United Nations cannot assist in the writing of a story of a great offense expiated by a great suffering.

Thus, the United Nations has been placed in an intolerable dilemma, from which it cannot escape except by appeal to international protection of human rights. The physical realities in South Africa are such that it is impossible to balance suffering and injustice caused in one place, against suffering and injustice averted elsewhere. The gathering storm clouds over the unhappy land of South Africa will not be scattered, nor will the generous and constructive forces there be awakened, if the role of the United Nations is confined to transferring power from the White minority to the Black majority. What passes as the democratic faith in many parts of the world is a creed which, as noted before, leaves without security all minorities and all special interests of unquestioned legitimacy. The triumph of African nationalism is not necessarily the triumph of the individual and of human dignity, and there is no assurance that the repressive racist Afrikaner regime of today will not be replaced by an equally repressive and revengefully racist African regime. The conflict and violence in South Africa spring as much from the fear of the White population as from the grievances of the Black population. The hope for a peaceful multi-racial society in South Africa, where Whites and Blacks can share political power in full justice, equality and mutual respect, cannot be anchored in any other foundation than in international protection of human rights and fundamental freedoms. Circumstances are forcing the hand of the United Nations in a direction which would make it possible for the world organization to guarantee the equal application of human rights and fundamental freedoms, without fear or favor to the sons and daughters of the different races, on which the destiny of South Africa rests.

CHAPTER XII

The Great Divide
between North and South

Nothing short of universal acceptance of the direct responsibility of the international community for the material welfare and social well-being of the human individual will avert the final reckoning that awaits a humanity which is too divided by national barriers and traditional allegiances to share its wealth and talent for the achievement of prosperity for all. Given the magnitude of the problem produced by the disastrous alliance of poverty and population in Asia, Africa and Latin America, all contemporary national and international efforts to relieve the hunger and misery which are the daily lot of more than half the world's population and to restore human dignity to the peoples that lack the basic necessities of life seem like an appalling irrelevancy. There is widespread agreement that unless the growing disparity in living conditions between North and South is appreciably reduced within a reasonably short time, darkness will descend upon the entire world. Like the proletariat in the Western countries in the beginning of this century, the peoples of the so-called developing areas must come into their share of the earth's bounty, or an international class warfare of colossal proportions will explode to shatter the peace of the globe. That the division of wealth broadly coincides with the division of race and color, only adds to the gravity of the great divide between the Northern and Southern Hemispheres.

On May 3, 1966, Secretary General U Thant told the Consultative Assembly of the Council of Europe that,

> it is the growing economic disparity of the nations of the world which faces us with our most serious source of tension and with the direct possibility of future calamity.

Despite international programmes for economic development and bilateral aid agreements, the plain fact is that
the rich industrialized countries of the world are growing
steadily richer and the less developed countries are, at
best, standing still. Taken in conjunction with the probable
growth of population over the next 30 or 40 years, this
trend opens up a most distressing prospect. The reports of
famine from various parts of the world and the evident
and increasing difficulties of many of the less developed
countries are only harbingers of the coming storm.

It is essential that our preocupation with our own immediate problems, or with more spectacular and short
term crises, should not make us deaf to these warnings.
If we do not pay heed to them there can be little doubt
that we are courting a disaster in which event the most
prosperous and stable countries may eventually be swept
away. We cannot allow it to be said of us by history that,
with all our knowledge and technological skill, we allowed
this long foreseable, and foreseen, calamity to overwhelm
us...[1]

There is no veneer thick enough to mask the sea of misery
that engulfs so many parts of the world. The International Bank
for Reconstruction and Development has divided the nations into
rich, middle-income, poor and very poor, with the latter two in
the overwhelming majority Its 1966 publications show that barely
ten percent of the world's population of over three billion, principally in the United States, Canada, Western Europe, Australia and
New Zealand, has an average national per capita annual income
of $1000.00 and over, while well over half the world's population,
mostly in Asia and Africa, has an average per capita income of
from $40.00 to $100.00 per year. In all, the statistics indicate that
two-thirds of the population of the world share less than one-
sixth of its income.[2]

Behind these statistics of deprivation are people who are
hungry, ill-fed, ill-housed, illiterate and disease ridden. Authoritative estimates place the number of people at the end of 1960
who suffered from active hunger or lack of sufficient calories at
roughly 500 million and those who suffered from malnutrition
or diet deficiencies in terms of vitamins, minerals and proteins,
at twice that number.[3] More than one billion persons were without

homes or living miserably in clearly substandard housing, while
many more lived in dwellings without even a minimum of the
amenities and conveniencies associated with modern housing.[4]
Even in the United States, nearly one house in every five in 1960
was without plumbing facilities or was officially considered "di-
lapidated."[5] Of a total of 206 million children of school age in
Asia, Africa and Latin America in 1960, only 110 million attended
primary school. Illiteracy among adults, or persons of 15 years
of age and upwards, extended to two-fifths of the total adult
population of the world, or more than 700 million men and women,
with women in the majority.[6] The life expectancy in the countries
with the lowest per capita income is still over 41.7 per cent, as
against 70.6 in countries with the highest per capita income. The
death of small children in the developing countries takes place at
a rate ten times higher than in the West.[7] In Brazil, for instance,
it has been estimated that during the span of one generation the
country loses no less than 32 per cent, almost one-third of its
potential productive capacity, as a consequence of premature
death.[8] The mortality rate among children in developing countries
suffering from protein-calorie deficiency alone is between 10 and
20 per cent.[9]

All indications point to an inevitable worsening of the situation in the future, due largely to the rapid growth in the world's
population at a rate that far outdistances any and all improvements in the living conditions of man. The Food and Agricultural
Organization's report of 1966 on *The State of Food and Agriculture* paints a grim picture of the consequences of a birth rate
that surpasses the production of food. Thus, while the world's
population in 1965/66 increased by about 70 million persons the
food output for the same year, because of droughts and weather
conditions, was no larger than that of the year before, or 2 per
cent less than in 1964/65. In the developing areas of Africa, Latin
America and the Far East, excepting mainland China, the decline
in per capita food production reached 4 to 5 per cent. This
amounted to a drop to 1957/58 levels, or the same as the "inadequate" level before the second World War. It is not merely a
question of poor harvests. When so many millions of people are
already suffering from hunger and malnutrition, there is little
margin against the effects of a poor harvest. If disaster was
avoided in large parts of the world in 1965/66, such as India and

other drought-stricken areas, it was because the large stocks of grain accumulated since the early 1950s, mainly in North America, provided a cushion against emergencies. But these stocks have been reduced to their lowest levels in well over a decade, and current production has proved unreliable.

The Malthusian specter of people outstripping the supply of food has never been more of a threat than it seems to be now. It has been estimated that the world population, approximately 3 billion in 1960, will rise to the order of 5.3 - 6.8 billion by the year 2000, with 6 billion as the most likely expectation.[10] According to this study projection, the major developed areas—Europe, the Soviet Union, North America, Australia and New Zealand—will have an increase of between 30 and 60 per cent of their 1960 population at the end of this century, while the less developed regions of the world will have an increase in the same period of between 95 and 150 per cent of their 1960 population. Mainland China alone is projected to have a population of more than 1.2 billion by the year 2000.[11] This accelerated rate of population growth has not only wiped out in large measure all increase in food production but threatens the world with an unparalled famine beginning in 1980. In Asia alone, the Food and Agriculture Organization has estimated, the total food supplies would have to be increased by 73 per cent by 1975, and by 228 per cent by the year 2000, if the nutritional level per capita were to be raised to the minimum necessary and, at the same time, provide for the expanding population.[12]

Reports to the 21-member United Nations Committee on Housing, Building and Planning, in September 1966, showed that in most developing countries the average rate of construction of housing was roughly two new dwellings per 1000 inhabitants per year. This rate of construction does not even remotely meet the needs for housing created by the massive flight of populations from the countryside to urban areas taking place on an ever increasing scale throughout the world, let alone the needs compounded by the rapid rise in population precisely in the areas where the housing situation is most acute.[13] The same is true of illiteracy. When the United Nations, in its resolution of 11 December 1963, proclaimed the World Campaign for Universal Literacy, it was estimated that in the existing circumstances approximately 20 to 25 million new illiterates would be added

annually to the adult population through the year 1970.[14] There
is no evidence to indicate that their numbers will be reduced by
the end of the decade, either absolutely or relative to the increase
in the world's population. Mexico, for example, which had experienced one of the most successful political and social revolutions of modern times, had more illiterates in 1966 than a quarter
of a century ago and more children out of school than ever.[15] The
same is true of the health situation in the world. The quality of
medical services cannot be readily improved when one doctor has
to service 30,000 or even 96,000 persons in the developing countries, as compared with one doctor per 1,000 inhabitants in the
West.[16] Given the diseases to which the hungry and ill fed succumb
and which are bred in conditions of squalor, together with the
increase in the birth rate, they only add up to hopelessness and
despair.[17]

The implications of the population explosion are clear. It has
been demonstrated that in a country where the rate of natural
increase comes to 2.5 per cent per year, for example, the equivalent of 10 per cent of the national income must go into capital
formation each year just to keep the standard of living from
declining. Considering that two-thirds of the people of the world
live in countries that have not yet reached a level of economic and
industrial development sufficient to assure their inhabitants even
a minimum measure of "freedom from want," the burden of
providing for increased numbers becomes unbearable. Thus Latin
America's total agricultural production rose by approximately 80
per cent between the pre World War II period and 1958/60, or at
a rate of 2.6 per cent per year. Yet, despite the fact that in the
aggregate this increase was considerable, and, indeed, greater
than that registered by the other regions of the world, it was not
enough to raise per capita production levels significantly, because
of the region's exceptional population growth during the same
period. In fact, while Latin America's aggregate agricultural
production index for 1958/60 was 20 per cent higher than the
index for the whole world, in terms of production per inhabitant,
the index for Latin America was 8 per cent lower than the world
average.[18]

Nature, history and economics have conspired to exact a heavy
toll from the underdeveloped areas of the world. They have
almost all started the race for economic and social development

with many handicaps. The approximately 120 countries and territories in this category are those which are found largely in the tropics and subtropics, where they are engaged in a permanent struggle against the forces of nature which have for so long barred them from the ascending curve of self-sustaining economic growth characteristic of the more temperate zones. Many are underdeveloped because their soil resources are poor. The United States and Canada, for example, possess 22.7 per cent of the world's cultivated lands, while Latin America, with just as many people to support, possesses only 6.5 per cent. Not all Asian, African and Latin American countries are blessed with rich mineral and other natural resources. Many are small, arid, or barely capable of producing scant crops and lean livestock. But even in those countries which are more richly endowed, their resources have not been put to their best use. These are the countries where steel and mechanical energy are relatively little used, where there is a shortage of efficient transportation and communication, and where the basic measure of a day's work is still, by and large, what a man can accomplish with his two hands and a few simple tools.[19]

"The human qualities that promote economic growth," we are told;

> are variously identified as knowledge and skills, technological capacity, efficiency, organizational capacity, initiative, energy and hard work, mutual trust and honesty, security and confidence in the future, inventiveness, mobility, 'universalism,' rationality, entrepreneurial ability, progressive outlook, ambition and drive, achievement, motivation, etc. But lists of desirable qualities do not generally give a very clear idea of the kinds of investment a country can and should make in the social field to promote economic growth. Governments cannot create such qualities by legislative fiat or budgetary appropriations. There are no operative branches of government in sociology and psychology disposing of funds to cultivate directly the desired qualities...[20]

These are products of natural environment and cultural and historic traditions, which are as decisive, if not more so, than all the other factors which make for economic and social growth or stagnation. The way people act, think and work is frequently more important than natural resources, geography, climate, rivers and oceans. Octave Galinier, a practicing French industrialist, attributes all the shortcomings of France's economic life to historical traditions which have taken deep root in his country. He goes so far as to contend that all outstanding industrial and business initiative owes its origin to Puritan Protestantism and that the pattern of cooperative and competitive enterprise was fashioned by the Protestant societies in Europe and North America, which had abandoned the attitudes and traditions that stifled individual initiative and responsibility. He accounts for the failure of the great civilizations in the East, Islam and the Mediterranean to produce mass industrial societies by their addiction to what he calls a neo-tribalism derived from a social tradition dominated by a master and slave, king and subject, and superior-inferior relationship and by the primacy of privilege. Only as they succeeded in abandoning old concepts of authoritarianism, Galinier maintains, were they able to broaden their economic life.[21]

To the extent that social and cultural traditions in the developing countries may be inimical to economic growth, it is part of the reality of the situation which can neither be ignored nor dismissed out of hand. Resistance is never stronger than when it is to change, and the ways of people must be approached with sympathetic understanding, or the price of change may prove too high. Despite the fact that in country after country in all parts of the world traditional habits of life are being uprooted and that the people of the developing nations are migrating by the millions from farm, hamlet and village to swell the ranks of the city dwellers, the social transformation which is taking place in Asia, Africa and Latin America is too anarchic to provide sure guidance. Two recent UNESCO surveys, for example, lay great stress on the importance of methods of economic assistance and on the need to take account of cultural factors as well as of human reactions. Inquiries into economic motivation and stimulation in developing countries and surveys of economic progress and its social implications in South and Southeast Asia, Africa, Australia, Peru, and among the Eskimos of Thule established the importance of viewing underdevelopment not primarily as a matter for the

economist, but for all who are concerned with social and economic
welfare, including anthropologists, sociologists and psycholo-
gists.[22] Thus the Food and Agriculture Organization has from
the very beginning emphasized the absolute necessity of enlisting
the cooperation of the people directly concerned in any and all
programs of rural development and insisted on the understanding
of the farmers who still form a majority of the world's population.[23] In the last analysis, the question of economic growth is
political and social and only secondarily technological. Centuries
of traditional culture cannot be undone overnight even in response to the most compelling economic needs.

Economic growth is a complex process that involves many
inter-related elements. Hunger and malnutrition, ignorance and
disease, poverty and stagnation are all at once cause and effect
which round out a vicious circle of factors opposing economic
progress. None of these evils can be successfully attacked in
isolation from one another. Disease, for example, is hard to
combat in conditions of hunger and malnutrition, and hunger and
malnutrition are hard to conquer in conditions of ignorance and
poverty. Far-reaching measures are needed to start the process
of economic development on a scale sufficiently large to breach
the walls of ignorance and poverty. But this is a task which all
too frequently exceeds the capacity of developing nations. However important their internal policies and actions for marshalling
their human and material resources for economic advancement
may be, their ability to force an exit from the vicious circle of
underdevelopment very often depends on the policies and actions
of others. Stability of primary commodity prices, for example, is
of crucial importance to the developing countries which, for the
most part, are the producers of these products. The sale of these
commodities in the world market provides them with most of the
capital for investment in roads, railways, harbors, airfields,
schools, hospitals, dams, irrigation projects and factories and industries of all kinds. The slightest drop in the price of their
products has a shattering impact on their economies, and a drop
of even one cent per pound of coffee, for example, can wipe out
the economic gains of a year in any one of the coffee-producing
countries. Indeed, the breadth of the impact of the severe fluc-
tuations in the prices of primary products has catapulted the
so-called commodity problem into one of the principal interna-

tional issues of the times. The economies of countries that depend for earnings on one or two primary products cannot absorb the shocks and uncertainties of world trade. "In the absence of major changes in national and international policies," we are told,

> countries which rely heavily on primary commodities for their earnings of foreign exchange will generally continue to be faced with the problem of insufficient and unstable export earnings to support an adequate and steady rate of economic development. Given the continued predominance of primary commodities in the exports of developing countries, it remains true that, if an early stimulus is to be provided to their export income, it must operate mainly through primary commodities; so, clearly, must any measures to reduce instability in their export earnings...[24]

But exports of primary commodities, even under the best of circumstances, cannot solve the problem of the trade gap of those countries. In the first place, international demand for many of these commodities has been increasing only moderately, far less than the increase in the needs of the developing nations for imports to achieve a satisfactory growth in income. Indeed, they are facing increasing competition from the growth of exports of primary commodities from developed countries. The consolidation of the protected market for domestic primary producers in the European Common Market, for example, has deeply cut into the export of agricultural products from developing countries. While exports of agricultural products from these countries declined in value between 1963/64, agricultural raw materials from developed market economies continues to rise at about 4 per cent per year.[25] Secondly, primary commodities are facing competition from more efficient synthetics. Malaysia's representative on the United Nations Economic Commission for Asia and the Far East, to cite one instance, declared at its 114th meeting in Wellington, New Zealand, on March 17, 1965, that natural rubber, his country's economic mainstay, had to face keen competition from synthetic rubber and that only with large-scale replanting with high-yield clones, improved tapping and processing methods and intensified research into various aspects of rubber production and use could natural rubber be made sufficiently competitive to discourage further investment in synthetic rubber manufacture in the world.[26] Together with the decline in prices for primary commodities, these factors account for the transformation of the developing countries' surplus of exports over imports in 1950 into a deficit in 1962 of $2.3 billion. According to figures cited at the 1964 United Nations Conference on Trade and Development, this deficit may reach the order of $20 billion by 1970.[27]

Practically all experts agree on the inescapable need to accelerate the industrial development of the developing countries and lay special stress on promotion and diversification of exports of manufactures and semi-manufactures as a source of foreign earnings.[28] Industrial development in developing countries is for the most part still in its incipient stages and, where more advanced, it is mainly inward oriented.[29] However, as in the case of primary commodity prices, industrialization and diversification of production are matters in which the determination of the developing countries is not decisive. They depend on an infrastructure they do not have; on the import of capital goods for which they cannot pay; on technical skills they do no have; and on opportunities for export they do not control. If, after so many generations in the role of producers of primary materials, developing countries cannot hold their own against agricultural products of developed countries, how can they hope to compete successfully against the manufactured and semi-manufactured goods that are the products of superior technology and long experience? One of the constant handicaps faced by developing countries when they attempt to take up the production of any new item of manufacture is that in many cases economies of scale cannot be achieved on the basis of small domestic markets, for the reason that in such circumstances production becomes uneconomical. On the other hand, small volume production makes it difficult to ensure the desired quality required by the sophisticated markets of the developed countries, whose access to the developing countries' manufactures and semi-manufactures is already strewn with enormous obstacles. Thus, the disparity between the export earnings and the import needs of the developing countries, lack of capital and the shortage of technical skills, and the host of problems of production and its rationalization close the vicious circle of poverty and stagnation from which these countries can never force an exit without assistance from abroad.[30]

Such assistance has, indeed, been forthcoming. Since the end of World War II, a basic tenet of international cooperation has been the moral duty of the developed countries to help the under-developed countries to increase their own rate of economic growth and correct the substantial disparities in income distribution in order to improve the standard of living of the broad masses. The years immediately following the end of the War witnessed a stirring of conscience toward the economic and social underdevelopment of the vast areas of the inhabited world and the urgency to bring to the teeming millions of people the food, health and housing, the knowledge, skills, opportunity, dignity and hope which they could not harvest with their own power and resources. The United States, as the wealthiest nation, was the first to embark on its own large program of economic aid to underdeveloped countries and served as a challenge to the international community as a whole. The past twenty years have chronicled various bilateral, regional and multilateral initiatives for bringing economic and social progress to underdeveloped countries, of which the Decade of Development which the United Nations General Assembly launched on December 19, 1961, has become symbolic of international cooperative effort in the economic and social spheres. The declared objective of the Decade of Development is the achievement of a five per cent rate of economic and social growth in the developing nations by the end of 1970, through the concerted efforts of the United Nations family of organizations and the efforts of individuals, groupings of people, nations and groups of nations throughout the world.[31]

Two decades of experience have failed to produce agreement on a general theory of economic assistance, any more than they have developed clear guidelines for success in the field. One thing, however, is beyond dispute: the response to the problem of under development has not even remotely been on a scale with the problem itself. In his Interim Report on the United Nations Development Decade of May 5, 1966, Secretary-General U Thant concluded as follows:

> In launching the Development Decade in 1961 the Governments and peoples of both developed and developing countries pledged themselves to strive to achieve accelerated economic growth and social progress. With this broad objective in mind, two specific targets were adopted by the

General Assembly—the achievement of a rate of growth in the developing countries of 5 per cent per annum by 1970 and an annual transfer of development capital from the developed to the developing countries equivalent to 1 per cent of the Gross National Product of the developed countries. Despite progress in some sectors, the pace of economic and social development in the first half of the Decade has been disappointing and neither of the goals set by the Assembly has yet been reached. Indeed, poverty, hunger and disease have increased in some areas during the first half of the decade. Unless the world community is prepared to give a massive new impetus to development, it is unlikely that the objectives of the Development Decade will be achieved by 1970. It lies within the power of Governments of both developed and developing countries to provide such an impetus. But to do so, they must be willing to follow up declarations of intent by the actual implementation of specific programmes and policies, many of which will involve some sacrifice, that alone can turn the aspirations embodied in the concept of the Development Decade into the reality of development itself . . .[32]

The developing nations have not been able to rise above the dead weight of their chronic poverty and anachronistic social structures,[33] nor the developed countries above their concern for their own interests and welfare. If the achievement of the goals of the Decade of Development demands the greatest efforts and sacrifices from the peoples and governments of the developing countries themselves, it is the contribution of the developed countries that will tip the scales between stagnation and growth, between increasing poverty and a measure of economic progress. "The stark fact which emerges intact from all the studies, reports and discussions devoted to the subject in the course of 1966," the Secretary General wrote in the Introduction to his Annual Report on the Work of the United Nations,

is that international aid is stagnating while the capacity of developed countries to provide such aid, measured in terms of an increase in their per capita incomes, has become greater.[34]

But aid is only part of the larger question, whether the world is capable of the social inventiveness and has the political will power to conceive and carry through large and sophisticated programs which are in balance with the problems they are designed to help solve. Can the world attack the problem of poverty within the framework of a traditional ethic that required internal social revolutions to undo? When the objectives and points of departure in all international economic relations are the needs of the state and its economic viability and competitive ability, steady and consistent initiatives to move events in the direction of prosperity for all can never be taken. Perhaps Senegal's Foreign Minister was right when, in his statement in the general debate on September 25, 1966, he suggested to the United Nations General Assembly that,

> it is necessary to lay the bases for a new world society, to make a new revolution, to overthrow all the practices, all the institutions, all the rules under which until now international economic relations have been organized, to the extent that these practices, these institutions and these rules enshrine injustice, exploitation and the establishment of an unjustified domination of the minority over the majority of mankind. It is not only a question of affirming the right to development, but also to take the measures that will enable us to exercise this right to development. We must build a new system based not only on the theoretical affirmation of the sacred rights of peoples and nations but based on the effective enjoyment of these rights. The freedom of peoples to self-determination, the sovereign equality of peoples, international solidarity—all of this will remain in vain and, forgive me, will remain hypocritical, so long as relations between nations are not examined in the light of economic and social facts. From this point of view, reality is in contradiction with principles. The new vision of the world which the United Nations Charter offered to the conscience of each one of us is still but a vision. It has not yet become international reality. The economic Bandung which we propose should enable us to draft a new economic charter for the world. We would meet not to present a ledger of com-

plaints, but to claim and demand that which is our due, more exactly that which is due to man, whatever his nationality, his race or his religion. We shall have to define a new revolutionary attitude which will make it possible, by starting with the somber realities of today, to move toward the realities which are more in accord with the ethics of the United Nations...[35]

It has yet to happen that the wealthy should willingly pool their resources with the poor in a great redemptive effort to relieve misery and want. There is no sign of the emergence of an international division of labor that would make developed and developing nations into partners in a great international enterprise and achieve what ought to have been the outcome of common sense and enlightened self-interest. Instead, the narrow concern of the economically advanced nations with their own immediate problems leads them into the pursuit of policies which contradict not only their declared intentions, but their own long-term interests.[36] We have already noted how the European Common Market has affected agricultural exports of developing countries, at the very same time when they have been urged to rationalize their agriculture and increase the proportion of their commercial agricultural production. Mention has also been made of the increasing competition from the production of many primary commodities in developed countries. Aside from direct and indirect effects of scientific and technical progress on the demand for primary products, their production in major industrial countries is supported on an extensive scale through domestic measures such as subsidies and the fixing of internal prices at above ruling import prices, as well as through direct barriers to imports. The result is that the market opportunities for external suppliers of like or competing commodities are invariably reduced. Similarly, while on the one hand there is general agreement that the economic salvation of the developing world lies in industrialization and diversification of production, access of its manufactured and semi-manufactured goods to the markets in the developed countries is limited, at best, and very often severely curtailed. No advanced industrial nation would, for example, let relatively easy and labor-consuming industries in some agricultural fields and light manufacturing, such as textiles, pass to developing nations. These unsophisticated industries are jealously held by the nations that have them not only by protective devices, but by discriminatory practices against competitors in the poor nations.[37] Reference may also be made to the fact that a good deal of the capital which flows into the developing countries is cancelled out by the growing burden of interest and other service charges on foreign capital.[38]

Still another example, attesting to the absence of properly interrelated measures reflecting the highly complex reality of a world in the process of development and the magnitude of the problem, is the so-called brain drain. A recent study, under the auspices of what was once the United Nations Special Fund, brought out the fact that the developing countries were losing talent to the rich industrial nations. Togo, for example, had sent more physicians and professors to France than France to Togo. There were more than 4000 foreigners practicing medicine in England; 5000 engineers from abroad were migrating annually to the United States. In the course of ten years ending in the middle of 1964, Argentina alone sent 13,800 highly trained immigrants to the United States. This brain drain, according to authoritative sources is as much deliberate as the result of objective conditions.[39] On September 1, 1966, Senator Walter F. Mondale of Minnesota, addressing the United States Senate, deplored the fact that the United States and other technologically advanced nations were attracting the most skilled manpower from developing nations and noted that this was one of the contributory factors which accentuated the growing gap between the rich and poor nations. He proposed a five point program which would mitigate the consequences of United States immigration and visa policies, which presently worked to the detriment of the developing countries, without offending the right of the individual to freedom of movement.[40]

To deal with the problem of the developing countries at a time when warnings pour in of coming catastrophe is inevitably to stress its somber aspects. United States Secretary of Defense, Robert S. McNamara, identified poverty as the basic cause of the violence around the world. In an address before the American Society of Newspaper Editors on May 18, 1966, at Montreal, he noted that all facts and figures pointed to an irrefutable relationship between violence and economic backwardness. Since 1958, he declared, 87 per cent of the very poor nations, 69 per cent of the poor nations, and 48 per cent of the middle income nations have suffered serious violence. And the trend of such violence is up, not down, he added:

> Given the certain connection between economic stagnation and the incidence of violence, the years that lie ahead for the nations in the southern half of the globe are pregnant with violence.[41]

Not only for the developing countries. For what happens in one part of the world sooner or later reverberates in all other parts of the world. And what is happening is nothing short of a gigantic political, economic and social revolution whose dimensions cannot be fully guaged and whose outcome cannot be predicted. Were it only a question of achieving the goal of an annual cumulative increase in gross national product of 5 per cent, for example, as set by the Decade of Development, the task of development might yet be manageable. Even though differences in money income may continue to grow greater between the developed and developing countries, the disparity in the human condition might be lessened by a coordinated approach on the part of all advanced countries to stabilize the prices of raw materials exported by poorer countries, to open the doors widely for their exports of low wage manufactures, to stimulate private investment, and to exhaust all inventive capabilities of foreign aid. However, as Secretary McNamara correctly pointed out,

> Development means economic, social, and political progress. It means a reasonable standard of living and the word "reasonable" in this context requires continual redefinition. What is "reasonable" in an earlier stage of development will become "unreasonable" in a later stage.[42]

Revolutions are generally founded upon hopes, not despair, and nations that are seeking to improve their economic lot are more prone to revolution than those sunk in lethargy. Dr. Paul Prebisch, Secretary General of the United Nations Conference on Trade and Development, told the Trade and Development Board on August 31, 1966, that one of the serious problems in the developing countries was the effect of technical progress on the lives of the people. He referred, among other things, to the fact that the application of modern technology to the media of mass information has had the result of spreading throughout the developing world social phenomena and consumption patterns typical of the advanced countries, which were patently beyond their reach.[43] It, therefore, may no longer be true that the real milestones of development are the big power dams, tall smokestacks and broad highways, but the factories that fashion local hides into shoes and sandals, the mills spinning locally grown cotton into cloth, or plants producing shingles for roofing and frames for windows.

If development means economic, social and political progress, the changes it requires and inevitably will bring are revolutionary—radically, violently and wrenchingly revolutionary. There can be no greater error than to see underdeveloped countries only as poor and overpopulated, with poverty as the prime source of suffering. The cry for social justice is heard as loudly as the cry for food. The need for social change is as marked as the need for economic progress.[44] The task of training untold millions of farmers in literacy, of dealing with the gathering of the rural dispossessed and distressed into urban multitudes, of disciplining city slum dwellers in the rigidities of factory work, of divesting landowner classes of ancient privileges and oligarchies of inherited and acquired power, and of overcoming all the many social ills that plague poor and rich nations alike, is too huge for any nation or group of nations to cope with unaided. Together, economic development and social progress call for a measure and degree of human solidarity which is nowhere on the horizon.

On September 15, 1966, Chairman of Comsat, James McCormack, told a group of educators at a seminar in New York on educational technology that it was now perfectly possible technically for all the world to have good schools, pure water, clean air and livable cities, but that the only problem was how to marshal the humane, economic and political machinery to manage the application of technology to the many needs of mankind. He was not convinced that technology necessarily enlivens the spirits or makes men moral or makes relations between men better.[45] Indeed, all the major technical developments of recent years have left strangely untouched most of the ordinary problems of living. The marvels of science and technology have failed to provide solutions to the most pressing economic and social problems. They made the most progress in areas where vested interests were not significantly affected, let alone jeopardized. Where such interests were affected or the conduct of affairs disturbed, innovation invariably encountered powerful obstacles. The traditional framework of international cooperation can never produce a common economic and social strategy necessary to cope with the human condition.

As in the political sphere of international relations, so in the economic and social spheres, the quest for international cooperation in the promotion of the common good invariably founders on the contradictions inherent in a world of sovereign nationstates each bent upon achieving maximum national advantage. All the impressive institutions of international economic and social cooperation which have been created in recent years cannot counteract the economic laws that inflict their own impassive punishment, nor repeal the inexorable consequences of adamant national self-interest. These institutions have been created to, operate within the framework of a system that was not designed to function efficiently without the compensators of supply and demand, competition and all the other laws of the market place. What, for example, is the use of sending technical experts and assistance to help develop the economy of the developing countries, when the economically advanced nations are not ready to buy the goods they then produce? If the only real advantage the developing countries may now have is low cost labor, this advantage is often cancelled out by Western barriers against low cost imports. Just as the confidence which the idea of *laissez faire* individualism inspired in the middle of the nineteenth century that the new economics would ensure the advent of a mutually interdependent world economy, a global community and permanent international peace soon had faded in the face of reality, so it is absurd to think that an international division of labor, which would bring into balance and harmony the conflicting economic and social forces, will emerge from the contemporary efforts to narrow the gap between rich and poor. The Welfare State was needed to enforce economic and social cooperation at home. Much more than what is in the offing will be needed to advance the world toward prosperity for all. International cooperation in the economic and social fields, too, must be freed from the shackles of national interest, by the assertion of the economic and social welfare of the individual human person as an immediate international responsibility and the direct object of all economic and social planning.

CHAPTER XIII

Visions and Realities

The late Secretary General of the United Nations, Dag Hammarskjöld, once observed that:

> ...if the law is the inescapable law of the future, it would be treason to the future not to state the law simply because of the difficulties of the present. Indeed, how could it ever become a living reality if those who are responsible for its development were to succumb to the immediate difficulties arising when it is still a revolutionary element in the life of society?[1]

The inescapable law of the future is international protection of human rights. It is the inexorable consequence of the formidable acceleration in scientific and technological progress and of man's reaching out for goals that have been set for him by his own nature. The law must be stated now, even though the distant rumble of impending change is not readily heard. When the issue is one of the survival of the race and of the conditions of its survival, the forward thrust of reason strikes out against the serene acceptance of the follies of man and refuses to endure in passive despair the evils born of harsh prejudices and stubborn irrationalities. It enjoins us to expose even the most plausible rationalizations and to strip of their elevated ambiguities even the most cherished ideals. We cannot enforce a just and enduring peace without sapping the foundations of some of our most cherished illusions, which commit us to a way of life as the sole and eternal verity. The path to a humane world order is today blocked by our obstinate and forcible clinging to a mass of ideas, representations, beliefs and judgements that make up the sub-rational forces of cohesion of the national political community and distort our vision of the larger world around us.

209

*"La guerre sera tant qui'l y aura des nations; elle cessera quand il n'y aura que des individus."** Thus wrote almost two hundred years ago Anacharsis Cloots, the Prussian-born nobleman of Gnadenthal, Baron Jean Baptiste du Val-de-Grace.[2] He who had disavowed the enlightened despotism of Frederick the Great to embrace the cause of the French Revolution, only to die on the Guillotine of Paris for his vision of a Universal Republic of Man founded on the Declaration of the Rights of Man, was quick to perceive the full consequences of modern nationalism, whose birth he had attended.

We have seen that, the basic goal of the state is the defense of its own welfare and the power methods by which it is ensured. Guided solely by the requirements of the national interest, the state, whether or not it represents the collective will of the citizenry or acts in response to internal pressures exerted upon it by particular interest groups masquerading as the majority, is more concerned with the exploitation of immediate advantages than with long-range world plans of interest to all. To the sovereign nation-state, its own needs and conscience are the ultimate criteria of right and wrong and of law and justice. Hence, the failure of any and all systems of international relations which rest on perpetually shifting balances and in which the element of power plays the decisive role to suppress the destructive forces that lead to war and international anarchy. Hence, too, the urgent need of creating conditions in which no state may breach the peace with impunity, nor block it without exceeding its legitimate functions.

To blunt the edge of nationalism and to do away with its excrescences and exaggerations, we must find the true incarnation of the international idea, which dictates the concerted effort toward the social advancement of the whole of humanity. The true and concrete incarnation of the international idea is man himself. Because there is but a single definition of man, so there can be but a single measure of man. Just as the basic units of physical measurement are length, mass and time, whatever the scales and however expressed, so the measure of man is basically the same everywhere. Its dimensions are the fixed drives of human nature and all the elemental pleasures and pains of the

---

* War will continue as long as there are nations; it will cease when there are only individuals.

flesh; the human spirit, with all its intuitions, feelings, fantasies and impulses, which seek the good, the true and the beautiful; and the power of the human mind, which is the basis of man's claim to dignity and worth, to freedom and justice. Sheer human interest can move the individual to reach out to those who are different from himself. It is only when individuals are grouped together under the banner of the nationalist creed that the differences between them emerge to divide them. In the final analysis, the human individual is the only arch that can hold up the bridge to span the great divide between the nation and the world.

As the need to encounter and respond to the fundamental problems of the age grows more urgent, the idea of international concern with the fate and welfare of the individual man, woman and child everywhere on earth comes forward not as a peacemeal answer to particular questions, but as a total conception of the good life of unchallengeable validity. Nothing reflects more accurately or expresses more forcefully the true aspirations of man than the enjoyment of the rights and freedoms set forth in the Universal Declaration of Human Rights and reduced to law in the International Covenants on Human Rights. Their international protection, in all its ramifications and with all it implications, suggests an eminently practical regulative principle of international relations. Ideas and ideals marching as if to war must, of course, prove themselves in action. But as a working hypothesis and as a philosophy of means and ends, international protection of human rights brings into international relations those dreams and hopes by which humanity moves from one historic epoch to another. No other conceivable governmental policy, at home and abroad, is better calculated to serve both advantage and justice than one consciously shaped by abiding concern for the rights and freedoms of man everywhere.

International responsibility for the promotion and defense of human rights is not only a basic principle which flows from the image of man in terms of the universal invoked in all great civilizations; it is a conclusion drawn from the interdependence of peoples and nations. The avowed purpose of the state—any state—is to serve the material, moral and spiritual well being of its peoples. Even though there is no single set of scales on which to weigh the well being of a country, the elements that go into the making of the good society are generally recognized and clearly distinguished. They are internal and external security and peace, economic development and social progress. And although it may be difficult to grasp the intricacies, the elusiveness and the paradoxes of another people's thoughts, the widening of man's horizons and the assurance of his worth and dignity have become universal aspirations. But their attainment and realization are beyond the unaided means of even the most powerful nation. Nature puts limits to the self-sufficiency of nations, and no one people has a monopoly in all fields of progress. Very often, excellence in one field is counterpoised by deficiencies in others. To call man's powers into full exercise; to heighten the sense of life in men; to provide opportunities for a life lived in the pursuit of values; to still the hunger, to banish the fear and to ease the unceasing battle of life requires the marshalling of the material and spiritual forces of all nations in a common endeavor controlled and directed by a clear and definite purpose.

International protection of human rights serves at once the interest of exalted idealism and of practical political objectives. It has much that is meaningful to say to peoples' dilemmas and exultations, and its actual and potential capacity to contribute to the solution of this century's formidable problems is unlimited. It is a notion that agitates deeply with its psychological, social, intellectual and political implications. International concern with the material and spiritual welfare of man in the concrete creates a common consciousness of right and wrong and provides a set of international rules of behaviour which rests on a well worked out conception of the world and man's place in it. It creates that necessary link between the individual and the international community without which the reconstruction of international relations on humane foundations is impossible.

Peace depends on the possibility of non violent change and the international constellation remains far and away the most important force for such change. The change that would set in motion all the other changes necessary to create a society of the human race is the change in the traditional structure of international relations and its emancipation from the limitations of class doctrines, political expediences and the pressure of national interests. It is a change which looks to a world of human dignity and equality, free from harassment by cruel governments, harsh societies, chronic economic ills and social woes. Only an international community with the will and the power to take up the cudgels on behalf of the human individual can hold out such promise. But to become a faith that would give life and strength to people, internationalism must be sustained by a philosophy capable of shaping experience into a developing narrative and supported by acts capable of evoking the deepest longings of the human mind and soul. There is no better way in which man can seek and find identification with the whole of humanity than by sharing in the grandeur, the adventure and the servitude, as well as in the advantages and benefits of internationalism, than as a subject and object of international relations. Therein lies the profound significance of international protection of human rights for the citizen, the nation and the international community. Therein lies the explanation of the crucial importance of every step toward the enlargement of the right and freedom of the human person to act out his role on the international scene independently of his nationality.

Throughout history, it has been the individual who has provided the forward momentum of freedom and liberty and who has served as the catalyst to set in motion events and developments that have changed the course of history. John Hampden's insistence, for example, that King Charles I could not, without the consent of Parliament, impose a levy on Buckinghampshire's landowners to provide a warship of 480 tons, with 180 men and guns "and the things necessary," led to a civil war that established his contention as a fundamental law of England. It was Oliver Brown, father of Linda Carol, the Negro girl of Topeka, Kansas, whose challenge to the Chaunnay County's Board of Education led to the unanimous Supreme Court decision of May 17, 1954, banning racial discrimination in public schools and sparked the civil rights revolution in the United States. On the international scene, too, the individual is fated to play the role of catalyst in mobilizing the reasoning forces of the world to affect basic structural changes in international relations. For only when the individual becomes a primary subject and object of international law and relations and is vested with substantive and procedural rights immune from the power of the state will the world arrive at the point of convergence of the interests of the individual, the community, the nation and the community of nations to herald a new dawn in the affairs of man.

The man we speak of is man in his national and cultural environment. Stripped of his environmental, national and cultural characteristics, spiritually adrift from his past and loosed from his traditional moorings, man loses his essential humanity. The evolution of the international community demands a background of certainties and the encompassing life of humanity with all its contrasts and all its contradictions. The historic forms of society cannot be dissolved, nor new ones created, either by abstract individualism or by abstract universalim. On this point Martin Buber warned us that,

> There is no practical universalism—universalism that is realizable though with the utmost effort—except that adumbrated by the prophets of Israel, who proposed not to abolish national societies together with their forms of organization, but rather to heal and perfect them, and thereby pave the way for their amalgamation.[3]

International concern with the fate of man does not seek to dissolve the bonds that bind the citizen to his state, nor to bar people from cultivating their traditions and cherishing their local patriotism. International protection for human rights stands for a true pluralism, in which man's beliefs and values can be subjected only to the minimum restraint required by respect for the human rights of others. Jaques Maritain envisions the pluralist world body politic as made up not only of the international and supra-national institutions created to serve it, but also, and first of all,

> of the particular bodies politic themselves; with their own political structures and lives, their own national and cultural heritages, their own multifarious institutions and communities—all this being enveloped, treasured, and held sacred by the same will which would tend, beyond all this, to a world-wide living together, and which would have achieved this aim by the foundation of a world political society...Only the world society taken as a whole both with the supra-national State and the multiplicity of nations, would be a perfect political society...[4]

Although international protection of human rights has yet to find what Lord Acton would call the prophet to proclaim and the champion to defend, it can boast of a background of increasing certainty. Almost four centuries ago, Hugo Grotius anticipated the possibility of such protection when he recognized as proper and lawful outside intervention on behalf of unjustly persecuted subjects.[5] He was of that school of natural law which conceived of the human person as the ultimate basis of international law and which centuries later inspired jurists to elaborate workable theories on the international legal status of the individual.[6] The several efforts over the past half century at international protection of the interests of minorities, labor, aborigines and underprivileged of many kinds;[7] the Nuremberg Judgement at the close of World War II;[8] the law of the European Communities and of international organizations regulating the legal status of their officials and emissaries;[9] the European Convention on Human Rights[10] and the Human Rights Convention of the Americas,[11] as well as the whole post-War movement under the aegis of the United Nations toward international protection of human rights,[12] represent a continuum from the rudimentary to the sophisticated rules of international law. Though the position of the individual as a subject of international law, even in those areas where he succeeded in breaking through the walls of a positivism which rests all customary international law on the will of the state, is still more of a postulate than a reality,

> it is noteworthy that as the international legal order has increasingly developed from a primitive to a more advanced stage, the closer the contact has grown between international law and the individual.[13]

An array of living forces is lining up behind the notion of international protection of human rights, determined to move toward the desired objective. Practicing lawyers and jurists in many parts of the world are responding to the need for the emancipation of the human person and raising him to the fullest status under the protection of the law of nations. Thus in June, 1961, the American Conference on World Peace Through the Rule of Law, held at San José, Costa Rica, agreed that,

> the effective protection of the fundamental human rights of the individual is the indispensable basis for achievement of a sound legal order based on peace and justice;

and recommended,

> that there be created a World Court of Human Rights with
> a carefully drafted jurisdiction which will respect the
> domestic jurisdiction of nations yet provide a forum to
> correct existing deficiencies in this important field.[14]

Similar conferences of continental scope held in Nigeria, India,
Thailand, Ceylon, Japan, Brazil and Italy yielded similar conclu-
sions and they were given universal expression in the Declaration
of General Principles for a World Rule of Law, adopted at the
First World Conference on World Peace Through The Rule of
Law in July, 1963, in Athens, Greece, as follows:

> All States and persons must accept the rule of law in the
> world community. In international matters, individuals,
> juridical persons, states and international organizations
> must all be subject to international law, deriving rights
> and incurring obligations thereunder...

> International law and legal institutions must be based on
> fundamental concepts of fairness, justice and human dig-
> nity...[15]

"It is Our earnest wish," Pope John XXIII declared in his
famed encyclical *Pacem in Terris,*

> that the United Nations Organization—in its structure
> and in its means—may become ever more equal to the
> magnitude and nobility of its tasks, and that the day may
> come when every human being will find therein an effective
> safeguard for the rights which derive directly from his
> dignity as a person, and which are therefore universal,
> inviolable and inalienable rights. This is all the more to be
> hoped for since all human beings, as they take an ever
> more active part in the public life of their own political
> communities, are showing an increasing interest in the
> affairs of all peoples, and are becoming more consciously
> aware that they are living members of a world com-
> munity.[16]

Within the United Nations and other intergovernmental bodies,
as on the outside, arguments in defense of the rights of man
and of his status as a subject of international law and international concern are frequently heard, even as nations defend the

right to be judge in their own cause. While it cannot be said that the debates in the international forums have produced, at least thus far, fierce contestants in a great and historic controversy, we perceive in the records definite glimpses of the self-assertion of the corporate will of nations and of the true conscience of mankind. The substantial concession made in the European Convention for the Protection of Human Rights and Fundamental Freedoms to the right of the individual to look to international organization for the ultimate defense of his rights and liberties, and similar concessions made in the International Convention on the Elimination of All Forms of Racial Discrimination, as well as in the Optional Protocol to the International Covenant on Political and Civil Rights,[17] are at once a witness against those so overawed by tradition that they dare not make a judgement, and a precursor of things to come. The expanding international cooperative activities in the economic, social, cultural and scientific fields carried on under the auspices of the United Nations family of organizations, by the various regional and sub-regional groupings, as well as under direct governmental sponsorship, have brought within the orbit of international concern practically all the cares and burdens of man. When these activities are inspired and informed by the concern of the community of nations with the fate of the human individual, whoever and wherever he may be, and are directed toward the goal of international protection of human rights, they provide a tremendous impulse to the movement for new forms of international organization and cooperation and for an international division of labor which alone can provide prosperity and abundance for all.[18]

We may not be able to predict the future, but we must try to mold it by directing events toward a goal which, though vast in scope and majestic in conception, is deeply rooted in the concrete interests of man and corresponds to his psychological resources. But a statement of goals is no substitute for innovation of formula for practical measures of attaining them. It must be accompanied by steady and consistent initiatives, as well as by resolute and ingenious action. Hence the supreme importance which attaches to the form and content of the measures taken by the United Nations to advance the cause of international protection of human rights. Unless the United Nations preserves an exquisite course of direction and strives to invest the idea of international protection of human rights with political power, it will neither seize the minds of men nor command their first allegiance.

The adventure and excitement of translating the objectives of the International Covenants on Human Rights and of the Optional Protocol into plans and the plans into action would in themselves provide a constructive outlet for the energies of even the most enterprising of people and open vast new fields to daring hopes and ideas. Though people hold to their ancient ways, yet the boundaries of public acceptance of new ideas are constantly extending. The United Nations must step boldly across the stage of history to wage the battle for a secure and bountiful peace. When the International Covenants emerge to confront reality, they must not be found wanting.

The tempo of history is constantly growing swifter. The greatest sin would be to fail to grasp the dream that is within our reach. We cannot wait for a concurrence of favorable circumstances to transform dreams into reality. Such a concurrence always seems to elude us, if for no other reason than that the affairs of men do not follow a structural pattern as rigid as that of the Shakespearean sonnet. The present stage of history is as favorable as any to a coalescence of humanity and the strengthening of international organization. This is the age of national freedom and emancipation. Within a few years' time the vindication of the principle of self-determination will be complete. The perils and opportunities of this overwhelming historic development are alike great. There is the danger that the new states, in their struggle for national consolidation and survival, will fall prey to the evils and excesses of a ruthless nationalism, with all its dark portends and mutual distrust, hatred, fear and competitive anarchy and thus add to the further dismemberment of the human family. But there is also in their way a great opportunity, now that they have attained independence and statehood, to turn their attention to the consolidation of mankind in a prosperous community of interdependent nations dedicated to the elevation of man and the administration of their common patrimony. Let their burden become their strength, to point the way to new forms of international association and cooperation. If freedom orients the will of the world, it has few other bulwarks than the rights of man.

Notes

NOTES TO CHAPTER I

1. Thus, according to many authorities, the rise of the modern, secular national state in the Middle East is changing profoundly the community role of Islam. The political and social revolutions are challenging many of the institutions of the *ancien regime* which are identified with the historic Muslim system,

> and it is therefore almost impossible to build a modern state and society without rejecting many institutions which in the past have been Islamic ... It is this situation that makes it difficult to state exactly what the role of Islam will be in the new Middle East that is gradually emerging. As a personal faith, Islam has vigor and vitality. As a constituent of the glorious civilization of the past, it is both a matter of pride and a subtle influence affecting the most modern-minded Muslim. But as a community structure, it has yet to find its new role in relation to the secular nationalism implicit in many modern Middle East developments ... John S. Badeau, "Religion in the Middle East," 25 *Social Education*, p.40 (1961.)

2. For a listing of peace plans and proposals throughout history, see Edith Wynner and Georgia Lloyd, *Searchlight on Peace Plans*, New York, E. P. Dutton & Co., 1944.

3. John Stuart Mill, *Vindications of the French Revolution of February 1848: Dissertations and Discussions—Political, Philosophical and Historical*, III, Boston, W. V. Spencer, 1868, p.382.

4. Following is a partial list of the works dealing with nationalism consulted: Lord Acton, *Essays on Freedom and Power*, edited and with a new introduction by Gertrude Himmelfarb, New York, A Meridian Book, 1955; Salo Wittmayer Baron, *Modern Nationalism and Religion*, New York, Harper & Bros., 1947; Crane Brinton, *The Shaping of the Modern Mind*, New York, Prentice Hall Inc., 1953; Jacob Burckhardt, *Force and Freedom*, edited by James Hastings Nichols, New York, Pantheon Books Inc., 1943; William Curt Buthman, *The Rise of Integral Nationalism in France, With Special Reference to the Ideas and Activities of Charles Maurras*, New York, Columbia University, Studies in History, Economics and Public Law, No. 455, 1939; Edward Hallet Carr, *Nationalism and After*, London, Macmillan Co., 1945; Ernest Cassirer, *The Myth of the State*, New Haven, Yale University Press, 1946; Edward T. Cargan, *The Intent of Toynbee's History*, Chicago, Loyola University Press, 1961; Herbert Adams Gibbons, *Nationalism and Internationalism*, New York, Frederick A. Stokes Co., 1930; Myron G. Gilmore, *The World of Humanism*, 1452-1517, New York, Harper & Bros., 1952; E. Harris Harbison, *The Age of the Reformation*, Ithaca, Cornell University Press, 1955; Carlton J. Hayes, *The Historical Evolution of Modern Nationalism*, New York, R. R. Smith Inc., 1931; Hans Kohn, *Idea of Nationalism: A Study in its Origins and Background*, New York, Macmillan Co., 1946; Hans Kohn, *The Twentieth Century*, New York, MacMillan Co., 1957; R. H. Lowie, *The Origin of the State*, New York, Harcourt,

Brace & Co., 1927; Arnold J. Toynbee, *A Study of History*, vol. XII (Reconsiderations), New York, Oxford University Press, 1961; Arnold J. Toynbee, *Hellenism*, New York, Oxford University Press, 1959; Alfred North Whitehead, *Adventures of Ideas*, New York, Macmillan Co., 1933.

5. Arnold J. Toynbee, *A Study of History*, IX, New York, Oxford University Press, 1954, pp.441-442.

6. It is difficult to select from the spate of books that have appeared in recent years those which best illuminate the subject of nationalism in the countries of Asia, Africa and other parts of the world which have emerged into independence since 1945. Among the more important consulted, mention may be made of the following: *The Politics of the Developing Areas*, edited by G. A. Almond and James Coleman, Princeton, Princeton University Press, 1960; Rupert Emerson, *From Empire to Nation: The Rise of Self-Assertion of Asian and African Peoples*, Cambridge, Harvard University Press, 1960; Jan Romein and Jan Eric Romein, *The Asian Century: A History of Modern Nationalism in Asia*, translated from the Dutch by Robert Clark, Berkeley, University of California Press, 1962; *Asian Nationalism and the West: A Symposium Based on Documents and Reports of the 11th Conference of the Institute of Pacific Relations*, edited by William L. Holland, New York, Macmillan Co., 1953; Bruce T. McCully, *English Education and the Rise of Nationalism in India*, New York, Columbia University Press, 1940; George McT. Kahin, *Nationalism and Revolution in Indonesia*, Ithaca, Cornell University Press, 1952; George H. T. Kimble, *Tropical Africa*, II, New York, The Twentieth Century Fund, 1960; Lord Hailey, *An African Survey*, revised edition, London, Oxford University Press, 1958; Virginia Thompson and Richard Adloff, *The Emerging States of French Equatorial Africa*, Stamford, Stamford University Press, 1960; Kwame Nkrumah, *Africa Must Unite*, New York, Frederick A. Prager, 1963; Tom Mboya, *Freedon and After*, Boston, Little, Brown Co., 1963; Alex Quaison-Sackey, *Africa Unbound*, New York, Frederick A. Praeger, 1963; *Arab Nationalism: An Anthology*, edited by Sylvia G. Haim, Berkeley, University of California Press, 1962; Anthony Nutting, *The Arabs: A Narrative History from Mohammed to the Present*, New York, Clarkson N. Potter, 1964.

7. For a complete listing, see *UN OPI, Press Release SA/216, 1 February 1967*. As of that date, the total membership of the United Nations was 122, as compared with 55 in 1946. Whereas in 1946 there were only three independent States in Africa—Ethiopia, Liberia and the Union of South Africa—at the end of 1966 the number stood at 35.

8. The figures are based on an unofficial compilation of census results and estimates in the *United Nations Demographic Yearbook 1963*.

9. See, for example, "Old-age Protection under Social Security Schemes," 82 *International Labour Review*, pp.542-571 (1960); "Medical-care Protection under Social Security Schemes," *Ibid.*, 89, pp.570-593 (1964); Subramanian N. Iver, "Degree of Protection under Family Allowances Schemes," *Ibid.*, 94, pp.477-486 (1966). President Lyndon B. Johnson gave succinct expression to the increasing reliance of the citizen upon his government when, in an address on April 3, 1965, to the Anti-Defamation League in Washington, D.C., he told the audience:

> Your Government is concerned not with statistics but with the substance of your schools, your jobs, your cities, your family-life, your country-side, your health, your hopes, your protection, your preparedness—and your rights and opportunities. (For text see *The New York Times*, February 4, 1965.)

Most of the Constitutions which have been written after World War II contain clauses relating to governmental responsibility in the economic, social and cultural spheres. Independently of constitutional provisions, the notion of governmental responsibility for economic and social welfare has been consecrated internationally in the Universal Declaration of Human Rights and in the International Covenant on Economic, Social and Cultural Rights. (For text of the Covenant, see *U.N.G.A. Res. 2200 (XXI), 16 December 1966*.) In the developing countries, state intervention in economic and social life is regarded as absolutely essential, not so much because it is ideologically desirable, but because it is inevitable if there is to be the swiftest possible development and if the meagre financial and technical resources are to be exploited to the full. Government can participate by owning certain parts of industry; or by creating the infra-structure which would guide the country into certain areas of development; or simply by working out an economic plan within which any development must be fitted. In any or all of these ways, government can maintain a course for the country, laying down the direction of development. Tom Mboya, *op. cit. supra,* note 6, pp.170-171.

10. Thus, in the course of the 1960 debate in the United Nations General Assembly on the then draft declaration on the granting of independence to colonial countries and peoples, India's Krishna Menon spoke for all the newly emergent nations when he said:

> We constantly say in India that on 15 August 1947 what happened was not independence, but we removed the main obstacle to independence, namely, foreign rule; independence had to be attained hereafter, that is to say, when people have adequate food, adequate shelter, adequate sanitation, adequate dignity, the capacity to exercise them—that is independence. *(A/PV 944:122.)*

In fact, Jawaharlal Nehru, who in 1938 was responsible for the establishment by the Congress Party in India of a Planning Committee to achieve the promotion of rapid and balanced economic development, was convinced that "national planning on a comprehensive scale could only take place under a free national government prepared to introduce fundamental changes in the country." Frank Moraes, *Jawaharlal Nehru,* New York, Macmillan Co., 1956, p.421.

11. In his closing speech at the Bandung Conference of 1955, the representative of Iran declared:

> History will recall the Bandung Conference as the first diplomatic manifestation of Afro-Asian solidarity and our conscious and determined will to begin a new era; the era of gradual emancipation from the enslaving old chains of fear and tyranny, of ignorance and want. Today we are proclaiming to the whole world the awakening of our two continents as a historical phenomenon of our time, our conviction that a completely independent and free Afro-Asia is possible and can by itself achieve such political, economic and social emancipation. *(Afro-Asian Conference, Bandung, 1955,* Speeches and Communiques, mimeographed.)

The so-called "anti-colonial" revolution is, of course, by no means exhausted by the assertion of political autonomy and independence. It is also a social and economic revolution, in which a small Westernized elite is seeking to bring their countries into the modern world, to create modern states and industrialized economies. As has often been the case in the West, the typical process of social revolution in Asia and Africa is to institutionalize power and vague ideas. In most of the developing countries there has been an effort to carry out a program of social and economic reform with a variation of the authoritarian technique, backed up by a highly articulate nationalism or a regional coloration. Their leaders have often protested that they could not possibly move their people forward within the framework of traditional democracy and sanctioned authoritarianism in the name of social and economic progress. See, for example, *The Ideologies of the Developing Nations,* edited with an introduction by Paul E. Sigmund, New York, Frederick A. Praeger, 1962, particularly Sukarno's "Lecture to the Students of Hassanudim University" of 1959; President Gamal Abdel Nasser's "The National Union Party"; President Mohammed Ayub Khan's "Pakistan Perspectives"; President Sekou Touré's "African Emancipation"; President Julius Nyere's "One-Party Rule"; and Kofi Baako's "Nkrumaism: Its Theory and Practice."

12. Lord Acton's observation that "whenever a single definite object is made the supreme end of the State, be it the advantage of a class, the safety or the power

of the country, the greatest happiness of the greatest number, or the support of any speculative idea, the State becomes for the time inevitably absolute," *Essays on Freedom and Power, op. cit., supra,* note 4, p.159, finds daily confirmation in virtually all areas of state relations everywhere on earth. Alexander Hamilton long ago noted that,

> Safety from external danger is the most powerful dictator of national conduct. Even the ardent love of liberty will, after a time, give way to its dictate. The violent destruction of life and property incident to war, the continual effort and alarm attendant upon a state of continued danger will compel nations the most attached to liberty to resort for repose and security to institutions which have the tendency to destroy their civil and political rights. To be more safe, they at length become willing to run the risk of being less free. Quoted by Edward Meade Earle, "American Military Policy and National Security," *53 Political Science Quarterly,* p.4, (1938).

NOTES TO CHAPTER II

1. For a history of the Kellogg-Briand Pact, see James T. Shotwell, *War as an Instrument of National Policy and its Renunciation in the Pact of Paris,* New York, Harcourt, Brace & Co., 1929. For text of the Pact see *Ibid.,* Appendix VI. See also Royal Institute of International Affairs, *Survey of International Affairs,* 1928, pp.1-36.

2. *Survey of International Affairs, op. cit.,* p.21.

3. James T. Shotwell, *op. cit.,* p.217.

4. F. P. Walters, *A History of the League of Nations,* London, Oxford University Press, 1952, II, pp.385-386.

5. Arbitration, of course, was a method of settling international disputes known to the ancient Greeks and Romans and even earlier. What the Hague Conference aimed at, was to place international arbitration on a permanent and world-wide basis. Between 1918 and 1941, for example, over 300 bilateral treaties creating permanent machinery for the settlement of disputes were concluded. Leo Gross, "Some Observations on the International Court of Justice," 56 *American Journal of International Law,* p.35 (1962). For a detailed history of arbitration see, J. H. Ralston, *International Arbitration from Athens to Locarno,* Stamford, Stamford University Press, 1929; A. M. Stuyt, *Survey of International Arbitrations: 1794-1938,* The Hague, Martin Nijhoff, 1939.

6. Charles Burton Marshall, *The Limits of Foreign Policy,* New York, Holt & Co., 1954, pp.111-112.

7. As of the end of 1962, only 34 contentious cases had been submitted to the International Court of Justice, 8 of which were stricken from its list for lack of jurisdiction, while 6 others were discontinued. See Shabtai Rosenne, *The World Court: What it is and How it Works,* Leyden, A. W. Sijthoff, 1962, p.218. There is general agreement that the Court, as the juridical arm of the United Nations, has not played a major and dynamic role in the settlement of international disputes. The late Dag Hammarsjold lamented the fact that States were not availing themselves of recourse to the Court but preferred settlement outside of it. *Introduction to the Annual Report of the Secretary-General on the Work of the Organization, 1 July 1954 - 15 June 1955,* General Assembly, Tenth Session, Official Records, Supplement No. 1, p.xiii.

8. For text, see *Yearbook of the United Nations, 1946-47,* p.612. On the practical implications of the Connally Reservation, the following comments by Professor Herbert W. Briggs are pertinent. Referring to the invocation by the United States of the Reservation in the *Inter-handel* case, which involved the Swiss Government and which entailed the restoration of property seized by the United States under the Enemy Alien Act, and otherwise refusing to submit the case to international arbitration or conciliation, Professor Briggs wrote:

The State Department is thus using the plea of domestic jurisdiction to reject arbitration ... Moreover, in refusing to comply with the conciliation provisions of the Treaty (with the Swiss) , the United States is attempting to set up its Constitution and laws as an excuse for failure to fulfil its international obligations. The legal insufficiency of such an argument is too well established in international law to require extended comment ... It ill-accords with United States professed advocacy of the rule of law in international relations and extends the stultifying effect of its domestic jurisdiction reservation to the compulsory jurisdiction of the International Court of Justice. "Toward the Rule of Law", 51 *American Journal of International Law.* pp.58-59, (1957).

As of the end of 1964, approximately 40 out of 115 States Parties to the Statute of the International Court of Justice—all Member States of the United Nations are *ipso facto* parties—had accepted the so-called compulsory jurisdiction clause (Article 36 (2)) , under which they recognize as compulsory *ipso facto* the jurisdiction of the Court in all legal disputes concerning: (a) the interpretation of a treaty; (b) any question of international law; (c) the existence of any fact which, if established, would constitute a breach of an international obligation; (d) the nature and extent of the reparation to be made for the breach of an international obligation. (For text of the Statute, see *United Nations Yearbook, op. cit.,* pp.843-850.) It should be noted, however, that acceptance of this clause is rarely unconditional. Aside from the condition of reciprocity, States Parties frequently exclude from the application of compulsory jurisdiction matters such as disputes relating to territorial status and questions regarded as being exclusively within the domestic jurisdiction of States. For an example of the former, ses the reservation of Guatemala in respect to the disputed area of Belize, *Ibid.,* p.610, of the latter; reservation made by India, *Ibid.,* p.609.

9. That control of armaments, let alone disarmament, implies and involves conceptions about the structure of international relations is abundantly evident from a reading of the history of disarmament negotiations, especially since the end of Word War II. A recent striking illustration is provided by the reaction of India, Japan, West Germany, Italy and other countries with potential nuclear capabilities to the proposed treaty to ban the spread of nuclear weapons, which has been the subject of serious negotiation between the United States and the Soviet Union. These countries have, to all intents and purposes, been asked to subscribe to a treaty under which they would surrender their rights to nuclear weapons but which would offer them no security against the possibility of nuclear attack or nuclear blackmail. Such a guarantee, especially in the case of such a non-aligned country as India, could come only in the general context of collective security, not in the specific context of a treaty so patently discriminatory in favor of the nuclear powers. Other objections to the proposed treaty relate to the question of international inspection and to the treaty's impact on the development of peaceful nuclear programs.

10. A most notable example is without doubt the Peace Corps movement. At the end of 1966, 18 countries had Peace Corps patterned on the idea which originated in the United States, while two others were about to act on it. Sponsoring a Peace Corps of one kind or another were Austria, Belgium, Canada, Denmark, France, Great Britain, Israel, Japan, Lichtenstein, the Netherlands, New Zealand, Norway, the Philippines, Sweden, Switzerland, the United States of America and West Germany. Finland and Italy were about to launch their Peace Corps. Together, they deployed about 19,000 volunteers in service in 95 States and territories in Africa, Asia and Latin America. (*The New York Times,* January 20, 1967.)

11. Article 1 (3) of the *Charter of the United Nations.* For text, see *United Nations Yearbook, op. cit.,* Appendix I.

12. *Constitution of the United Nations Educational, Scientific and Cultural Organization, Ibid.,* pp.712-717.

13. In an article in *The New York Times Magazine* of September 17, 1961, former Under-Secretady of State for International Organization, Harlan Cleveland, wrote that on the average, one major intergovenmental conference gets under

way every day of the year, each with an instructed American delegation. He noted that a total of 394 such conferences were held in 1960, while 352 were held in the first eight months of 1961. A total of 400 inter-governmental conferences were scheduled for 1962. These conferences covered a variety of subjects, from international control of atomic energy, to the price of zinc, and from conservation of Atlantic tuna, to the control of desert locust.

14. From an address to the Hungarian Academy of Science in Budapest. *(UN OPI Press Release SG/1529,* 2 July 1963.) It should be noted that the proliferation of international meetings and conferences has been the subject of increasing concern and debate in the United Nations. The "booming business called international conference" has been severely criticized and led to the adoption of repeated resolutions on the subject. See, for example, the statement made by the United States representative on the Budgetary Committee of the 1963 General Assembly. United States Mission to the United Nations, *Press Release No. 4279,* October 25, 1963; also, *U.N.G.A. Res. 2239* (XXI) of 20 December, 1966.

15. See, for example, Francis Rosentiel, *Le Principe de "Supranationalité,"* Paris, Editions A. Pédone, 1962; Marc-Stanislas Korowicz, *Organisations Internationales et Souveraineté des Etats Membres,* Paris, Editions A. Pédone, 1961; C. A. W. Manning, *The Nature of International Society,* New York, Wiley, 1962.

16. This accounts for the fact that, whereas in political intercourse national governments display excessive sensitivity when it comes to defending their "domestic domains," the same governments have been tolerating within the framework of the expanding international organizations outside interference in their budgetary, exchange and trade policies and accepting encumbrances entailed in bilateral and multilateral technical and economic assistance programs. The operations of such international agencies as the International Monetary Fund, GATT, the Organization for European Economic Cooperation and the several Technical Assistance agencies of the United Nations produce new legal situations and new legal categories.

17. It is a universally accepted fact that the explosion of a sufficiently large number of nuclear bombs at any point on earth, dispersing long-lived isotopes in the air, can poison the entire globe. Human interference with his environment and man's increasing control over natural forces have been producing effects that not only cross national boundaries and sectional frontiers, but reach ever more from continent to continent. The question of pollution, of every kind, is an outstanding example. It has reached a magnitude which compels increasing international attention. Truly, as Halford Mackinder, England's great geographer, warned at the beginning of this century, the world's people are living "in a closed system in which they can do nothing of which the repercussion does not come back upon them from the very anti-podes."

18. The books and monographs on the North Atlantic Treaty Organization are so varied and extensive that it is difficult to single out any for special mention. Among the books consulted are: Robert Strausz-Hupe, James E. Dougherty and William R. Kintner, *Building the Atlantic World,* New York, Harper & Row, 1963; Margaret E. Ball, *NATO and the European Movement,* New York, Frederick A. Praeger, 1959; Alastair Buchan, *NATO in the 1960's: The Implications of Interdependence,* revised edition, New York, Frederick A. Praeger, 1963; Robert Kleiman, *Atlantic Crisis: American Diplomacy Confronts a Resurgent Europe,* New York, W. W. Norton & Co., 1964; Ben T. Moore, *NATO and the Future of Europe,* New York, Harper & Row, 1958; F. E. Mulley, *The Politics of Western Defense,* New York, Frederick A. Praeger, 1962.

19. This is especially true of the United States and England, which have been the most persistent champions of NATO and the idea of Atlantic Community to which the late President John F. Kennedy gave most eloquent expression in his Paulskirche speech in Frankfurt a/M on June 26, 1963. (For text, see *The New York Times,* June 26, 1963.) As far as the United States is conecrned, to question NATO is to place in doubt, according to many observers, the very premise of America's post-World War II international posture. There is no doubt as to the symbolic significance of NATO in marking the unmistakable metamorphosis of American

foreign policy in rejecting 150 years of isolation. NATO was the first American peacetime assumption of military responsibilities outside its hemisphere, and its continued strategic importance to the defense of United States interests has been repeatedly reaffirmed. See, for example, President Johnson's letter of March 23, 1966, to President Charles de Gaulle. (*The New York Times,* March 25, 1966).

20. General de Gaulle's refusal to accede to the nuclear test ban treaty of 1963 has been regarded as the most forceful assertion of France's independent national policy. On that occasion President de Gaulle, in a speech in Lyon on September 28, 1963, featured as a major statement of policy, declared that France would not be bound by the United Nations, NATO, or a United Europe in anything that concerned her national interests. (*The New York Times,* September 29, 1963.) In fact, France has since the beginning of 1959 progressively reduced her participation in NATO, commencing with the withdrawal that year of her Mediterranean fleet from even fictive NATO control, until the removal on July 1, 1966, of all her forces committed to NATO from the latter's command. The final link of France with the integrated military organization of NATO was severed on Apdil 1, 1967, when the flags of fifteen NATO nations, which for sixteen years fluttered over the Supreme Headquarters of the North Atlantic Treaty Organization at Rocquencourt, outside Paris, were hauled down, and all but that of France were unfurled over NATO's new headquarters in Belgium.

21. Thirteenth Press Conference, Paris, (Text supplied by the Embassy of France, Press and Information Service, New York, *Speeches and Press Conferences,* No. 239, February 21, 1966).

22. The question of nuclear arms control has divided the Atlantic Alliance for many years and there is no satisfactory solution in sight. The full implication of the proposed non-proliferation treaty, for example, is to reduce America's allies to permanent dependence on the United States and to make them acquiesce in American strategy. Whatever the reality of the situation may be, nations cannot for reasons of security and national prestige accede willingly to an act of self-abnegation and place their fate blindly in the hands of even the most trusted ally. Thus, according to the views of many observers on the scene, all the efforts to fashion NATO into an integrated military and political alliance are bound to end in frustration until the nuclear weapons nettle is firmly grasped. See, for example, F. W. Mulley, *op. cit.,* note 18, *passim;* see *also* Robert Kleiman, *Ibid, passim.*

23. For many years, for example, the United States has persisted in its views that the goals of Soviet policy were forever the same in Western Europe and elsewhere and held fast to the notion of an international Communist conspiracy. General de Gaulle has not been alone in his reevaluation of the military threat of the Soviet Union and in his analysis of the political, economic and social evolution of the Communist countries in Europe. Thus at the December, 1966, meeting in Paris of the North Atlantic Council, Belgian Foreign Minister Pierre Harmel proposed that a new study be undertaken to reevaluate the Alliance in terms of changes since 1949. Not only has his proposal been accepted, but the Belgian initiative was broadened to include efforts to bring about a detente and a parallel reduction of armaments between NATO and the Warsaw Pact countries. On January 24, 1967, M. Harmel told the Belgian-American Society in Brussels that he hoped to see progress in the Atlantic Alliance toward a European security conference, a non-aggression treaty with the Warsaw Pact countries, and a general solution of the political problems dividing Europe. (*The New York Times,* January 25, 1967.)

24. When the United States finally came around to agree on the need to recognize and encourage a relaxation of relations with the Soviet Union and the Eastern bloc, West Germany was beginning to wonder whether the United States was not preparing to sacrifice German reunification for the sake of American-Soviet amity. Bonn reacted indignantly, for example, when President Johnson failed to insist on action leading to the reunification of Germany in his speech in New York on October 7, 1966, in which he announced his policy aimed at easing tensions with Eastern Europe. (For text, see *The New York Times,* October 8, 1966.) Much of West Germany's opposition to the proposed nuclear non-proliferation treaty stems from the suspicion that the United States is far more interested in reaching

an accord with the Soviet Union on banning the spread of nuclear arms than in gratifying West Germany's interests in the matter. A great deal of importance has been attributed in West Germany to an article in the June, 1965, issue of *Foreign Affairs* by the chief United States disarmament negotiator at Geneva, William C. Foster, in which he wrote that a nuclear non-proliferation treaty was worth pursuing even at the expense of eroding the North Atlantic Treaty Organization. It had reached a point where President Johnson's personal intervention was needed to assure the West Germans that Mr. Foster's views were not shared by the American Government. *(The New York Times,* April 28, 1967.) Nevertheless, all indications point to increasing pressures rising within West Germany for a new policy to replace the former total reliance upon the United States for the promise of reunification.

25. "The Americans may be our allies," it is often heard in Europe, "but when it comes to business they are not our friends." Thus, for instance, *The Financial Times* of London of April 8, 1965, had this to say in connection with the Labor Government's decision to scrap the strike aircraft TSR2 in favor of the cheaper American F 111:

> There are two consequences of the situation which should be accepted openly. The first is that Britain is now dependent on the United States to supply it with advanced weapons in the conventional as well as the nuclear sphere. We must rely on the good will of the Administration, for example, to equip our forces in Malaysia with equipment as up-to-date as that supplied by Russia to the Indonesians. This is not a pleasant fact to swallow.

> The second consequence is that what has happened in the case of aircraft may happen in the case of other technically advanced industries unless action is taken in good time. The very size of the United States market gives American firms an inbuilt advantage, and the only way for European firms to match it is to pool their resources. Attempts which are now being made to establish joint aircraft development programs with France should be extended soon to other industries and other countries. It the countries of Europe do not get together, they will be beaten separately in one advanced field after the other.

Prime Minister Wilson spoke in similar vein when he addressed the Consultative Assembly of the Council of Europe on January 23, 1967; in the course of his speech he said:

> Let no one here doubt Britain's loyalty to NATO and the Atlantic Alliance. But I have also always said that that loyalty must never mean subservience. Still less must it mean an industrial helotry under which we in Europe produce only the conventional apparatus of a modern economy while becoming increasingly dependent on American business for the sophisticated apparatus which will call the industrial tune in the 70's and 80's. (For text, see the *London Times,* January 24, 1967.)

The question of a "technology gap" between Europe and the United States was raised again in connection with the proposed nuclear non-proliferation treaty. Early in 1967, there was a flood of articles in the European press on the subject, in which the view was expressed that if the non-nuclear countries subscribed to the treaty, they might find themselves ultimately denied the use of atomic energy for peaceful purposes, leaving the present nuclear powers to monopolize the economic benefits accruing from the peaceful use of atomic energy. (For a survey of how the question of the technology gap appears to Europeans and Americans, see *(The New York Times,* (International Edition), March 14, 1967.)

26. *The New York Times,* April 7, 1964.

27. *The New York Times,* May 8, 1964.

28. For example, at a luncheon meeting on May 9, 1964, of Belgian-American associations in Brussels, Secretary of State Dean Rusk suggested the importance of closer coordination of the policies and efforts of the NATO nations outside the

North Atlantic area, in order to prevent Communism from expanding its domain over the less developed countries and called for assistance from all NATO members for South Viet-Nam in the struggle against Communist aggression there. *(The New York Times,* May 10, 1964). The Secretary of State expressed similar sentiments in even stronger terms at subsequent NATO meetings, especially at the meeting of the NATO Council in December, 1966. *(The New York Times,* 16 December, 1966.) The European allies not only rejected the general idea of collective security in Asia, but any effort to link NATO with the United States military position there. Thus in 1965, NATO's Secretariat prepared a legal opinion, which ruled that Hawaii was not included within the territorial guarantees of the North Atlantic Treaty.

29. In his *Politics Among Nations* (New York, Alfred A. Knopf, 3rd ed. 1960), Hans Morgenthau maintains that historical experiences of states during the past century do not substantiate the conception made popular in recent years that "war is made in the minds of men." However, he admits that ideological conflict has grown in importance with the passage of time and that the ideology of Communism is a more important consideration than has been the case with other ideologies of the past. "Nations," he writes,

> now oppose one another as standard bearers of ethical systems ... The moral code of one nation flings the challenge of its universalism into the face of another, which reciprocates in kind. Compromise, the virtue of the old diplomacy, becomes the treason of the new ... While all politics is necessarily pursuit of power, ideologies render involvement in that contest for power psychologically and morally acceptable to the actors and their audience" (p.61).

In the same vein, Quincy Wright writes:

> As civilization has advanced, it has become more and more necessary that war should be fought for ideas ... No other state can be expected to assist in a war for England or France, but in a war for liberty allies may be available ... While political values have differed with form of government and geographical position, all the great powers have considered the maintenance of their power position of primary political value. As a result, world politics have continued to be power politics. The great powers have continued to subordinate considerations of welfare, political tradition and national ideals to the diplomatic and military requirement of power. *A Study of War,* Chicago, Chicago University Press, 1942, I. p.159.

That the great powers dominating the world scene are also vehicles of competing ideologies is not peculiar to the twentieth century. Thus, it has been pointed out that the reason why the French Revolution's impact was far greater than that of the other movements against the old hierarchical order of things in Europe was that France was the great power and its influence was great. According to Professor R. R. Palmer, the French were never primarily concerned to promote revolution abroad. Still less were the other radical manifestations the result of some occult conspiracy by secret societies controlled from Paris. He emphasizes the conflict in the minds of the French leaders between patent national advantage and fidelity to the revolutionary cause; between the questions of foreign policy impinging upon French domestic policies and national interests; between full scale exploitation of Batavian, Helvetic and Cisalpine satellites and attempts to win their political sympathies, and concludes that the French actions on these and other questions cannot be explained by an inner need to spread the new doctrines. R. R. Palmer, *The Age of the Democratic Revolutions: A Political History of Europe and America, 1760-1800,* vol. II, Princeton, Princeton University Press 1964.

30. From the Statement issued by the Conference of Representatives of Communist Parties in Moscow, November, 1960. (For text, see *The New York Times,* December 7, 1960.)

31.   Point 14 of the "Twenty-one Conditions" for membership in the Communist International adopted by the Second Comintern Congress in August, 1920, in Moscow, provided:

> Every party which wishes to join the Communist Internatioial is obliged to give unconditional support to any Soviet republic in its struggle against counter-revolutionary forces. Communist parties must carry on unambiguous propaganda to prevent the dispatch of munitions transports to the enemies of the Soviet republics; they must also carry on propaganda by every means, legal or illegal, among troops sent to strangle workers' republics. *A Documentary History of Communism,* edited with introduction, notes and new translations, by Robert V. Daniels, New York, Random House, 1960, II, p.89.

> The unquestioning acceptance of the decisions of the International in accordance with Point 16 required of all Communist Parties applied to the Soviet Union as the only Soviet Republic in existence for more than two and a half decades. Daniels refers to the oft-quoted admonition of Lenin, to the effect that the proof of a good Communist was his loyalty to the Soviet Union—the socialist fatherland. *Ibid.,* p.96.

32.   The tensions which characterized Soviet-Yugoslav relations prior to the excommunication of Yugoslavia from the Communist International, included the following issues: Tito's ambitious plans for a Southeast European Federation, which was to include Roumania (and ultimately Hungary and a Communist Greece) and which had the support of Bulgarian Communist and Comintern leader Georgii Dimitrov; his plans for the rapid industrialization of Yugoslavia and his unwillingness to serve as a mere source of raw material for the Soviet Union; his reluctance to accept Moscow's terms for the establishment of Soviet—Yugoslav joint-stock companies; and his practice of keeping Soviet personnel in Yugoslavia under the surveillance of his secret police. All those and other issues were indicative of Tito's desire to be master in his own country, although he and his followers professed loyalty to Moscow even after their excommunication. See John S. Rechetar, *A Concise History of the Communist Party of the Soviet Union,* New York, Frederick A. Praeger, 1960, p.249. For text of the resolution of June 28, 1948, of the Communist Information Bureau "Concerning the Situation in the Communist Party of Yugoslavia," see Robert V. Daniels, *op. cit.,* II, pp.169-174.

33.   Following the workers' uprising in June, 1956, in Poznan, Poland, Wladyslaw Gomulka, who had been in the Soviet Union's disfavor for his nationalistic leanings, was reinstated as Secretary General of the Polish Workers' Party. On October 20, 1965, he addressed the Central Committee, in the course of which he stated:

> What is immutable in socialism can be reduced to the abolition of the exploitation of man by man. The roads of achieving this goal can be and are different. They are determined by various circumstances of time and place. The model of socialism can also vary. It can be such as that created in the Soviet Union; it can be shaped in a manner as we see it in Yugoslavia; it can be different still. Only by way of the experience and achievements of the various countries building socialism can the best model of socialism under given conditions arise." Robert Daniels, *op. cit.* p.327. For documentation on the Hungarian uprising in October, 1956, see *Ibid.,* pp.240-249. Regarding Soviet-Chinese relations, see below, pp.29-30.

34.   The case of Roumania is especially instructive. Unlike Yugoslavia, which had set forth ideological doctrines of its own and introduced basic changes in Communist practice, Roumania's assertion of sovereign independence in her political, economic and defense policies has been patently nationalistic in tone and inspiration. In April, 1964, the Central Committee of Roumania's ruling party authorized the publication of a statement and policy analysis, which has come to be regarded as a historic manifesto of national Communism. The statement asserted as an absolutely binding principle that each Communist-ruled country must be

sovereign over its economic life and must not be forced by any supra-national body to take action against its own will. "The idea of a single planning body for all Comecon countries," the statement declared, "has the most serious economic and political implications. The sovereignty of the socialist state requires that it holds in its hands all the levers for managing economic and social life." It insisted upon the complete independence of every Communist party and absolute equality. "There does not and cannot exist," the statement continued, "a 'parent' party and a 'son' party, parties that are 'superior' and parties that are 'subordinate,' but there exists the great family of Communist and Workers parties, with have equal rights." Internationally, the statement asserted the freedom of each Communist-ruled country to conduct its foreign relations and Roumania's independent position in the Sino-Soviet conflict. (See *The New York Times*, April 27, 1964. A brief analysis of the statement by Harry Schwartz is contained in *The New York Times* of May 5, 1964.) This position was reaffirmed by Roumanian Communist Party leader Nicolae Ceausescu in a major address in Bucharest on May 14, 1966, (For text see *The New York Times*, May 17, 1966) and by the Central Committee of the Party on October 14, 1966. (*Ibid.*, October 15, 1966.)

35. The Soviet Union has come close to executing a design blue-printed one hundred years ago by Nicolas Danilevsky in a book entitled *Russia and Europe* published in 1869, which has long been accepted as the Bible of Pan-Slavism. Danilevsky advocated the formation of an all-Slav federation, embracing practically the whole part of Eastern and Southeastern Europe which the Red Army had occupied at the close of World War II, excluding Poland and the Russian zones of occupation of Germany and Austria, but including Greece, Constantinople and the Straits. As envisioned by Danilevsky, the proposed federation, of which Russia was to be the leader, was to consist of eight units. The largest of them, of course, was to be Russia, including Finland, the Baltic provinces, White Russia, the Ruthenian parts of Bukovina and Hungary, and Bessarabia. The second unit was to be a Serb-Croat-Slovene Kingdom, comprising roughly the area of the Yugoslav State of 1939, together with Istria and Trieste which Yugoslavia has always claimed. The third unit was to be a Czech-Moravian-Slovakian Kingdom very much like the pre-War Czechoslovak Republic, except that Carpatho-Ruthenia was to be incorporated into Russia. The fourth unit was to consist of Bulgaria, including the larger parts of Rumelia, and Macedonia. The fifth, sixth and seventh units were to consist, respectively, of Greece, Hungary and Roumania, while the eighth unit was to comprise a region round Constantinople, together with territories on both sides of the Straits. Although Danilevsky had excluded Poland, or those parts of Poland that were under Austrian and Prussian rule, he had no doubts that sooner or later that country would become part of the proposed federation. The formation of the federation, according to Danilevsky, was conditional upon a general war in which Russia would emerge victorious. A detailed critique of the Danilevsky book, upon which the present summary is based, appeared in the *Twentieth Century and After* December, 1945, under the title *The Bible of Pan-Slavism*.

36. For text see *The New York Times*, September 5, 1964.

37. From the text of the Soviet Union's Communist Party Draft Program for the Twenty-Second Congress. (For text see *The New York Times*, August 1, 1961.)

38. The Chinese Communist Party has accused the Soviet Union of betraying the revolutionary movement to advance her nationalist interests and of practicing great power politics at the expense of the whole "socialist camp." This was the burden of the letter sent on June 14, 1963, by the Central Committee of the Chinese Communist Party to the Soviet Union's Communist Party Central Committee (For text, see *The New York Times*, July 5, 1963), and of the article published on September 6, 1963, by the Chinese Communist Party organs *Jenmin Jih Pao* and *Hung Chi* on the origins and development of the ideological differences between Moscow and Peking. The article reads:

...The facts of the past seven years have amply proved that the present differences within the international Communist movement are differences between the line of adhering to Marxism-Leninism and the line of clinging to revisionism; between the revolutionary line and the non-revolutionary and counter-revolutionary line, and between the anti-imperialist line and the line of capitulation to imperialism. They are differences between proletarian internationalism and great power chauvinism, sectarianism and splitism ... (For text see *The New York Times,* September 14, 1963.)

In turn, the Soviet Union has accused the Chinese Communist leadership of harboring ideas divorced from "actual reality, a dogmatic, bookish approach to problems of war, peace and revolution," and of being willfully engaged in activities which are undermining the unity of the Socialist commonwealth and grossly violative of all norms of relations between fraternal countries. In a statement in the September 21, 1963, issue of *Izvestia,* which denounced China's attitude toward the nuclear test ban treaty, China was accussed of having gone beyond the doctrinal dispute to outright hostility against the Soviet Union and its people. Referring to the *Jenmin Jih Pao* statement cited above, *Izvestia* went on to say:

The September 1 statement of the PRC Government, like the entire big propaganda campaign started lately by the Chinese leadership, is no longer a comradely discussion between Communists but actions of people who have set the aim of discrediting at any cost the C.P.S.U. and the Soviet Union, of splitting the Communist movement and undermining the unity of anti-imperialist forces... All this shows that the leaders of the C.P.C. have transcended the boundaries of comradely party discussion and are now waging an open political struggle against the C. P. S. U. and the other Marxist-Leninist parties, a struggle for their special goals... The Soviet Government would like to stress that it is impermissible to transfer differences in ideological questions, disagreements arising among parties, to relations between the Socialist states—to use them as a pretext for fanning nationalism and chauvinism, mistrust and dissension among the peoples of these states ... (For text, see *The New York Times,* September 23, 1963.)

The Sino-Soviet split continued to widen in the next several years. All attempts to heal the breach between the two Communist powers ended in failure. In March, 1966, the Chinese Communists rejected an invitation from the Soviet Communist Party to attend its Twenty-third Congress and accused the Soviet Union of collaboration with the United States in a "holy alliance against China." (*The New York Times,* March 3, 1966.) A conciliatory statement by Soviet Communist Party Secretary Leonid I. Brezhnev at the Twenty-third Congress of the Communist Party in the Soviet Union, (For text, see *The New York Times,* March 30, 1966) and another by Soviet Premier Aleksei N. Kosygin to the Supreme Soviet on August 3, 1966, were answered by China with a repetition of old charges. Said Premier Kosygin:

In its policy in respect to the Peoples' Republic of China, the Soviet Government will continue to proceed from the sincere striving of our party and people to restore friendly relations and unity with Peoples' China on the principled basis of Marxism-Leninism and proletarian internationalism. This position meets the interests of Socialist countries, including the interests of the Chinese people itself, the interests of the general struggle against imperialism, for peace and social progress. (For text see *The New York Times,* August 4, 1966.)

In reply, the 11th plenary session of the Eight Central Committee of the Communist Party of China, which was held in Peking from August 1 to August 12, 1966, issued an communique which stated, *inter alia,* that

The new leading group of the Communist Party of the Soviet Union has inherited Krushchev's mantle and is practicing Krushchev's revisionism without Krushchev. Their line is one of safeguarding imperialist and colonialist domination in the capitalist world and restoring capitalism in the Socialist world.

The leading group of the C. P. S. U. has betrayed Marxism-Leninism, betrayed the great Lenin, betrayed the road of the great October Revolution cause of the international proletariat and of the oppressed peoples and oppressed nations, and betrayed the interests of the great Soviet people and the people of the Socialist countries.

They are uniting with U. S.—led imperialism and the reactionaries of various countries and forming a new holy alliance against Communism, the people, revolution and China. But this counter-revolutionary alliance, holy alliance is doomed to bankruptcy and is already in the process of disintegration... (For text, see *The New York Times*, August 14, 1966.)

This verbal barrage was followed by violent and brutal demonstrations outside the Soviet Embassy in Peking early in September, 1966, and the expulsion of Russian and other foreign students later that month. The Soviet Union retaliated by ordering the expulsion of all Chinese students who were given until October 31, 1966, to leave the country. On February 16, 1967, the Soviet Communist Party openly appealed for the overthrow of the leadership of Mao Tse-tung and the return of China to the Socialist community. In an editorial in the February 16, 1967, issue of *Pravda*, the Chinese leadership was accused of conducting an anti-Soviet campaign with the deliberate purpose of goading the Soviet Union into breaking diplomatic relations and assuming the responsibility for the consequences of such a step. "The facts show," the editorial added,

that the people who today direct the policy of China set before themselves the goal not only of bringing up the Chinese people in a spirit of enmity toward the U.S.S.R., but of aggravating Soviet-Chinese relations to the limit and, in the final count, to bring them to a complete break... If we omit the series of wars and the periods of direct aggression against the Soviet Union... it will be possible to say that never before has such a fierce campaign been conducted against it as the one launched by the present leaders of China... There is no doubt that the Mao Tse-tung group will not be able to deceive endlessly the Chinese people and the Chinese Communists... (See *The New York Times*, February 16, 1967.)

39. On November 6, 1964, on the eve of the 47th anniversary of the Bolshevik Revolution, Leonid I. Brezhnev, First Secretary of the Soviet Communist Party, declared:

...In their relations with the Socialist countries, the Communist Party of the Soviet Union and the entire Soviet people are guided by the principles of Socialist internationalism, by the desire to strengthen fraternal friendship, cooperation and mutual assistance on the basis of full equality, independence and a correct combination of the interests of each country with the interests of the entire Socialist world. The world Socialist system is a social, economic and political community of free and equal peoples... (*The New York Times*, November 7, 1964.

On several occasions in 1965 and 1966, the Soviet Communist leader reiterated the Soviet Communist Party's avowed opposition to any trend toward hegemony in the Communist world.

40. See, for example, O. Edmund Clunn, *Twentieth Century China*, New York, Columbia University Press, 1964: Robert S. Elegant, *The Center of the World: Communism and the Mind of China*, New York, Doubleday & Co., 1964; C. P. Fitzgerald, *The Birth of Communist China*, New York, Frederick A. Praeger, 1966; Dun J. Li, *The Ageless Chinese*, New York, Charles Scribner's Sons, 1965; Klaus Mehnert, *Peking and Moscow*, translated from the German by Leila Vennewitz, New York, G. P. Putnam's Sons, 1963; George Paloczi-Horvath, *Mao-Tse-Tung: Emperor of the Blue Ants*, New York, Doubleday & Co., 1963.

41. For a better understanding of the background of the border conflicts between China and the Soviet Union, see Owen Lattimore, *Studies in Asian Frontier History*, New York, Oxford University Press, 1963; Francis Watson, *The Frontiers of China: A Historical Guide*, New York, Frederick A. Praeger, 1966.

42. *The New York Times* (International Edition), March 9, 1963, quoting an editorial from the March 7, 1963 issue of *Jenmin Jih Pao*.

43. *The New York Times*, September 2, 1964. This may explain the Soviet initiative of September 21, 1964, in proposing the inclusion in the agenda of the 19th session of the United Nations General Assembly of an item entitled: "Renunciation by States of the use of force for the settlement of territorial disputes and questions of frontiers. (*A/5751*, 21 September 1964.) Since then, Soviet spokesmen have repeatedly referred to the frontier difficulties with China and reiterated their warnings of the consequences. On June 1, 1966, for example, Soviet President Nikolai V. Podgorny told the people of Khabarovsk near the Chinese border that the Soviet Union was alert and determined to protect the Far Eastern territories against any invaders. He went on to say:

> The Khabarovsk territory is a border zone. The soldiers of the Far Eastern Military District, the sailors of the Pacific Fleet and our valiant border guards are faithfully guarding this vibrant region, created by the hands of our forefathers and covered with the sweat and blood of our people. (*The New York Times*, June 2, 1966.)

On February 16, 1967, an editorial in *Izvestia* accused China of carrying on propaganda against the Soviet Union based on "nationalistic and even racialist tones," and warned that,

> Advancing territorial claims against the Soviet Union, the leadership of the Chinese Communist Party pursued the purpose of fanning still further the chauvinistic mood of the Chinese people. (*The New York Times*, February 16, 1967.)

44. Robert N. Carew Hunt, *The Theory and Practice of Communism*, 5th edition, New York, Macmillan Co., 1957, pp.204-207.

45. Draft Program for the 22nd Congress of the Communist Party of the Soviet Union, *op. cit.* On the subject of the new man to be brought forth by Communism, see Bukharin and Preobraschensky, *ABC of Communism*, quoted by Sherman H. M. Chang, *The Marxian Theory of the State*, Chester, Pa. John Spencer Inc., 1931, pp.59-60; and Engels, *Landmarks of Scientific Socialism, Ibid*, pp.134-135. For having described the 'homo sovieticus' of 1964 in the flesh, Yugoslavia's Mihajlo Mihajlov was sentenced to nine months in prison. On April 30, 1965, a Yugoslav District Court sentenced him to the prison term for having offended the Soviet Union in his *Moscow Summer 1964*, a two-part report on his visit there. This report was published by the *New Leader* of New York in a special issue of March 29, 1965. A third installment, which was never published in Yugoslavia, appeared in the June 7, 1965, issue of the *New Leader*. See also Klaus Mehnert, *Soviet Man and his World*, translated from the German by Maurice Rosenbaum, New York, Frederick A. Praeger, 1962.   !

46. See, for example, Charles A. Beard, *The Idea of National Interest: An Analytical Study in American Foreign Policy*, New York, Macmillan Co., 1934. For a study of the symbols and arguments employed by American statesmen and publicists for territorial expansion and political domination of the Western Hemisphere, from the outbreak of the American Revolution to the Presidency of Franklin Delano Roosevelt, see Albert K. Weinberg, *Manifest Destiny: A Study of Nationalist Expansion in American History*, Baltimore, The Johns Hopkins Press, 1935. See also Dean Acheson, "Ethics in International Relations Today," an address delivered by the former Secretary of State on December 9, 1964, at Amherst College, Mass. See *The New York Times*, December 10, 1964.

47. Thus in a letter dated August 23, 1963, to Senator J. W. Fullbright, Chairman of the Senate Foreign Relations Committee, concerning the partial nuclear test ban treaty that was up at the time for Senate ratification, former President Dwight D. Eisenhower noted that

> The people of many countries see the cold war only as a conflict between two powerful, ambitious and greedy colossi. They are frightened ... (*The New York Times*, August 24, 1963.)

48. "Our most creative achievements of statesmanship (The Marshall Plan, for example) are not acts of generosity. Generosity is probably beyond the moral capacity of collective man," Reinhold Niebuhr wrote. *Reinhold Niebhur on Politics*, edited by Harry R. Davis and Robert C. Goods, New York, Charles Scribner Sons, 1960, p.308. The Food-for-peace program, to cite another example, had its origins in American agricultural surpluses. The surplus could not be put on the market without upsetting the delicate price balance, while storing it proved costly and burning it was practically and morally wrong.

49. In the United States, for example, George Kennan and Walter Lippman have for years been pointing out that American diplomacy was suffering from an excess of moral fervor. The United States assumed the role of opponent to international Communism out of concrete self-interest based on the recognition that world Communism was the vehicle for a new form of political imperialism that could menace American national security. But the way the role has been played conveyed the impression that the United States acted out of a missionary impulse. In his statement before the Senate Foreign Relations Committee in Washington on February 20, 1967, Professor Henry Steele Commager declared:

> One explanation of our obsession with Communism and more particularly now, with "Communist aggression" in Asia is to be found, I think, in a deep and persistent trait of the American mind: the belief in Old World corruption and New World innocence. The men who won the independence of America from the mother country were convinced that the Old World was abandoned to tyranny, misery, ignorance, injustice and vice and the New Yorld was innocent of these sins ...
>
> The notion of an international Communist conspiracy, which a good many Americans still cling to, fits neatly into this shibboleth of Old World wickedness and New World virtue. And so, too, our habit of throwing a mantle of morality over our own wars. We do tend, perhaps more than other nations, to transform our wars into crusades ... (For text see *The New York Times*, February 21, 1967.)

50. Quoted by Alexander Dallin, *The Soviet Union at the United Nations: An Inquiry into Soviet Motives and Objectives*, New York, Frederick A. Praeger, 1962, p.205. It was also quoted by Costa Rica's Foreign Minister, Ortiz Martin, in his statement to the United Nations General Assembly in 1961. (*A/PV.1073:118.*) The year before, then Premier Nikita Krushchev warned the General Assembly at its 882nd plenary meeting on October 3, 1960, that:

> If the machinery which is called upon to solve major international issues with due regard for the interests of all States, if this United Nations machinery—the Security Council and the Secretariat—resolve these questions to the detriment of the socialist and neutralist states, then, naturally, these countries will not recognize such decisions and will rely on their own strength to defend the interests of their States, the interests of peace. (*A/PV. 882:53*).

51. For text, see *The New York Times*, April 21, 1961. The assertion of national self-interest is not the prerogative of the Great Powers. When, on December 18, 1961, India was called upon by the United Nations Security Council to account for her military action against the Portuguese in Goa, the Indian representative told the Council:

...Let us not forget, we are living in the twentieth century and the greatest thing that has happened in this twentieth century is that no longer can colonialism be tolerated, whether in Asia, in Africa or in Latin America or anywhere else.

That is the situation with which we are faced. It must be realized that this is a colonial question. It is a question of getting rid of the vestiges of colonialism in India. That is a matter of faith with us. Whatever anyone else may think, Charter or no Charter, Council or no Council, that is our basic faith which we cannot afford to give up at any cost...*(S/PV.987:40.)*

NOTES TO CHAPTER III

1. The historic variability of the concept of the brotherhood of man, as of man himself, for example, makes it an infirm principle for the living present. It cannot be raised to an operating force in international relations. However broad its range, the modern notion of the brotherhood of man rests upon the acceptance of certain basic values and attitudes concerning the duty of men to one another and to themselves, which in fact bars many peoples from membership in the world fraternity.

Nor can we look to religion and its moral and ethical preachments, even though the kinship between all religions is nowhere so marked as on the ethical level. Despite the great progress made by the ecumenical movement, religions are more divided by that which their priests assert to be divine, than united by what their prophets preach as humane. It is instructive to note the warning contained in the Decree on Ecumenism adopted by the Ecumenical Council, Vatican II, and proclaimed on November 21, 1964, by Pope Paul VI, that the Catholic doctrine be clearly presented in its entirety, as "nothing is so foreign to the spirit of ecumenism as a false irenicism, in which the purity of Catholic doctrine suffers loss and its assured genuine meaning is clouded." Chapter II. (For text see *The New York Times*, November 22, 1964.) Paragraph 25 of Chapter III enjoins as follows:

> Now that we have briefly set out the conditions for ecumenical action and the principles by which it is to be directed, we look with confidence to the future. This sacred Council exhorts the faithful to avoid superficial and imprudent zeal for this could only hinder real progress toward unity. Their ecumenical action must be fully and sincerely Catholic, that is to say faithful to the truth which we have received from the Apostles and fathers of the church, in harmony with the faith which the Catholic Church has always professed, and at the same time directed toward that fullness to which Our Lord wills his body to grow in the course of time. *(Ibid.)*

Besides, as Ernst Troeltsch has pointed out, the pure will and devotion to an ideal world which is sufficient for righteousness in religion, cannot limit or shape history. He recalls that

> Earthly history remains the foundation and the presupposition of the final personal decision and sanctification; but in itself it goes on in its way as a mixture of reason and natural instinct, and it can never be bound in any bonds except in a relative degree and for temporary space. Ernst Troeltsch, *Christian Thought*, London, University of London Press Ltd., 1923, p.68.

From the practical point of view, the major religions have yet to establish an international ethos which could serve as a common foundation of a world community. In many parts of the world, especially in the newly-independent countries of Asia and Africa, there has been a renascence of the old religions in the form of their identification with nationalism. Thus in 1960, the Burmese Parliament amended the Constitution to make Buddhism the state religion and reaffirmed the strong ties between Buddhism and nationalism in Burma. *Governments and Politics in Southeast Asia*, edited by George McT Kahin, 2nd edition, Ithaca,

Cornell University Press, 1964, pp.105-106. In Indonesia, the Islamic organizations have played an important part in the independence movement and have remained a strong unifying factor in the nation's politics. *Ibid.*, pp.194-195. Buddhism has been a focus for political and religious agitation in South-Vietnam, *Ibid.*, pp.418-422, while the clergy has been an active political force in Ceylon and Pakistan, *Ibid.*, p.213. In the Middle East, religion very often reinforces political loyalties. *The Politics of the Developing Areas, op. cit.*, supra I, note 6. In sub-Saharan Africa, African nationalists have attached great importance to the organization of African separatist churches, *Ibid.*, p.334.

Undoubtedly, the major religions have been deeply concerned with the question of international peace and world order. See, for eample, the Proceedings of the World Convention of Religions on the Foundations of Peace, which was held in London from August 18 to August 24, 1950; "International Affairs—Christians in the Struggle for World Community: An Ecumenical Survey prepared under the auspices of the World Council of Churches," in *The Christian Hope and the Task of the Church*, New York, Harper & Bros., 1954. The Encyclical Letter *Pacem in Terris* of Pope John XXIII has provided the basis for extended discussion of the fundamental problems of the human condition in the twentieth century by people of all faiths, or of no faith, and has been hailed as a political testament of the highest order. However, as Ernst Troeltsch has argued, neither the great universal religions, nor scientific enlightement, nor the inter-change of philosophic thought have changed the fact that material interests and elementary passions, rather than higher spiritual purposes and values, remain the bonds of cohesion wherever people unite.

2. For a picture of the economic plight of Europe on the eve of the Marshall Plan in 1947, see Joseph M. Jones, *The Fifteen Weeks*, New York, The Viking Press, 1955; also *Outline of European Recovery Program*, 80th Congress, First Session, Committee on Foreign Relations, December 17, 1947.

3. "No one can say with certainty how real was the Soviet menace in 1949. But, although Soviet intentions could not be assessed, Soviet military capabilities and the general outward thrust of Soviet policy made the menace appear real enough to the statesmen of the West." Robert Strausz-Huppe, James E. Dougherty and William R. Kintner, *op. cit.*, supra, II, note 18.

4. The Organization for European Economic Cooperation (OEEC) was established on April 16, 1948, for the purpose of facilitating, with Marshall Plan aid, the restoration and modernization of the war-ravaged economies of Europe. The parties to the Convention which created the OEEC were: Austria, Belgium, Denmark, France, Greece, Iceland, Ireland, Italy, Luxembourg, Netherlands, Norway, Portugal, Sweden, Switzerland, Turkey and the United Kingdom, with the United States and Canada as associate members. That the OEEC had accomplished successfully its main objectives and had set the stage for the development of the European Economic Community, are beyond dispute. But it is also true that the OEEC worked within the traditional framework of international organization and that its objectives were limited in conception and in time. The Convention of April 16, 1948, contained no firm commitment to the idea of a single market or the creation of an intimate union of economies as had been hoped for by the United States and the protagonists of European movement. For text of the Convention, see United States Department of State, American Foreign Policy, *Basic Documents*, I, pp.992-1000; for a precise review of the work of the OEEC, see M. Margaret Ball, *op. cit.*, *supra II*, Note 18, pp.227-252.

5. On March 17, 1948, Belgium, France, Luxembourg, the Netherlands and the United Kingdom entered into a Treaty of Economic, Social and Cultural Collaboration and Collective Self-Defense, which established the so-called Western European Union. The treaty was directed primarily against any future German aggression. In the course of the next several years, the character and purpose of the Western European Union changed radically by the inclusion of the Federal Republic of Germany and the creation of the OEEC, the Council of Europe and NATO. For

text of the Treaty, signed at Brussels, as amended, see *International Regional Organizations: Constitutional Foundations,* edited by Ruth C. Lawson, New York, Frederik A. Praeger, 1962, pp.154-170.

6. Established by the Treaty of Westminster of May 5, 1949, the Council of Europe's aim, as provided in Article 1 (a) of the Statute, "is to achieve a greater unity between its Members for the purpose of safeguarding and realizing the ideals and principles which are their common heritage and facilitating their common economic and social progress." For text of the Statute, see Ruth C. Lawson, *op. cit.,* pp.25-40.

7. The North Atlantic Treaty was signed on April 4, 1949. Its objectives are set fourth in Article 5, which provides:

> The Parties agree that an armed attack against one or more of them in Europe or North America shall be considered an attack against them all; and consequently they agree that, if such an armed attack occurs, each of them, in the exercise of the right of individual or collective self-defense recognized by Article 51 of the Charter of the United Nations, will assist the Party or Parties so attacked by taking forthwith, individually and in concert with the other Parties, such actions as it deems necessary, including the use of armed force, to restore and maintain the security of the North Atlantic area. For text of the Treaty, see Ruth C. Lawson, *op. cit.,* pp. 5-83.

As we have noted in Chapter II, the distinguishing feature of NATO, which makes it different from similar treaties in the past, has been the institutionalization of the methods of cooperation, especially the integration of the armed forces of NATO's members, against which President de Gaulle had launched his severest criticism of the Alliance.

8. Richard Coudenhove-Kalergi, *Kampf um Europa: Aus meinem Leben,* Zurich, Atlantis Verlag, 1949. The idea of European unity, of course, goes back to Roman days. The Roman Empire made an economic, political and cultural unity of the whole Mediterranean basin and bequeathed a tradition which survived for almost two thousand years and which has taken on many forms. See, for example, René Albrecht Carrié, *One Europe: The Historical Background of European Unity,* New York, Doubleday & Co., 1965. Plans for the unification of Europe have come down to us which date back six and seven centuries and have been advanced by the strong, as well as the weak, the idealist and political practitioner, the saint and the sinner. See Edith Wynner and Georgia Lloyd, *op. cit., supra,* I, note 2. In the epilogue to his *History of Nineteenth Century Europe,* New York, Harcourt, Brace & World, 1933, Benedetto Croce envisioned the coming of European unity as follows:

> ...And just as seventy years ago, a Neopolitan of the old Kingdom or a Piedmontese of the sub-alpine Kingdom became an Italian without becoming false to his earlier quality but raising it and resolving it into his new quality, so the French and the Germans and the Italians and all the others will raise themselves into Europeans and their thoughts will be directed towards Europe and their hearts will beat for her as they once did for the smaller countries, not forgotten now but loved all the better... This process of European union, which is directly opposed to nationalist competition and has already set itself up against it and one day will be able to liberate Europe from it altogether tends at the same time to liberate her from the whole psychology that clings to this nationalism and supports it and generates kindred manners, habits and actions. And if this thing happens, the liberal ideal will be fully restored in men's mind and will resume its ideal (p.360.)

9. Richard Mayne, *The Community of Europe: Past, Present and Future,* New York, W. Norton & Co., 1963, p.79.

10. See Ernest B. Haas, *The Uniting of Europe: Political, Social and Economic Forces, 1950-1957,* Stamford, Stamford University Press, 1959, *passim;* Hans A. Schmitt, *The Path to European Union: From the Marshall Plan to the Common*

Market, Baton Rouge, Louisiana State University Press, 1962, *passim;* Arnold J. Zurcher, *The Struggle to Unite Europe, 1940-1958,* New York, New York University Press, 1958, *passim.* As in the case of NATO, it is very difficult to single out for special reference any particular book or books from the many which have been appearing in increasingly large numbers in the United States and abroad. The books listed above, have been consulted by the author more frequently than others.

11. For text, see *Keesing's Contemporary Archives,* 1950, p. 10701.

12. For text, see Ruth C. Lawson, *op. cit.,* pp.69-107; for a fuller treatment of the Community, see Henry L. Mason, *The European Coal and Steel Community: Experiment in Supranationalism,* The Hague, Martin Nijhoff, 1955; see also Hans A. Schmitt, *op. cit.*

The Council of Europe established by the Treaty of Westminster on May 5, 1949, emerged substantially as but another intergovernmental agency in which the States Parties retained their sovereign independence and freedom of action. This juridically attenuated instrument of cooperation could hardly be said to transcend national barriers and to serve as an institutional expression of the idea of a united Europe. Perhaps its most important contribution has been as a forum for discussion of Europe's fate and future. It certainly was a far cry from the hopes articulated by the Congress of Europe held at the Hague in May, 1948, which demanded economic integration—the amalgamation of national economies, uniform currencies and the free circulation of capital and labor, as well as political union, and the immediate convocation of a European Parliament, recruited from the national legislatures or elected by them. Hans Schmitt, *op. cit.,* p.39.

13. For text of Premier René Pleven's speech of October 28, 1950, before the North Atlantic Treaty Organization Defense Committee on the question of a European Defense Community, see *Keesing's Contemporary Archives, op. cit.,* p.11037. It should be noted that the concept of a European Army first took shape in discussions in the European Assembly at its second session in 1950. A resolution by Winston Churchill called for the creation of integrated forces. Guy Mollet of France thought the European Army to be an indispensible condition to the rearmament of Germany, on which the NATO members had agreed in principle in September, 1950, as a result of the Korean conflict and the uncertainties of Soviet intentions at the time in Central Europe. Hans Schmitt, *op. cit.,* pp.43-44.

14. For text, see Royal Institute of International Affairs, *Documents on International Affairs, 1952,* pp.116-170; For discussion of the negotiations, see Hans A. Schmitt, *op. cit.,* pp. 205-229. Article 38 of the Treaty called for a democratically elected assembly to explore the matter of coordinating sector integration in a political federation.

15. For text, see Basil Karp, "The Draft Constitution for a European Political Community", VIII *International Organization,* (1954).

16. Hans A. Schmitt, *op. cit.,* p.213 *et seq.;* also, Ben T. Moore, *op. cit., supra,* II, note 18.

17. For the texts of the resolutions and a summary of the debates of the Intergovernmental Conference that hammered out the plans for the two Communities, see *Keesing's Contemporary Archives, 1956,* p.15030; see also Hans A. Schmitt, *op. cit.,* pp.231-245, and Ben T. Moore, *op. cit.,* pp.116-145. For a comprehensive study of Euratom, see Kalus E. Knorr, *Euratom and American Policy,* Princeton, Princeton University Press, 1956. For the abridged text of the Treaty of Rome which created the European Economic Community, see Ruth C. Lawson, *op. cit.,* pp.116.145.

18. *The New York Times,* July 25, 1966.

19. *Agricultural Policies in Europe and North America*: 5 reports covering 1956-1961, published by the Organization for European Economic Cooperation, Ministerial Committee for Agriculture and Food, Paris. See also, Michael Tracy, *Agriculture in Western Europe,* New York, Frederick A. Praeger, 1964.

20. Lord Robbins, *Politics and Economics: Papers in Political Economy,* New York, St. Martin's Press, 1963, p.132.

21. Jacques Maritain, *Man and the State,* Chicago, Chicago University Press, 1951, p.190.

22. The Treaty entered into force July 1, 1967. For text see IV *International Legal Materials: Current Documents,* pp.776-800 (1965).

23. From the statement by General de Gaulle at his May 15, 1962, Press Conference in Paris. (*The New York Times,* May 16, 1962.)

24. See Roy C. Macridis, *De Gaulle: Implacable Ally,* New York, Harper & Row, 1966.

25. *The New York Times,* January 26, 1962.

26. *The New York Times,* October 12, 1962. In fact, the smaller countries of the Common Market, according to many authorities, look upon England's entry into the Community as a necessary guarantee against domination by their more powerful partners. See, for example, Professor Geyl's final G. M. Trevelyan memorial lecture at Cambridge University on March 8, 1963, in which the University of Utrecht Professor explained the importance of Britain's membership in the European Economic Community and which was widely reported in the British press on March 9, 1963.

27. It is not yet clear what kind of nationalism is emerging in West Germany and what direction it is likely to take. It is being fed my many springs and nutured by memories of the past, and frustrations and grudges of the present. German irredentism, for example, has as much to feed on today as it did during the years between the two World Wars, with the country divided into East and West Germany and the Oder-Neisse frontier challenged. A speech on May 18, 1964, by Hans Christoph Seebohm, Minister of Transport in the Government of Ludwig Erhardt, at the annual meeting of the Sudeten German Refugees Association in Nuremberg, in which he called for "the return of the Sudeten German homeland to the Sudeten German people" on the basis of the Munich Pact of September 30, 1938 (*The New York Times,* May 20, 1964) caused shock and surprise. Although the Minister was officially rebuked and his statement disavowed by the Federal Republic (*Ibid,* May 23, 1964), the incident awakened suspicion not only of Germany's territorial claims, but of the strength of the extremist elements behind them. The subsequent showing of the officially-dubbed neo-nazi National Democratic Party in the State parliamentary elections, only added to the forebodings. In November, 1966, the National Democratic Party won 8 of the 96 seats in Hesse and 15 of the 204 seats in Bavaria. On April 23, 1967, the Party scored also in the Rhineland-Palatinate, where it won 4 out of 100 seats, and a similar number in Schleswig-Holstein, out of a total of 72 seats. (*The New York Times,* April 24, 1967.) These and other factors, some of them beyond West Germany's control, have made it very difficult to discern clearly the long-range trends in that country. And for that reason alone, it may be too early to assess whether Germany's economy and political life have been so completely integrated into the economy and political life of Western Europe, as to reduce the possibility of an independent German nationalist policy in the future to an improbability.

28. On January 22, 1963, the French and West German Governments concluded a treaty of friendship and cooperation designed to end "400 years of war and disputes" between the two nations and link them in close collaboration in major policy fields. It provides for a wide range of coordinated action in foreign affairs and defense, in matters of education and youth, and social and family affairs, and calls for meetings at least twice a year between the nations' chiefs of state and government, and four times yearly between the ministers responsible for the several areas of cooperation; monthly meetings of experts in the field of foreign policy, economics and cultural affairs, and bi-monthly meetings of the military chiefs of staff. Among other things, the treaty provides that the armed forces of the two nations will engage in joint training and manoeuvres and coordinate their research, development and production of conventional arms. (Cooperation in the manufacture of nuclear weapons is specifically excluded.) In the field of education, the treaty provides that diplomas of each country will be recognized by the other; that a broad program of scholarship and student exchanges will be instituted and that the teaching of the French language in German schools and of the German

language in French schools will be extended. For text of the Treaty see, *Journal Officielle*, Law No. 63-604, 27 June 1963.

On the occasion of the ratification of the treaty by the French Parliament on June 14, 1963, President de Gaulle hailed it as a "world revolution" and "one of the great things of history." It followed the ratification by the Parliament of the Federal Republic of Germany, which hailed the treaty as an expression of the will of the two peoples which for centuries faced one another with mistrust or emnity, to remove all national opposition between them. However, like all other treaties concluded between governments, the treaty of friendship between the two countries did not automatically close the door on the past and open a new era. Difficulties which had arisen in the relations between France and Germany in recent years have often led observers to minimize the impact of the treaty and to reserve judgement regarding its future possibilities for constructive change.

29. The Federal Republic is committed to the reunification of Germany as a fundamental and uncompromising national policy. The vision of a reunited Germany is kept alive in the hearts and minds of the German people and it has found its most poignant expression in the so-called "Hallstein doctrine," which not only rejects the legitimacy of the East German regime, but seeks to discourage others from recognizing it. The reunification of Germany is a problem which lies at the heart and core of the division between East and West. The prize of a Germany reunited and committed to one side or the other is too great to be abandoned by either of the major contestants. Meanwhile, neither East nor West can afford to see its part of Germany, as it were, fall to the other without inviting disaster to their respective military and political positions. But, above all, there is the fact that few nations have ever acquiesced in their division by a foreign mandate. On the occasion of the tenth anniversary of the reestablishment of German sovereignty in 1965, the Bonn Government declared:

> In these ten years since the achievement of sovereignty, the Federal Republic of Germany has achieved a firm and acknowledged place among the free nations of the world. But the great goal of reunification still lies unachieved before us. We must and shall pursue this goal tirelessly. We hope confidently for the support of the three Western powers, which declared themselves expressly in the treaty on Germany (Paris Treaties) for reunification. (*The New York Times*, May 6, 1965.)

If the reunion of West and East Germany is finally realized, the healing of the German split is bound to set in motion developments of momentous consequence to the world. On this point, General de Gaulle's remark at his March 25, 1959, news conference in Paris is as relevant as ever. Said de Gaulle:

> The reunion of the two parts into a single Germany which would be entirely free seems to us the normal destiny of the German people, provided they do not call into question their present frontiers in the west, the east, the north and south, and that they move toward integrating themselves one day in a contractual organization of all Europe for cooperation, liberty and peace. (*The New York Times*, March 26, 1959.)

30. In November, 1959, Great Britain, Austria, Denmark, Norway, Portugal, Sweden and Switzerland initiated in Stockholm a treaty creating the European Free Trade Association, for the purpose of bridging the gulf that had developed between themselves and the Common Market countries, by providing for the gradual elimination of tariffs between their own members and between them and the Common Market, but maintaining their own separate tariffs toward the outside world. Unlike the Common Market, the Association was conceived as a commercial bloc tied together by the removal of tariffs, without any ideological commitment or surrender or sovereign freedom of action. (For text of the European Free Trade Association, see *United Nations Treaty Series*, v. 370:3.)

31. To the political division between East and West, must be added the economic division between Eastern and Western Europe. In January, 1949, the USSR, Albania, Bulgaria, Czechoslovakia, East Germany, Hungary, Poland and

Roumania, informally established the Council for Mutual Economic Aid, known as Comecon. Originally created in response to the Marshall Plan and O.E.E.C., which the Soviet bloc rejected, Comecon did not emerge into its full importance until 1956 when the Common Market was about to be inaugurated and Comecon's potentialities for integrating Eastern Europe's economy were increasingly developed. On December 14, 1959, the countries concerned formalized these developments by agreeing in Sofia on a Charter of the Council for Mutual Economic Assistance. For text see Ruth C. Lawson, *op. cit.*

32. It should be recalled that the underlying idea behind the concept of Atlantic Community is that Western Europe as a collective entity is indispensible to the creation of a trans-Atlantic partnership and that trans-Atlantic partnership is indispensible to the survival and prosperity of the free world. In spite of the disarray in the Atlantic Alliance and the questioning of many of its premises, the validity of the concept will have force until the conditions which first gave birth to it have fundamentally and permanently changed.

33. For text, see *The New York Times*, January 15, 1963.

34. For text, see Embassy of France, Information Service, New York, *Speeches and Press Conferences*, No. 186, January 28, 1963. For an account of the negotiations on British entry into the Common Market, see Nora Beloff, *The General Says No: Britain's Exclusion from Europe*, Gloucester, Mass, Peter Smith, 1964; also, Drew Middleton, *The Supreme Choice: Britain and Europe*, New York, Alfred A. Knopf, 1963.

The 1958 experience to which France's Foreign Minister has alluded, refers to the British attempt to build a Europe-wide trading community and thus preserve the post-War experiment in European economic cooperation, as well as the traditional patterns of international commerce. While France led the opposition, all the members of the Common Market were determined to preserve the integrity of the Treaty of Rome and its internal and external consequences. Although the fears on the part of at least some Common Market members that their commercial competitive advantages might be dissolved in the larger free trade area proposed by Great Britain could be allayed, the principles involved in the Rome Treaty could not be readily compromised. The primacy of the political objectives attached to the Common Market and the mainly economic and commercial purposes behind the British effort proved irreconcilable then and frustrated all subsequent efforts at cooperative co-existence between the Common Market and the European Free Trade Association. The political objectives of the European Economic Community compelled it to move in a continuous line of clear and logical development toward European political integration and made it inhospitable to any and all suggestions which did not parallel it. In the end, Great Britain was compelled to reverse her position when, in the summer of 1961, she applied for membership in the Common Market. The other members of the Free Trade Association soon followed suit.

Whether or not the changes Great Britain has been undergoing since the French veto of January 14, 1963, are acceptable or not, the British lion has recognized the Common Market as the focus of power in Europe and is determined to come out of his exclusive lair "to join the pack." On May 2, 1967, Prime Minister Harold Wilson told the House of Commons of the decision of the Government "to make an application under Article 237 of the Treaty of Rome for membership of the European Economic Community." This time, the British approach to the Common Market has been set within a broad historical context. Addressing the Consultative Assembly of the Council of Europe on January 23, 1967, in Strasbourg, Prime Minister Wilson declared that

> Over the next year, the next ten years, the next twenty years, the unity of Europe is going to be forged, and geography, history, interest and sentiment alike demand that we play our part in forging it—and working it. (For text, see *The Times, London*, January 24, 1967.)

And yet all protestations that Great Britain is prepared to move boldly toward Europe and to accept the discipline of the Rome Treaty have failed so far to placate the opposition of General de Gaulle, whose major concern remains the question of what kind of Europe it will be if Britain does succeed in joining the Common Market, what dominant interests will move an enlarged Community, what role it will play in the world and what kind of relations it will forge with the United States. On May 16, 1967, General de Gaulle spoke at length on the implications of Great Britain's re-application for Common Market membership, in the course of which he emphasized that the real question of Great Britain's membership was its effect on the nature of the European Economic Community and that he was not sure whether it would not bring in its train "destructive upheavals" and undo the work of the past. Said General de Gaulle:

> ...I have spoken of destructive upheavals within the Common Market. We all know that it has taken ten years to construct it and also an untiring effort of cooperation on the part of the Six ... When they have finished building the edifice, they will have to live together in it, that is, from year to year, to submit to the rules, compromises and sanctions which have and will have been decided.

> ...The Common Market is a sort of Miracle. At this point to introduce new massive elements, among those which have been so painfully agreed upon, would clearly mean putting into question the whole structure and its components and raising the problem of a completely different undertaking... The idea and the hope which led the Europeans to unite was no doubt the idea and the hope of forming a group which would be European in every respect. That is to say, one which would not only carry its full weight in trade and production, but would also be capable of dealing politically for itself and by itself vis-à-vis whomsoever it might be. Given England's special relationships, those of the British with America, the obligations as well as the advantages for them, given the existence of the Commonwealth and the privileged relationships they have with England and given that the British still bear, or think they must still bear, special obligations in various parts of the world, which distinguish them fundamentally from the Western nations ... The admission of England at this time, would necessitate in fact

> building a totally new edifice and in razing what has just been built. (For text, see *The New York Times,* May 17, 1967.)

In a statement issued on April 26, 1963, the International Chamber of Commerce, meeting in congress in Mexico City, declared:

> Economic regionalism must not be allowed to become economic nationalism on a larger scale.

> The regional groupings of our time, whether already achieved or in the process of formation or only tentatively envisaged do not exclude the conviction that barriers of trade must ultimately give place to a broader and freely evolving division of labor between nations ...

> The economic assumptions underlying freedom within regions may soon be seen to apply with equal force to freedom throughout the world ...

> Everywhere there is a growing awareness that no nation or group of nations can go it alone without drifting into a backwater away from the mainstream of human progress. (For text see *The New York Times,* April 27, 1963.)

In his Message to Congress on January 25, 1962, in which he stated the case for a Trade Expansion Act to take the place of the Trade Agreement Act of 1934, eleven times renewed, President John F. Kennedy declared:

> ...The growth of the European Common-Market—an economy which may soon equal our own, protected by a single external tariff similar to our own—has progressed with such success and momentum that it has surpassed its original timetable, convinced those initially sceptical that there is now no turning back and laid the groundwork for a radical alteration of the economics of the Atlantic alliance ...

The purpose of this message has been to describe the challenge we face and the tools we need. The decision rests with the Congress. That decision will either mark the beginning of a new chapter in the alliance of free nations—or a threat to the growth of Western unity. The two great Atlantic markets will either grow together or they will grow apart. The meaning and range of free economic choice will either be widened for the benefit of free men everywhere—or confused and constricted by new barriers and delays. (For text see 'The New York Times,' January 26, 1962.)

The Trade Expansion Act was defined by President Kennedy as a "bold new instrument of American trade policy" and was aimed primarily at ensuring that United States exports will not be seriously damaged by the creation of privileged trading blocs, in the first place the European Economic Community. But its purpose was also to promote a free and open world commerce. It gave the President of the United States unparalleled tariff-cutting authority and the necessary freedom to negotiate with other trading powers tariff reductions such a free and open world commerce demanded. For more than four years these negotiations, which have come to be as the Kennedy Round, were being carried on in the context of the General Agreement on Tariffs and Trade (GATT), until they were brought to a successful conclusion in the evening of May 15, 1967. (For statement of GATT's director-general regarding the tariff accord, see *The New York Times,* May 16, 1967.)

While it is generally agreed that the tariff agreement will stimulate the rising volume of trade between the industrialized and affluent nations, it is still open to question whether and to what extent it may compensate for the divisive factors inherent in the rise of the European Economic Community as an independent power in its own right in competition with other power centers in the world.

On April 1, 1962, President Tito of Yugoslavia spoke for most of the socalled non-aligned nations when he declared:

The question of the Common Market, as well as of closed markets in general, causes concern not only to my country but also to all other countries which are outside economic bloc divisions. It is obvious that we cannot remain idle and that we have to undertake certain measures in order to protect ourselves from various discriminatory tendencies displayed by States belonging to closed markets toward third countries.

This question was discussed during my visit to Cairo and the Sudan. As this affects not only non-aligned but also other countries, it is necessary to undertake common action. This action will not be aimed at establishing a third closed market of uncommitted or non-aligned countries, but toward more intensive and better organized trade exchange and cooperation among non-aligned countries. (Statement of April 1, 1962. For text see, *Yugoslav News Bulletin,* published by the Yugoslav Information Center, New York, April 2, 1962.)

37. *Moore's Digest of International Law,* Vol. VI, p.552.

38. For text see Ruth C. Lawson, *op. cit.,* pp.339-344.

39. For text see, *Annals of the Organization of America States,* Vol. VI (Special Number) 1954, Appendix B, p.116.

40. From an address before the American Society of International Law, April 22, 1914, cited in *Hackworth's Digest of International Law,* Vol. V, p.440.

41. See Chapter II, note 46, *supra.*

42. For text see *The New York Times,* May 3, 1965.

43. These five Latin American countries voted for a Mexican resolution calling for the immediate withdrawal of United States troops from the Dominican Republic and against the establishment of an inter-American Force. (*The New York Times,* May 11, 1965.) For a discussion of the Dominican situation in the United Nations Security Council, see *S/PV. 1196, 1198, 1200, 1202, 1203, 1204, 1208, 1209, 1214, 1215, 1216, 1217, 1218, 1219, 1223,* For the statement of Ambassador Adlai Ste-

venson, presenting the case for the United States, see *S/PV.1196;* for the statement of Ambassador Velasquez of Uruguay, see *S/PV. 1198.* For a terse, although not necessarily wholly objective, analysis of the whole question, see Theodore Draper, "The Dominican Crisis; A Case Study in American Policy," *Commentary,* December, 1965.

44. Just over a century and a half ago the great Latin American liberator, Simon Bolivar, called a congress of the American States at Panama to form an integrated league of sovereign states in the Western Hemisphere and met with resistance, especially on the part of the larger countries south of the Rio Grande. Geographical barriers, political animosities, differences in size and wealth, history, traditions and culture combined with a class structure that is hostile to change, to keep the Latin American nations apart. In fact, the stimulus toward regional cooperation, even in the economic field, was provided from abroad, largely by the United Nations Economic Commission for Latin America and the Alliance for Progress. See, for example, *Cooperation between the Secretariats of ECLA and of other Inter-American Agencies,* (*E/CN.12/674,* 9 May 1963, *passim*); *Trade Expansion and Economic Integration among Developing Countries* (*TD/B/85,* 30 August 1966, p.27.) For recent works on Latin America's political, economic and social problems, see Milton Eisenhower, *The Wine is Bitter,* New York, Doubleday & Co., 1963; Gerhard Masur, *Nationalism in Latin America: Diversity and Unity,* New York, Macmillan Co., 1966; John Gunther, *Inside South America,* New York, Harper & Row, 1967; Tad Szulc, *The Winds of Revolution: Latin America Today and Tomorrow,* New York, Frederick A. Praeger, 1963; *The Politics of Change in Latin America,* edited by Joseph Maier and Richard W. Weatherhead, New York, Frederick A. Praeger, 1964. See also, *The Politics of Developing Areas, op. cit., supra* I, note 6.

45. For text of the Declaration of American Chiefs of State, see *The New York Times,* April 14, 1967. See also the Declaration of Bogota of August 16, 1966, in which the Presidents of Chile, Colombia and Venezuela and the personal representatives of the Presidents of Ecuador and Peru proposed steps for promoting social progress and regional economic integration in anticipation of the meeting at Punta del Este of American Chiefs of State. (U. N. Doc. *A/6410,* 8 September, 1966.)

46. For text, see Ruth C. Lawson, *op. cit.,* pp.364-368.

47. The region was united from the middle of the 16th century until 1821 under the Captaincy General of Guatemala. In November, 1824, the delegates of the five Provinces promulgated the Constitution which established the Federal Republic of Central America. It lasted only 14 years and dissolved in the face of the reluctance of the component republics to cede even a minimum of sovereignty to the larger political body which was necessary for its growth and survival. Another attempt at some form of political integration was made in 1907 under the Treaty of Washington, which ended in similar failure. See Thomas L. Karnes, *The Failure of Union: Central America,* Chapel Hill, University of North Carolina Press, 1961.

48. For text, see Ruth C. Lawson, *op. cit.,* pp.347-360.

49. *The New York Times,* November 12, 1963.

50. *Africa Must Unite, op. cit., supra* I, note 6. See also his statement "United We Stand," at the Conference of African Heads of States and Governments at Addis Ababa in May, 1963. (*Proceedings of the Summit Conference of Independent African States,* Addis Ababa, May 1963, I:2, *Gen/Inf. 7.*)

51. For text, see *Ibid.,* I:1. For background information on the question of Pan-Africanism, see *Pan-Africanism Reconsidered:* Papers Delivered at the 1960 Conference of the American Society of African Culture, Berkeley, University of California Press, 1962; *New Forces in Africa:* A Symposium, edited by William H. Lewis, Washington, Public Affairs Press, 1962; Vernon McKay, *Africa in World Politics,* New York, Harper & Row, 1963; Colin Legum, *Pan Africanism: A Short Political Guide,* revised edition, New York, Frederick A. Praeger, 1965; Alec Quaison-Sackey, *op. cit., supra* I, note 6.

52. It should be noted, however, that much of the appeal of Pan-Africanism rests on the proposition that it is the only force that can overcome the centrifugal forces inherent in Africa's geographic, tribal, linguistic, religious and other historic differences. At the Summit Conference in Addis Ababa, which promulgated the Charter of African Unity, Ghana's Dr. Nkrumah warned:

> There is hardly any African State without a frontier problem with its adjacent neighbors. It would be futile for me to enumerate them because they are already familiar to us all. But let me suggest to Your Excellencies that this fatal relic of colonialism will drive us to war against one another as our unplanned and uncoordinated industrial development expands, just as happened in Europe. Unless we succeed in arresting the danger through mutual understanding on fundamental issues and through African Unity, which will render existing boundaries obsolete and superfluous, we shall have fought in vein for independence. Only African Unity can heal this festering sore of boundary disputes between our various states. Your Excellencies, the remedy for these ills is ready to our hand. It stares us in the face at every customs barrier, it shouts to us from every African heart. By creating a true political union of all the independent states of Africa, we can tackle hopefully every emergency, every enemy and every complexity. This is not because we are a race of supermen, but because we have emerged in the age of science and technology in which poverty, ignorance and disease are no longer the masters, but the retreating foes of mankind. We have emerged in the age of socialist planning, when production and distribution are not governed by chaos, greed and self-interest, but by social needs. Together with the rest of mankind, we have awakened from Utopian dreams to pursue practical blueprints for progress and social justice. *(Proceedings of the Summit Conference of Independent African States, op. cit.* 1:2, *GEN/ INF/33.)*

53. From an address to a ten-day International Economic Symposium on problems of emerging Africa. *(The New York Times,* July 30, 1962.) In a paper prepared for the June, 1960, Conference of the American Society of African Culture, *Pan-Africanism or Nationalism,* David Apter and James Coleman stated:

> African political leaders were forced by circumstances to emphasize "national" rather than Pan-African goals and symbols during both the period of agitation for independence and the period of nation-building after independence. The social revolution they sought to achieve after attaining the "political kingdom" of independence required national unity, respect for authority, positive loyalty and a sense of shared purpose, all of which made it "absolutely essential for leaders to create national symbols, national institutions, and a sense of national identity." Also, both the Socialist and democratic ideals of the new states tended to reinforce nationalism and maintain the nation-state as a separate entity. When Socialism becomes official state policy, the government becomes deeply committed to preserving the state and using it to achieve socialist goals. When democracy is practiced, the people tend to organize, campaign and vote on national issues and symbols to which voters become attached through habit and tradition ... Quoted in Vernon McKay, *op. cit.,* pp.130-131.

54. See Ruth C. Lawson, *op. cit.,* pp.295-296.

55. For text of the African Charter of Casablanca, see *Ibid* pp.303-306.

56. *Ibid,* pp.295-296.

57. *Ibid,* pp.306-312.

58. *Proceedings of the Summit Conference of Independent African States, op. cit.* 1:2.

59. *Ibid, GEN/INF 4.* As in the case of Latin America, all efforts at regional integration are concentrated primarily in the economic field. The United Nations Economic Commission for Africa, in cooperation with the Organization of African

Unity, has divided the continent into four sub-regions which are regarded as economically viable and within which economic and particularly industrial development is to be planned on an integrated basis—a northern sub-region comprising six countries, a western sub-region comprising fourteen, a central sub-region of six, and an eastern sub-region of nine countries. In addition, old monetary or economic areas, going back to colonial times, have served as a basis for sub-regional common markets such as the proposed East African Economic Community which would include, in addition to the original three parties—Kenya, Uganda and Tanzania—also Zambia, Malawi, Ethiopia, Burundi, Mauritius and Madagascar; the Equatorial Customs Union, and the West African Customs Union. *Trade Expansion and Economic Integration among Developing Countries, op. cit.,* pp.27-29.

60. Again, whatever progress has been made toward regional cooperation on the Asian continent has been in the economic field, principally under the auspices of the United Nations Economic Commission for Asia and the Far East. *Ibid.* pp.32-33.

61. A theme which runs through so many comments on the Arab world is that, although the countries of the Middle East, with one exception, have the same religion and the same civilization, it has proved difficult for these states to translate this common outlook into measures of concrete economic or political cooperation. Like Pan-Slavism, Pan-Arabism has served as a handmaiden to politics within the Arab world and has been fed more on grievances against Israel than on affirmative purposes. See, for example, *The Middle East in Transition,* edited by Walter Z. Laqueur, London, Routledge & Paul, 1958, *passim;* Emil Lengeyl, *The Changing Middle East,* New York, Oxford Book Co., 1960; *Arab Nationalism: An Anthology, op. cit., supra* I, note 6, *passim.*

NOTES TO CHAPTER IV

1. For references to the debates on Articles 52-54 in plenary and in Committee III and Sub-Committees, consult Index, *United Nations Conference on International Organization, Documents.*

2. Until that time, the inter-American system was the only important regional grouping of consequence which challenged in many ways the idea of universalism. In fact, it was the Latin American nations which at San Francisco defended the cause of regionalism and which were responsible for the present wording of Articles 52, 53 and 54 of the United Charter, assigning an importance to regional organizations beyond that contemplated in Chapter VIII of the Dumbarton Oaks proposals. Many international lawyers have long ago regretted the fact that the Latin American countries have through their statesmen and international lawyers developed for a hundred years doctrines which they felt were destined to weaken norms and institutions of general international law. A warning to this effect was made as recently as March, 1963, at a Round Table Meeting of Scholars, convoked at San José, Costa Rica, by the Carnegie Endowment for International Peace, in cooperation with the Department of Legal Affairs of the Pan-American Union. For a brief report, see 58 *American Journal of International Law,* p.126, 1964. For a brief general discussion of the weakening factor of regionalism in respect to universality of international law, see, for example, Gesina H. J. Van der Molen's paper, "The Present Crisis in the Law of Nations" in *Symbolae Verzijl,* The Hague, Martinus Nijhoff, 1958, pp.238-254.

3. *A/SR. 144,* p.159.

4. Neither the Security Council nor the General Assembly has attempted to define the scope of Article 52. The first time the regionalism issue was debated in the Security Council was in 1954, in connection with Guatemala's complaint of aggression against Honduras and Nicaragua and implicating the United States. Brazil and Colombia submitted a draft resolution which would have referred the Guatemalan complaint to the Organization of American States for urgent consideration, which Guatemala rejected. The arguments in the Security Council revolved

about the propriety of the Security Council acting against the wishes of a member State by asking it to take its troubles, as it were, elsewhere. The United States argued that while each State Member had the right to ask the Security Council for an urgent meeting, the substance of the issue determined whether or not it could not be better dealt with, in the first instance, by a regional organization. Brazil and Columbia argued that since the Organization of American States had already been seized with the situation, it was reasonable that the Council should wait for the report of the Organization before deciding on the adoption of the agenda which, in this instance at least, meant the admission of the Guatemalan complaint. Other members of the Council thought that Council action on the Guatemalan complaint, in competition with the organization of American States, would upset the balance established in Article 52 of the Charter between the United Nations and the regional organizations. The Soviet Union was alone in its views that the Security Council was competent to act on the complaint and vetoed the draft resolution of Brazil and Colombia. (See *S/675*, 20 June, 1954.)

More than ten years later, the Soviet Union supported the majority of African States Members, which had asserted that the Organization of African Unity alone was the proper organ to deal with the Congo question, to the exclusion of the United Nations. The question arose in connection with the complaint of eighteen African States of December 1, 1964, against the United States and Belgium, accusing the two States of aggression following the parachuting on November 24, 1964, into Stanleyville, Congo, of Belgian paracommandos, carried by United States aircraft, in an attempt to rescue the lives of a thousand foreigners belonging to ten different nations, who had been held as prisoners of war or hostages by the rebel authorities there. The action was taken with the consent of the Congolese Government headed at that time by Moise Tshombe. The question was debated in the Security Council intermittently from December 9 through December 30, 1964. The burden of argument of the African States, supported by the Soviet Union and Czechoslovakia, was that the Congo was an African problem and could be solved only by Africans, and that those outside Africa who intervened on behalf of the Tshombe Government, did so against the wishes of the overwhelming majority of Africans which had preempted the question by appropriate resolutions taken by the Organization of African Unity. On December 24, 1964, the late Adlai Stevenson stated:

> I heard also some strange doctrines asserted here, provoked, I hope, more by emotion than by mature reflection. For example, that African States can intervene against their neighbor African State while denying the right of other States to answer the neighbor's call for help. (*S/PV. 1185*, p.16.)

For further details, see *S/PV. 1177/1189*. The most recent case before the Security Council which involved the question of "conflict of jurisdiction" between the United Nations and the regional organizations was that of the Dominican Republic in 1965.

The issue of regionalism figured prominently in the debates at the sixteenth session of the General Assembly in 1962, in connection with Cuba's charges of aggression against the United States. Many delegations took exception to the expulsion of Cuba from the Organization of American States, as inconsistent with the purposes of the United Nations Charter. The intervention of the representative of Ceylon during the debate on the Cuban complaint in the General Assembly's Political Committee articulated a point of view which was shared by many delegations. Said Ambassador Malalasekera:

> What concerns my government in this issue is that to our great regret and sorrow the decisions taken at the Punta Conference affect the fate not only of the members of the OAS but also of every nation represented in this Chamber ... If the end aimed at is merely the exclusion of Cuba or any other member State from a club of nations, we have no quarrel with it ... Any alliance of nations can make its own rules for membership, and, of course, any of its members may insist on its legal rights under that membership. But if the end aimed at is sanctions—as some States have interpreted the issue—then we come up against the very provisions of the Charter, namely,

Article 52 ... The decisions arrived at Punta del Este are—to use the popular word—"incompatible" with that Article and, in the view of my delegation, incompatible with the spirit of the Charter itself ... In making these observations, we need hardly add that we speak as a non-aligned nation whose sole interest is that a strong and effective United Nations should govern the world. Having no great armies or navies ourselves, Ceylon's security rests entirely on a United Nations whose supreme over-riding authority is our only guarantee of national survival in a heavily armed world.

We, and perhaps many other delegations, will feel more secure if—as we hope—some day, perhaps at the next session of the General Assembly, we may have a full and all-out discussion of the relations of regional organizations to the United Nations—perhaps a Secretariat study of how they complement each other and of the circumstances in which they can become incompatible. Perhaps this study could be undertaken by the International Law Commission.

In making this statement we realize that it is a far-reaching proposal. We make it because we cannot conceal our deep anxiety regarding a trend which is manifesting itself in the world, in which regional organizations are drifting into an aggrandizement of those powers which should rightly be the exclusive political preserve and prerogative of this world Organization. This, of course, is due to the fact that precisely defined juridical norms do not exist. As this debate has shown abundantly, the time has come to deal with this problem in an organized juridical manner. We make the proposal because of this and we very much hope, therefore, that this study will be undertaken ... (*A/C.1/PV.1240*, 2 February, 1962, pp.28-30-36.)

In the economic and social fields, too, the issue of regionalism has frequently emerged as both a practical problem and a doctrinal question. We quote at random the Twenty-Eighth Report of the Administrative Committee on Coordination of the United Nations Economic and Social Council of May 6, 1963, which contains the following conclusion:

The decentralization of the activities of the United Nations, instances of which in the field of public administration have so frequently been noted in this report, is a means to increase the intensity, the pertinence and the realistic character of international collaboration to the solution of the problems of the developing countries, and of the specific problems of the newly independent States. But the universal character and aims of the United Nations imply that at headquarters level should be brought out the common elements of an inter-regional character, that are quite numerous in the field of administrative science, techniques and procedures. This balance, once admitted, implies practical consequences that have been otlined in the report when examining each particular field of the international work. (*E/3765*, Annex L, p.59.)

5. *Introduction to the Annual Report of the Secretary-General on the Work of the Organization*, 16 June 1956—15 June 1957. (*A/3594*/Add. 1.)

6. For a ready reference to United Nations activities, see *Everyman's United Nations: The Structure, Functions and Work of the Organization and its Related Agencies during the Years 1945-1962 and a United Nations Chronology for 1963*, 7th edition, October 1964, U.N. Publication 64. I. 9.

7. This refers to the decision which enables the General Assembly to deal with an issue when, in the presence of a serious threat to the peace, action is paralyzed by a veto in the Security Council. U.N.G.A. Res. 377 (V) , 3 November 1950.

8. See Chapter XI.

9. In an address at the University of Chicago on May 1, 1960, the late Dag Hammarskjöld stated:

> ...The experiment carried on through and within the United Nations has found in the Charter a framework of sufficient flexibility to permit growth beyond what seems to have been anticipated in San Francisco. Even without formal revisions, the institutional system embodied in the Organization has undergone innovations explained by organic adaptation to needs and experiences...Dag Hammarskjöld, *Speeches and Statements*, edited by Wilder Foote, London, the Bodley Head, 1962, p.256.

10. It is generally conceded that the resolution of the so-called Cuban missile crisis in 1962 was facilitated by the United Nations and that the confrontation between the United States and the Soviet Union was eased by the intervention of the Security Council.

11. It must be noted, however, that the withdrawal in May, 1967, of the United Nations Emergency Force from the Egyptian-Israeli frontier at the request of the United Arab Republic Government and the immediate compliance of the Secretary General of the United Nations with that request raised many doubts as to the reliability of the United Nations as guardian of national frontiers. (For background information concerning the events in May, 1967, see U.N. OPI., Press Release EMF/449, 3 June 1967.)

12. See, for example, Report of the Special Committee on Peace-Keeping Operations, *Comprehensive Review of the Whole Question of Peace-Keeping Opeartions in all their Aspects*, (A/6654, 17 May 1967.)

13. United Nations General Assembly, First Session, 1946, *Official Records*, Plenary Meetings, Second Plenary meeting, London, 11 January 1946.

14. United Nations General Assembly, Second Session, Eighty-Second Meeting, 17 September 1947.

15. *S/PV.933:23*.

16. U.N.O.P.I. Press Release PM/4219, 10 June 1963.

17. From an address at Mt. Holyoke College, Hadley, Mass. (U.N.O.P.I. Press Release SG/1512, 31 May 1963.)

18. See *supra*, p.245. Note 4.

19. Replying to questions concerning his request for the resignation of the late Dag Hammarskjöld as Secretary General of the United Nations, former Premier Nikita Krushchev told the United Nations Correspondents Association in New York that the failure of the United Nations to adopt his proposal for a three-member United Nations Executive Board—the so-called Troika Proposal-would perpetuate the world organization's "imabalance" against the Soviet bloc and would force the Soviet Union "to uphold our interests outside the United Nations by relying on our own strength." (*The New York Times*, October 8, 1960.)

20. United States Mission to the United Nations, *Press Release No. 3875*.

NOTES TO CHAPTER V

1. A thousand visible and invisible bonds are constantly being woven, which bind different parts of humanity. They range from formal and informal groupings of people across national frontiers sharing common interests and purposes, to systematic intellectual cooperation which, in the words of Rene Maheu, Director General of UNESCO, "is daily becoming more widespread in its range, more diversified in quality and more organized in depth," and which "forms the technical foundation of the first true and universal civilization." (From his address to the Economic and Social Council of the United Nations, forty-first session, 7 July 1966. *UNESCO/DG/1966/6*, p.2.) These bonds may be fragile and easily break even under the slightest tensions provoked by conflicts of national interests. But they are not incompatible with the national interest, or they could not flourish in peace-time.

2. G. S. Viereck quotes the secret head of British war propoganda in America during World I as having told him after the War was over that,

> You cannot make an effective appeal to the masses without arousing primitive instincts and prejudices. Without hate, there can be no propaganda. Give me something to hate, and I guarantee to organize a powerful propaganda campaign anywhere within 24 hours. *Spreading Germs of Hate,* New York, Liveright Publishing Corp., 1931, p.16.

3. The growth of the French monarchy for almost eight centuries was founded on the development of royal justice, which the people trusted more than the courts of the feudal lords.

For England, see H. E. L. Holdsworth, *Sources and Literature of English Law,* Oxford, Clarendon Press, 1925, pp.188-192; *History of English Law,* 7th revised edition, London, Methuen & Co., Ltd., 1956, pp.25-26.

4. Kant's system rested upon the doctrine of moral personality as the ultimate unit of human society. His idea of free moral personality as the condition of any ethical action, laid the truest philosophical ground for democratic tolerance, equality of opportunity and for the protection of the conditions necessary to all free self-development. In brief, the Kantian principle that every man is to be regarded as an end in himself is a form of the doctrine of the Rights of Man. For an analysis of Kant's Essay, "Toward Perpetual Peace," see Carl J. Friedrich, *Inevitable Peace,* Cambridge, Harvard University Press, 1948. See also, Bertrand Russel, *A History of Western Philosophy,* New York, An Essandres Paperback, pp.711-712.

5. Article 1 (3) of the Charter of the United Nations.

6. Treaty of Westminster, see *supra* III, note 6; also, European Convention on Human Rights, official edition of the Council of Europe.

7. Inter-American Convention on Human Rights. For text, see *Final Act of the Fourth Meeting of the Inter-American Council of Jurists,* Pan-American Union, Washington, D.C., January 1960.

8. Charter of the Organization of African Unity, see *supra* III, note 44.

9. *Draft Convention on Human Rights and the Central American Court,* New York, Freedom Through Law Inc., 1964.

10. For text, see *The New York Times,* April 11, 1963. For a brief analysis of the Encyclical, see Rev. J. Joblin, "The Papal Encyclical, *Pacem in Terris,*" 88 International Labour Review, pp.1-15 (1963).

11. U.N.O.P.I. Press Release SG/1078, 6 December 1961.

12. See, for example, the statement of Morris Abrams, United States Representative on the Commission of Human Rights, Twenty-third Session, 1967. (*E/CN. 4/SR, 899,* pp.4-7.)

NOTES TO CHAPTER VI

1. It must be noted, however, that the provisions of the United Nations Charter in respect to human rights are not, in the words of the late Sir Hersh Lauterpacht, "an artificial innovation which is out of keeping with the essential purpose of international law, with the modern tendencies of its development, and with the sources from which it has drawn its vigour and its dignity." *International Law and Human Rights,* New York, Frederick A. Praeger, 1950, p.145. More than half of this pioneering book is devoted to tracing the United Nations' Charter commitment to human rights to their sources in law and in history.

2. United Nations General Assembly, First Session, *Official Records,* Plenary Meetings, 8th Plenary Meeting, 15 January 1946, pp.123-124.

3. *Ibid,* First Plenary Meeting, 10 January 1946, p.41.

4. *Ibid,* Fourteenth Plenary Meeting, 18 January 1946, p.209.

5. *Ibid,* Eleventh Plenary Meeting, 17 January 1946, p.170.

6. The subject of blind obedience and the duty of the human conscience has since time immemorial exercised the minds of philosophers, jurists and moralists alike. Still, the line between civil and uncivil disobedience remains as uncertain as ever, both in theory and in practice. See, for example, *A Matter of Life,* edited by Clara Urquhart, Boston, Little, Brown & Co., 1963; H. Mark Roelof, *The Tension of Citizenship: Private Man and Public Duty,* New York, Rheinhart Co., 1957; Leonard W. Doob, *Patriotism and Nationalism: Their Psychological Foundations,* New Haven, Yale University Press, 1964; Harold Laski, *The Danger of Obedience and Other Essays,* New York, Harper & Bros, 1930. To what extent the Nuremberg Judgement, the Eichmann trial and the trials in Germany and abroad of Nazis accused of crimes against humanity have brought some clarity to the subject is still undertermined. The first paragraph of Article 6 of the Charter of the Nuremberg Tribunal affirmed the responsibility of the individual in the commission of international crimes. The Genocide Convention sanctioned for the first time the international punishment of crimes committed against persons on any national territory. The trials of Nazi criminals carried out the principle of individual responsibility in practice. Together, they give totally new dimensions to the problem of individual conscience in the face of governmental policies. Robert K. Woetzel, in his *The Nuremberg Trials in International Law,* New York, Frederick A. Praeger 1960, admits that international incidents since 1946 have contradicted the Nuremberg judgement. Nevertheless, he adds,

> there are no conflicting decisions of other international tribunals, nor acts of the international community expressing opposite opinion, or an overwhelming practice of nations that would invalidate the law of Nuremberg... It stands strong and undiminished in its legal significance, constantly reaffirmed by the nations seeking peace in this world and the protection of individual liberties. (p.243.)

Pieter Drost, in his *The Crime of State,* Vol. I, Humanicide, Leyden A. W. Sijthoff, 1959, asserts that just as there is a violation of basic human values, such as integrity, liberty, security and dignity of person, when a common crime is committed by a private person, so violations of these rights by an official of the state constitutes "humanicide" and must be punished accordingly. He states further that such crimes of state should be punished internationally, not only because they may endanger international peace and security, but also because the state authorities are often beyond the reach of national law and jurisdiction.

7. The Soviet Union has been consistent in its emphasis on national sovereignty and opposition to compulsory international jurisdiction. Its concept of domestic jurisdiction has been almost unlimited and it has vigorously opposed any effort to define in advance the precise bounds of this reserved domain, arguing that the notion of domestic jurisdiction was embedded in positive international law, that it went hand in hand with the idea of state sovereignty and that the need for invoking its protection could not be predetermimed but depended on the nature of concrete disputes. See, Zigurd L. Zile, "A Soviet Contribution to International Adjudication: Professor Krylov' Jurisprudential Legacy," 58 *American Journal of International Law,* pp.359-388, (1962); Alexander Dallin, *The Soviet Union and the United Nations, op. cit., Supra* II, note 50; M. S. Rajan, *United Nations and Domestic Jurisdiction,* New York, Longman, Green & Co., 1959. Thus Soviet representatives at the United Nations have been intolerant of proposals which envisage even the barest international supervision over international treaties on human rights, let alone of suggestions that would give individuals international procedural rights to assert their liberties before international bodies. In December, 1965, however, political circumstances compelled the Soviet Union to vote in the General Assembly for international implementation machinery for the enforcement of the International Convention on the Elimination of all Forms of Racial Discrimination and for the right of individual petition. It retreated to its traditional conception of enforcement of international law by the self-restraint of the participants in international intercourse, when in December, 1966, it succeeded in eliminating the

element of compulsion in the implementation machinery for the enforcement of the International Covenant on Civil and Political Rights and abstained on the Optional Protocol to the Covenant dealing with the right of individual recourse to international bodies to seek redress for violations of human rights. (For the text of the International Convention on the Elimination of All Forms of Racial Discrimination, see *U.N.G.A. Res. 2106 (XX)* of 21 December 1965; for text of the International Covenant on Political and Civil Rights and of the Optional Protocol, see *U.N.G.A. Res. 2200 (XXI)* of 16 December 1966.)

8. The countries which have consistently supported liberal and workable international measures for the enforcement of human rights have been few and far between. In general, few Member States have been concerned with the question of human rights at the level of decision or of policy-making, and have given it low priority. As a former adviser to the United States Delegation to the General Assembly, who served on the Third Committee which deals with human rights questions, remarked:

> Countries should be encouraged to assign competent and well-informed people to international human rights work. International Organizations can only be as effective and imaginative as the delegates participating in them. Until the human rights field is treated by governments with the importance it merits, it will be hard really to move ahead. Richard B. Bilder, "The International Promotion of Human Rights: A Current Assessment," 56 *American Journal of International Law,* p.733 (1962.)

The sins of ommission and commission on the part of Member States, especially of the Great Powers, have been great. Thus, the policy of the United States between 1953 and 1958 in the matter relating to the international covenants on human rights has caused a former United States Deputy Permanent Representative to the United Nations to note:

> The abandonment by the United States of support for enacting human rights into binding international legal obligations has arrested progress toward one important, though little noted, long-term objective: that of making individuals as well as states, subjects of international law. Ernest A. Gross, *The United Nations: Structure for Peace,* New York, Harper & Row, 1962, p.106. For details, see Moses Moskowitz, *Human Rights and World Order,* New York, Oceana Publications, 1958, pp.55-79.

With the advent of the Kennedy Administration in 1961, the United States position vis-a-vis the whole question of the treaty-approach to human rights changed radically, both at home and at the United Nations. See, for example, Ambassador Arthur J. Goldberg's testimony before a Sub-Committee of the Committee on Foreign Affairs of the United State Senate on February 23, 1967. (For text, see United States Mission to the United Nations, *Press Release/USUN-18,* February 23, 1967. See also his address before the Annual Meeting of the Conference of United Nations Representatives, UNA—USA, (*Press Release/USUN-27,* March 21, 1967).

9. See *The Ideologies of the Developing Nations, op. cit., supra,* I, note 11, *passim.*

10. For the debates in the Third Committee of the Fifth Session of the General Assembly, 1950, of the question of self-determination, see (A/C. 3/SR. 302, 309-311, 315.)

11. This has become as if part of a creed and has been repeated at virtually every gathering of Asian and African States. See, for example, the resolution of the Second Conference of Independent African States at Addis Ababa in April, 1960, on the eradication of colonial rule of Africa.

12. U.N.G.A. Res. 1514 (XV), 14 December 1960. For a general discussion of the subject, see Rupert Emerson, *Self-Determination Revisited in the Era of Decolonization,* Cambridge, Center for International Relations, Occasional Papers in International Affairs, No. 9, 1964.

13. For text, see United States Mission to the United Nations, *Press Release No. 4480,* December 12, 1964.

14. *Five Year Perspective, 1960-1964,* E/3347/Rev. 1, April 1960, paragraph 90. In 1963, the representative of the United States on the Coordinating Committee of the Economic and Social Council expressed surprise at a statement which had appeared in the introduction to Section VII of the Secretary-General's Annual Report on the Work Programme of the United Nations in the Economic, Social and Human Rights Fields and its Budgetary Requirements, which stated that projects in the field of human rights were "obviously not amenable to evaluation on the basis of their contribution to progress toward the objectives of the United Nations Development Decade, which are essentially of an economic and social nature." *(E/3788,* p.45.) The representative of the United States said that it was a surprising statement and denoted a narrow legalistic approach to human rights which appeared to overlook completely the relationship between freedom and development, and which failed to take into account the new energies released in individuals and nations as they grew in freedom. It might not be possible to evaluate the contribution of human rights to development in terms of money, he added, but there was no doubt that it was enormous. The identification of human rights with the key objectives of the Development Decade, such as freedom from hunger, would not only give fresh impetus to economic and social development in the Decade, but might also give new life and drive to human rights projects throughout the United Nations system. *(E/AC.24/SR.238,* p.5.)

15. See Chapter XI.

16. See *supra,* Note 7.

17. A/SPC/SR.385;14, 16 October, 1963.

18. For the most recent listing of United Nations activities in the human rights field, see *Work Program of the United Nations in the Economic, Social and Human Rights Fields and its Budgetary Requirements,* (E/4331/Add. 16, May 1967.)

19. This is generally true of most United Nations activities, especially in the economic, social and related fields. On December 13, 1966, the General Assembly adopted a resolution relating to a general review of the programs and activities in the economic, social, technical cooperation and related fields of the United Nations, the specialized agencies and other institutions and agencies related to the United Nations system and recalled that the work in these areas

> which has expanded rapidly, grown more complex and changed its nature, has evolved over a period of more than twenty years on the basis of unrelated proposals rather than in accordance with a coordinated plan,

and that

> this situation, among other factors, has impaired not only the ability of the Economic and Social Council to coordinate the work of the United Nations family of organizations in these fields but also the ability of Member States from that work . . . (U.N.G.A. Res. 2188 (XXI), 13 December 1966.)

20. In connection with the 20th anniversary of the Universal Declaration of Human Rights, the General Assembly, (in Resolution 2080 (XX) of 20 December 1965), approved the convening in 1968 of an International Conference on Human Rights in order to:

> a) Review the progress which has been made in the field of human rights since the adoption of the Universal Declaration;

> b) Evaluate the effectiveness of the methods used by the United Nations in the field of human rights, especially with respect to the elimination of all forms of racial discrimination and the practice of *apartheid*;

> c) Formulate and prepare a program of further measures to be taken subsequent to the celebrations of the International Year for Human Rights. *(U.N.G.A. Res. 2080* (XX), 20 December 1965.)

21. *UN ECOSOC Res. 624 B* (XII), 1 August 1956; *728 B* (XXVIII), 30 July 1959; *888 B* (XXXIV), 24 July 1962; and *1074 C* (XXXIX), 28 July 1965. For a critical appraisal of the reporting system, see Moses Moskowitz, *supra*, note 8, Chapter VI.

22. For the most recent periodic reports, as of the end of February, 1967, see *E/CN.4/892* and Addenda 1-26, (political and civil rights); and *E/CN.4/917* and Addenda 1-19 (economic, social and cultural rights.) Commission on Human Rights, Report on the Twenty-Second Session, 1966. (*E/4184*, Resolution 12 (XXII.)

23. Commission on Human Rights, Report on the Twenty-Third Session, 1967 (*E/4322*, Resolution 16 (XXIII.)

24. Report of the *Ad Hoc* Committee on Periodic Reports, 1966, (*E/CN.4/876*.)

25. Report of the *Ad Hoc* Committee on Periodic Reports, 1967, (*E/CN. 4/939*.)

26. Moses Moskowitz, *op. cit.*

27. Arcot Krishnaswami, *Study of Discrimination in the Matter of Religious Rights and Practices*, (*E/CN.4/Sub.2/200/Rev. 1*, concluding paragraph.)

NOTES TO CHAPTER VII

1. For texts, see *U.N.G.A. Res. 2200* (XXI). 16 December 1966. The substantive articles of the Covenant on Economic, Social and Cultural Rights include provisions recognizing the right to work, to social security, to adequate standards of living and freedom from hunger, and to health and education. The Covenant on Political and Civil Rights provides for the right to life and liberty, security and privacy of the person. It guarantees the right to a fair trial, prohibits slavery, and provides protection against arbitrary arrest or detention. It recognizes freedom of thought, conscience and religion; freedom of opinion and expression; the right of peaceful assembly, and freedom of association. Other articles provide for freedom of consent to marriage and for the protection of children and guarantee the preservation of the cultural, religious and linguistic heritage of minorities.

Two distinct sets of implementation clauses are provided for the Covenants. The Parties to the Covenant on Economic, Social and Cultural Rights would report to the Economic and Social Council on measures adopted and progress achieved toward the realization of those rights. The Council would promote appropriate international action to assist the States Parties in those fields. The measures of implementation of the Covenant on Political and Civil Rights would be carried out primarily by a Human Rights Committee composed of 18 persons elected by the States Parties. The Committee would consider reports submitted by the States Parties and may address general comments to the States as well as to the Economic and Social Council. The Committee would also receive complaints of violations of the Covenant from States Parties recognizing its competence for that purpose and act upon such complaints in accordance with a prescribed procedure. The Committee would attempt to establish the facts, and an *ad hoc* conciliation commission might be established, with the prior consent of the States concerned, to offer good offices with a view to reaching a friendly solution on the basis of respect for the rights recognized in the Covenant.

Under the Optional Protocol, which would come into force when 10 States Parties to the Covenant have accepted it, the Human Rights Committee might receive and consider communications from individuals claiming to be victims of a violation by a State Party of any of the rights set forth in the Covenant.

2. On the general question of the importance of international covenants on human rights, see Moses Moskowitz, *op. cit.*, VI, Note 8, ch. VII, *passim*.

3. *Ibid*, p.50.

4. The only time the United Nations intervened actively to redress a situation involving violations of human rights was in 1963 when it disptached a Fact Finding Mission to South Viet-Nam to inquire into allegations concerning the persecution

of Buddhists by the South Vietnamese Government. However, the circumstances under which the Fact Finding Mission came into existence—the invitation extended by the President of South Viet-Nam to the President of the General Assembly to send such a mission and the dispatch of the Mission without benefit of a General Assembly resolution establishing its juridical foundations and mandate—coupled with the fact that no action was taken by the General Assembly or any other organ of the United Nations on the Report of the Mission, largely because of the intervening coup d'etat in South Viet-Nam which claimed the life of President Ngo Dinh Diem, disqualifies the case from serving as a precedent for United Nations action in defense of human rights. For details, see *The Violation of Human Rights in South Viet-Nam: Report of the United Nations Fact-Finding Mission to South Viet-Nam, (A/5630,* 7 December 1963.) It may be noted that on December 13, 1963, the Soviet Delegation to the XVIII Session of the General Assembly made an official statement declaring that the sending of the Mission to the South Viet-Nam should not be considered a precedent for the future. (Press release dated December 13, 1963, by the USSR Mission to the United Nations.)

5.   The Secretary General of the Council of Europe, M. Polys Modinos, acknowledged that what the Council had accomplished at the regional level through its European Convention on Human Rights, which has been in force since 1953, and through its guarantees, its Court and its Social Charter could not be fully effective unless it was in some way integrated into a universal system of protection of human rights. Statement at the Twenty-Third Session of the Commission on Human Rights, 1967, *(E/CN.4/SR. 897,* p.5.)

6.   Regarding the importance of international institutions and procedures for enforcement of human rights, particularly the right of individual petition, see H. Lauterpacht, *International Law and Human Rights, op. cit., supra, VI,* Note 1; Carlos García Bauer, *Los Derechos Humanos, Preocupación Universal,* Guatemala City, Editorial Universitaria, 1960, pp.227-274; Moses Moskowitz, *op. cit., supra, VI,* Note 8, pp.105-151; W. Paul Gormley, *The Procedural Status of the Individual before International and Supranational Tribunals,* The Hague, Martinus Nijhoff, 1966.

7.   *UN OPI Press Release/GA/3098,* 22 October 1965.

8.   *UN OPI Press Release SG/SM/393,* 15 November 1965.

9.   *The New York Times,* September 30, 1963.

NOTES TO CHAPTER VIII

1.   The adequacy of the world's natural resources in the face of rapid population expansion was among the subjects of discussion at the Second World Population Conference held in Belgrade, Yugoslavia, from 30 August to 10 September 1965. The majority of the discussants agreed that population growth could eventually outrun natural resources. *(E/CONF.41/3,* I, (Summary Report), pp.305-316.)

The question of the balance between population and resources is still very much a matter of speculation. In the first place, no inventory has yet been made of the world's resources to set the population limits of the earth. An effort to this effect was decided upon by the United Nations in 1966. (See the Secretary-General's report, *Implementation of a Five-year Survey Programme for the Development of Natural Resources, E/4281,* 4 November 1966.) Secondly, there is great uncertainty as to the adaptability of the technology-deficient, high-density regions in the world to modern science and technology. Thus, an inventory of natural resources in Africa, published by UNESCO in 1963, pointed out that "studies in soil conservation in semi-humid and humid tropical regions have shown the possible harmful effects in Africa of highly mechanized agriculture." *(A Review of the Natural Resources of the African Continent,* UNESCO 1963, p.13 and chapter 6, *The Soils of Africa, passim.)* In certain areas, however, scientists have not hesitated to pass final judgement. There is general agreement that water, for example, can no longer be regarded as an inexhaustible resource. The United Nations Conference on the Application of Science and Technology for the Benefit of less Developed Areas of 1963 laid great stress on the urgency of immediate action to preserve the world's water supply. It recommended that governments should without delay enact legislation for an optimum allocation of water among different uses and ensure that the water development policy of the country embraced both water and soil conservation and served to minimize the pollution of surface and underground resources. *United Nations Conference on the Application of Science and Technology for the Benefit of Less Developed Areas, (E/3772:9,* 21 May 1963.)

Certainly, there is a limit to the acreage of land that can be brought under cultivation, even under optimum conditions. Whereas in 1955, for example, there was 1.25 acres per head of population, it was only 1.8 in 1959. It is estimated that in the year 2000, this figure will be reduced to .50 of an acre and to about .25 of an acre fifty years later. (*Ibid,* Paragraph 67.)

2. As Harrison Brown has so aptly noted,

> There are, of course, physical limitations of some sort which will determine the maximum number of human beings who can live on the earth's surface. But at the present time we are far from the ultimate limit of the number of persons who could be provided for. If we were willing to be crowded together closely enough, to eat foods which would bear little resemblance to the foods we eat today, and to be deprived of simple but satisfying luxuries such as fireplaces, gardens and lawns, a world population of 50 billion would not be out of the question. And if we really put our minds to the problem we could construct floating islands where people might live and where algae farms could function, and perhaps 100 billion persons could be provided for. If we set strict limits to physical activities so that caloric requirements could be kept at very low levels, perhaps we could provide for 200 billion persons. *The Challenge of Man's Future,* New York, The Viking Press, 1954, pp.220-221. See also, Robert Rienow and Leona Train Rienow, *Moment in the Sun,* New York, Dial Press, 1967.

Part of the problem of population expansion is the explosive growth of cities and metropolitan agglomerations, which is rapidly changing the world from a rural and agricultural society to a predominantly urban one. All demographic forecasts concur in showing that urban growth will proceed at an ever accelerating pace in the foreseeable future, as people around the world are on the move in pursuit of what they believe will be a better life, greater opportunity and improved health and education which city life might provide. While the total world population is expected to double by the end of this century, the urban population is expected to increase fourfold by the year 2000. An increase of such magnitude cannot but completely change the whole pattern of human settlement.

> Superimposed on a situation already very critical is a heavy concentration of population in large cities which tends to monopolize a disproportionate share of a country's resources; congestion, lack of housing and services, social stress; inadequate economic basis; obsolete administrative systems; competition of man with the machine for urban space, air and water, and the expectation of evergrowing mechanization; these are some of the conditions which impose a complete rethinking of the problem, a careful assessment of its causes and the urgent elaboration of integrated policies and programs. *United Nations Conference on the Application of Science and Technology,* etc. *op. cit.,* Paragraphs 146 and 147.

See also Charles Abrams, *Man's Struggle for Shelter in an Urbanizing World,* Cambridge, M. I. T. Press, 1964; Serge Chermayeff and Christopher Alexander, *Community and Privacy: Toward a New Architecture of Humanism,* New York, Doubleday & Co., 1963; Donald E. Carr, *Death of the Sweet Waters,* New York, W. W. Norton & Co., 1966; Lincoln H. Day and Alice Taylor Day, *Too Many Americans,* Boston, Little, Brown Co., 1964; Barry Commoner, *Science and Survival,* New York, The Viking Press, 1966; John Perry, *Our Polluted World,* New York,

Franklin Watts, 1967. For a listing of United Nations activities in the area of environmental problems, see *Programme of the United Nations in the Economic, Social and Human Rights Fields and Its Budgetary Requirements,* 1967, *(E/4331/ Add 7, 10, 12 and 17.)*

3. *Six Billions To Feed,* Food and Agriculture Organization, World Food Problems, No. 4, Rome 1962, p.3; see also Chapter XII below.

4. On June 30, 1966, President Johnson told an audience in Omaha, Nebraska:

> Most of the world's population is losing the battle to feed itself. And if present trends continue we can now see the point at which even our own vast productive resources, including the millions of acres of farm lands that we now hold in reserve, will not be sufficient to meet the requirements of human beings for food. (*The New York Times,* July 1, 1966.)

5. For greater details, see *World Population Prospects Up To The Year 2000 (E/CN.9/186,* 20 January 1965.)

6. See Chapter XII below.

7. *Report on the World Social Situation, 1963, (E/CN.5/Add. 2,* p.2.)

8. *UN OPI, Press Release ECAFE/221,* 2 January 1964.

9. *The New York Times,* January 21, 1964.

10. The problem of isolating the automation-manpower relationship from other vital factors still remains largely unsolved and the conclusions thus far reached may be compounded, in the words of United States Secretary of Labor, W. Willard Wirtz, "very little of reliable analysis and very largely intuition." (From a statement made in Washington. D.C. on December 9, 1964. *The New York Times,* December 10, 1964.) This was substantially confirmed by the Presidential Commission on Technology, Automation and Economic Progress in its Report of February, 1966. Charles E. Silberman and the Editors of Fortune, *The Myths of Automation,* New York, Harper Row, 1966. A contrary point of view is presented by Ben B. Seligman in his book, *Most Notorious Victory: Man in an Age of Automation,* New York, Glencoe Free Press, 1966. The American Foundation on Automation and Employment—an organization established early in 1962 in New York under the joint sponsorship of United States Industries and the International Association of Machinists—has been concerned with developing ways to ease the impact of automation on workers whom it displaces and is carrying on a widespread educational campaign at home and abroad. (See, for example, *Focus on Automation; The Management View, The Labor View, The International Questions,* published by the Foundation in 1963 and containing addresses at a Foundation—sponsored meeting in Geneva, Switzerland, December 13, 1962.) However, placed in the broader setting of the problem of marshalling the humane, economic and political machinery and resources for the application of science and technology to the many needs of mankind, automation does loom large as a great human problem in the future. Like science and technology in general, which has brought both good and evil, so automation can mean hardship as it holds out the potentiality for increased abundance. See, for example, *Man and His Future,* edited by Gordon Wolstenhohne, Boston, Little, Brown & Co., 1963.

11. "A Naturalist Looks at Overpopulation", in *Our Crowded Planet: Essays on the Pressures of Population,* edited by Fairfield Osborn, New York, Doubleday & Co., 1963, p.211.

12. "Too Many People", *Ibid.* p.225.

13. "The Good Life", *Ibid,* p.220.

14. Shepard B. Clough, *Basic Values of Western Civilization,* New York, Columbia University Press, 1960, p.122.

15. See P. W. Bridgman, *The Way Things Are,* Cambridge, Harvard University Press, 1959, pp.316-325.

16. "Too Many People", *op. cit.,* pp.224-225.

17. The widespread concern with the population expansion problem is manifested by the increasing preocupation with it by national and international author-

ities. For a review of the activities of the United Nations and its organs and agencies in this area, see Population Commission, Report of the Thirteenth Session, 1965, *(E/4019)*. For greater details, see the following reports and proposals of the Secretary-General: *Regional Demographic Activities, (E/CN.9/192)* ; *Long-Range Programme of Work in the Fields of Population, (E/CN.9/196); Work Programme and Priorities for 1965-66, (E/CN.9/197.)*

18. In 1963, the rate of increase was 0.9%, or half the world average. (*The New York Times*, February 2, 1964.)

19. *World Population Prospects Up To The Year 2000, op. cit.,* Section IV.

20. *Ibid*, Section VI.

21. There seems to exist a great deal of apprehension among Japanese in government, medical and welfare circles lest the continuation of the low rate of population increase might lead to national suicide. Japanese demographic experts believe the present birth rate may not be high enough to sustain a stable population. (*The New York Times*, February 2, 1964; August 7, 1966.)

22. One of the tenets of Marxism has been that the Malthusian theory is a vicious capitalistic plot to limit the proletariat and stifle revolution. When mainland China in 1961 changed its policy in respect to birth control, it was vehemently denounced in the Soviet Union. (See, for example, an editorial in *Izvestia* of September 12, 1963, reported in *The New York Times*, September 14, 1963.) At the Second World Population Conference in Belgrade in 1965, the representative of the Soviet Union, V. E. Ovsienko, argued that national economies should be developed in harmony with the needs of the people, rather than having the numbers of people controlled in order to harmonize with economic growth. *(UN OPI Press Release SOC/3404,* 6 September 1965); see also the statement by Soviet Academician E. K. Fedorov at the United Nations Conference on the Application of Science and Technology to Developing Areas, *(E/3772,) op. cit.,* pp.127-129.

23. Thus reports from Australia have spoken of increasing national concern over the decline in the birthrate since 1961, in a country which has subsidized immigration from Europe to populate a continent as large as the United States. (See, for example, *The New York Times*, August 8, 1966.) Similar reports have come from Canada of a declining birth rate and of increasing attention to immigration. (*The New York Times*, August 7, 1966.) The steadily declining birth rate in the countries of Eastern Europe, where it has reached the bottom of the world scale, persuaded the Communist regimes to engage in a campaign to curb at least some of the freedoms, such as legalized abortions, which have been factors in the population decline. (*The New York Times*, October 23, 1965.)

NOTES TO CHAPTER IX

1. Quoted in Inis L. Claude Jr., *National Minorities: An International Problem*, Cambridge, Harvard University Press, 1955, p.9.

2. Thus, even such a liberal statesman and humanitarian as the late President Edouard Benes of Czechoslovakia favored assimilation as a national policy. He held the view that Jews, for example, must either assimilate or emigrate. Kurt Stillschweig, "International Protection of Human Rights," IX *Historia Judaica*, p.49, (1947.) Even in a relatively well-integrated country like the Turkish Republic, there are on the statute books many specific bans on political articulations regarded as endangering national unity. A law of association dating back to the Ottoman period and in force with little modification to the present day prohibits political associations based on distinctions of race, language, religion, locality or social class. *The Politics of the Developing Areas, op. cit., supra* I, note 6. The editors note that,

> While everybody is keenly aware of the existence of these various groups, any open reference to such distinctions in the press or in public speech would meet with cries of indignation. (p.431.)

The United States, the classic land of diversity, has not escaped the pressures of assimilation either. For many years the United States has gloried in the description of its society as the "great melting pot." This, of course, was never true. The racial, ethnic and national groups that came to the United States did not fly apart, as it were, after they had settled in the country. They clove to each other for self-protection against other groups that had preceded them, as well as against those that followed them. However, as these conditions slowly abated, the pressures of assimilation increased in force and dimension. The more the idea of America's diversity was publicly accepted, the more the "melting pot" reality asserted itself. See, for example, Joshua A. Fishman's three-year survey entitled, *Language Loyalty in the United States,* London, Mouton & Co., 1966; Nathan Glazer and Daniel Patrick Moyniham, *Beyond the Melting Pot: The Negros, Puerto Ricans, Jews, Italians and Irish of New York City,* Cambridge, Harvard University & M. I. T. Press, 1963; also, Reinhold Niebuhr and Alan Heimert, *A Nation so Conceived: Reflections on the History of America, from its Early Visions to its Present Power,* New York, Charles Scribner's Sons, 1963, *passim.*

3. Switzerland, of course, is the classic example.

4. According to the *Encyclopaedia Brittanica,* about 600,000 Armenians, or one third of their number in Turkey, were slain. Others have put the figure as high as one-million or more.

5. "As an aggregate result of Hitler's 'repatriation' policies (1939-44) ; German flight from the Red Army (1944-45) , and outright expulsion and organized transfer (1944-50) , almost all German enclaves in European countries were practically eliminated. On the whole, over thirteen million Germans were, in one way or another, removed from various European countries." Joseph B. Schechtman, *Post-War Population Transfers: 1945-1955,* Philadelphia, University of Pennsylvania Press, 1962, p.363.

6. "The exchange of population between the Soviet Union and Poland and between the Soviet Union and Czechoslovakia, involving over 2.5 million people, united all Ukrainians, White Russians and Lithuanian minorities with their main bodies, the Ukrainian, White Russian and Lithuanian Soviet Republics. On the other hand, Poland became a state inhabited almost entirely by Poles." *(Ibid,* p.364.)

Still unsolved is the question of the 400,000-strong Hungarian minority in Czechoslovakia, the 1.6 million Hungarians in Roumania and the 500,000 Hungarians in Yugoslavia, who together constitute the largest minority bloc left in Europe. An abortive attempt by Bulgaria at a wholesale transfer of the Turkish minority left the problem festering. *Ibid,* Chapter VII; see also Anhtony T. Bouscaren, *International Migrations since 1945,* New York, Frederick A. Praeger, 1963, Ch. V.

7. The Soviet Union identifies 109 separate ethnic nationalities within its borders UN OPI, *Press Release STAT/304,* 13 August 1964. The Release reviews highlights in the United Nations *Demographic Yearbook 1963.)* Students of Soviet policy seem to be in general agreement that up to the 17th Soviet Communist Party Congress in 1934 any deviation toward nationalism, either local or Greater-Russian, was regarded as a departure from Leninist internationalism. "The Seventeenth Congress withessed the turning point in Stalin's nationality policy. Prior to 1934, he had condemned Russian great power chauvinism as the principal danger; now local non-Russian national deviations were condemned as equally dangerous. This marked the beginning of Stalin's orientation toward Russian nationalism." (John S. Rechetar, *op. cit., supra* II, note 32, p.234.) Stalinism claimed to represent the "international proletariat" at the same time that it based itself on a revival of Russian chauvinism and cruelly punished any genuine defense of the national identity of its non Russian subject peoples. It permitted and even encouraged Russian nationalism, while condemning that of the non Russians as "bourgeois nationalism," *(Ibid,* p.214. See also Robert N. Carew Hunt, *op. cit., supra,* II, note 44 p.219 *et seq.)* The conclusion that assimilation is on the rise in the Soviet Union has been reached by many observers and specialists on the nationalities problem. See, for example, proceedings of the Conference on the State of Ethnic Minorities in the Soviet Union, which was convened by Brandeis University, 30 October—2 November 1965. The proceedings are scheduled for publication in 1968.

8. *The New York Times,* August 1, 1961.

9. For a variety of historical, political and sociological reasons, Jews have been included among the ethnic minorities whose Russification has received priority. See, for example, William Korey, *The Legal Position of the Jewish Community of the Soviet Union: An Inquiry,* a paper read at Brandeis University Conference above.

10. See, for example, Theodore Shabad's dispatch from Talinn, Estonia, to *The New York Times* of July 20, 1965, in which he speaks of efforts made by Estonians to curb immigration of Russians into their country.

11. *Documents of the 22nd Congress of the CPSU. Report on the Program of the Communist Party of the Soviet Union, 1961.* New York, Crosscurrents Press, 1961, p.116.

12. Professor John A. Armstrong, at the Conference on the State of Ethnic Minorities in the Soviet Union, *op. cit.*

In a dispatch from Kiev dated April 19, 1966, the United Press International reported that the Kremlin had opened a campaign against anti-Soviet nationalist organizations that were alleged to have been infiltrating the Soviet Union since the end of World War II. (*The New York Times,* April 20, 1966.) On May 24, 1966, Peter Grose reported to *The New York Times* to the effect that the minority nationalities, especially the Ukrainians, remained a focus of dissidence and the object of attention on the part of emigre nationalist movements. (May 31, 1966.)

13. See, for example, letter dated 25 November 1961 from the Permanent Representative of the United States of America to the United Nations addressed to the President of the General Assembly, *(A/4985.)* In this 12-page letter, the late Adlai Stevenson charged the Soviet Union of pursuing policies and practices toward her minority nationalities and ethnic groups reminiscent of the worst forms of imperialistic and colonialist practices of the past and cited Soviet sources in substantiation.

14. See Owen Lattimore, *op. cit., supra* II, note 41; Francis Watson, *Ibid.*

15. *Supra,* pp.29-30 and notes.

16. Thus on April 2, 1963, the Soviet Union addressed a note to China in which it warned against Peking's efforts to make racism the basis of Chinese Communist tactics. (*The New York Times,* April 4, 1963.) In reply to this and a subsequent note, leading party newspapers in China accused the Soviet Union of propagating "white racism" and being an "apologist for neo-colonialism." (*Ibid,* October 23, 1963.)

17. In recent years the rivalries among the Croats, Serbs, Slovenes and other ethnic groups in Yugoslavia's heterogeneous population have been on the increase. In the spring of 1967, an argument between Croat and Serbian academicians about diphthongs and Serbian phrases was enough to bring to the surface ancient rivalries and more recent grievances dividing some or all of the six republics which make up Yugoslavia. A *Declaration on the Name and Position of the Croatian Literary Language* issued on March 16, 1967, by a number of Croatian cultural organizations, asking that Croatian be recognized as a separate language, instead of as a component of Serbo-Croatian, the principal language of the country, led to charges and counter charges of Serbian domination and regional nationalism and their combined threat to the integrity of the Yugoslav State. On March 26, 1967, President Tito warned that he would not tolerate anything that could lead to a revival of the old divisions between brother peoples of Yugoslavia. (*The New York Times,* March 27, 1967.) He repeated that warning time and again in the following days, as he had so often in the past on other occasions. Speaking at the centennial celebration of the Academy of Sciences and Arts in Zagreb, in November, 1966, the Yugoslav President pleaded for the need for cooperation and tolerance among Serbs, Croats and other nationalities. (*The New York Times,* November 11, 1966.)

In addition, Yugoslavia and Bulgaria have for more than sixty years been on the opposite sides of the Macedonian question, which has troubled the relations between the two countries whatever their internal regimes may have been. (See for example, *The New York Times*, April 3, 1964; February 16, 1965; September 18, 1966; November 20, 1966 and December 7, 1966.) There is also the question of the Albanian and Roumanian minorities in Yugoslavia, which from time to time comes into the open. (*The New York Times*, September 7, 1966.)

18. For texts, see *Cyprus: Presented to Parliament by the Secretary of State for the Colonies, the Secretary of State for Foreign Affairs and the Minister of Defence by Command of Her Majesty*, July, 1960, London, H. M's Stationery Office, Cmnd 1093.

19. For an authoritative statement of the background of the Cyprus problem, see *Report of the United Nations Mediator on Cyprus to the Secretary-General (S/6253, 26 March, 1965.)*

20. For the most recent statement of the position of the Cyprus Government, see (*E/4306*, 8 March 1967, pp.10-25; for the position of the Turkish Government, see *E/4306/Add.3*, 27 April 1967.)

21. Before we leave the continent of Europe, it is instructive to note that ancient ethnic divisions and animosities persist even in the most libertarian countries. Thus, for example, after more than 130 years of common nationality, the Flemish and Walloon communities in Belgium are as divided as ever over their rights and aspirations in the Kingdom. The fight of the Flemings, who are in a numerical majority, to preserve the integrity of their culture and to stop the expansion in Flanders of the French language which predominated for almost a century, and the fear of the Walloons of the ever-growing influence of the Flemings in Belgian political and economic life is a permanent threat to the unity of the nation. Bloody riots and other hostile acts have accompanied extremist demands for the division of the Kingdom into two autonomous Dutch-speaking and French-speaking states under a federal system of government. (For background information see, Shepard B. Clough, *A History of the Flemish Movement in Belgium*, New York, Richard R. Smith Inc., 1930; Maurice Pierre Herremans, *La Wallonie*, Bruxelles, Meurice, 1951.) There is no doubt that a careful cataloguing of the ethnic and territorial problems in Europe, from the Basque and Catalonia in Spain, to Greece, and from there across the continent to Wales would fill many pages. Thus on March 18, 1966, the Federal Court in Lausanne found three men guilty of terrorism in promoting the secession of the French-speaking population from the predominantly German Swiss Canton of Bern created more than a hundred and fifty years ago by the Treaty of Vienna in 1815. (See *The New York Times*, March 19, 1966.)

22. The Politics of the Developing Areas, *op. cit.*, p.416.

23. See *Ibid*, pp.239-246. For a more detailed discussion of the Indian nationalist movement, see A. R. Desai, *Social Background of Indian Nationalism*, Bombay, University of Bombay Publications, Sociology Series, No. 2, 1948; P. B. Sitaramaya, *The Nationalist Movement in India, Bombay*, Padma Publications, 1947; V. P. Varma, *Modern Indian Political Thought*, Agra, Lakshmi Narain Agarval, 1961; Michael Edwards, *Asia in the European Age, 1948-1955*, New York, Frederick A. Preager, 1962. See also *supra*, I, note 6.

24. *The New York Times*, January 27, 1960.

25. *Major Governments of Asia*, edited by George McT Kahin, second edition, Ithaca, Cornell University Press, 1963; Hugh Tinker, *India and Pakistan: A Political Analysis*, New York, Frederick A. Preager, 1962.

26. Hugh Tinker, *op. cit.*, p.137.

27. *Major Governments of Asia, op. cit.*, p.302.

28. Differences over the Constitution, especially over the question of residual authority of the Indian Government, led to a breakdown of negotiations and the resumption of guerilla fighting in September, 1964. Since then various attempts to negotiate a settlement, directly between the Indian Government and Naga insurgents and through the mediation of third parties, have yielded no results. On April 11, 1967, India's Foreign Minister told the Parliament that Naga groups were seeking arms and ammunition in China and training in sabotage and

guerilla techniques there to continue their fight for independence. (*The New York Times,* April 12, 1967.) For a statement of the Naga insurgents' case by one of their leaders, see A. Z. Phizo, *The Fate of the Naga People,* a report by the President of the Naga National Council, London, 1960 (mimeographed). Irregular reports are issued by the Indian Baptist Church Convention, which in 1964 established a peace mission to bring about a peaceful settlement of the Naga dispute. The Nagas are overwhelmingly Christian.

The Indian Government has faced other tribal rebellions. The most important of these has been the secessionist movement in the Mizo region in the State of Assam, where the Government was compelled to concede autonomy to the tribal districts in that State. On January 13, 1967, the Government announced that within six months Assam would be reorganized into two units—the plains and the hill districts—of equal status, with their own legislative assemblies and councils of ministers, but with a common governor and high court. (*The New York Times,* January 14, 1967.)

29. See *The New York Times,* March 10, 1966.

30. *The New York Times,* November 2, 1966.

31. Master Tara Singh, who in 1960-1961 dramatized the militant Sikh demands by fasting, is quoted to have said:

> We have adopted the linguistic principle because it suits us. We know that a genuinely Punjabi-speaking state will be such that the Sikh religion will be safe in it. Hugh Tinker, *op. cit.,* pp.138 and 155.

It should be noted that barely a month had passed since the division of Punjab when the Sikhs made new demands upon the Indian Government. These included the abolition of the common governership and High Court which linked the two states of Punjabi Subha and Hariani, and the incorporation into Punjabi Subha of certain border areas and the federally administered city of Chandigarh, joint capital of the two states. Threats of self-immolation on the part of Sikh leaders in support of their demands ended on December 26, 1966, in a tenuous agreement, according to which the demands for control of the Chandigarh would be arbitrated by Prime Minister Indira Gandhi and the other area disputes settled by a special commission. (*The New York Times,* December 27, 1966.)

32. For a clear exposition of India's struggle for national unity and against the centrifugal forces in her society, see Selig S. Harrison, *India: The Most Dangerous Decades,* Princeton, Princeton University Press, 1960.

33. *Major Governments of Asia, op. cit.,* sections on India and Pakistan. See also Baron Christopher Bromhead Birdwood, *India and Pakistan*: *A Continent Decides,* New York, Frederick A. Praeger, 1954.

34. These conclusions are compelled by a study of the more important statements made over the past twenty years in the Security Council and General Assembly of the United Nations by the representatives of India and Pakistan. See, for example, Palmer D. Edwards, *Law and Civilization,* Washington, D.C. Public Affairs Press, 1959; J. B. Das Gupta, *Indo-Pakistan Relations,* New York, Gregory Lunz, 1958; J. S. Bains, *India's International Disputes,* New York, Asia Publishing House, 1962.

35. The most serious clashes in more than a decade, they broke out within a week of the discovery of the theft on December 26, 1963, of a strand of hair of the Prophet Mohammed from a Mosque in Srinigar, Kashmir's capital, where the holy relic had been safeguarded for three centuries. For months thereafter refugees on both sides of the East Pakistan border were fleeing in opposite directions in the wake of much devastation resulting from the communial riots. For the official versions of the events, see releases issued by the Information Service of India at the Indian Embassy in Washington and by the Indian and Pakistani Missions to the United Nations in New York.

For text of the Tashkent Declaration, see (*S/7221,* 25 March 1965.) Subsequent events only showed that the understanding reached at Tashkent, like all other efforts which preceded it, failed in wrenching the Kashmir problem into a new path. From 1947 to February 1964, more than 100 meetings of the Security Council were devoted to the Kashmir dispute. (*S/PV. 1091:42.*)

36. *The Politics of the Developing Areas, op. cit.,* pp.153-246, *passim;* J. S. Bains, *op. cit.,* Chapter IV.

37. In January, 1965, Sir Lalitha Rajapakse, President of the Ceylon Buddhist Congress, was quoted as affirming that,

> The State must actively favor Buddhism and the Buddhists until they regain the dominant place they held in the kingdom of Kandy before the British came to this region and deposed the kings in 1815. (*The New York Times,* January 6, 1965.)

Evidence of Buddhist ascendancy may be seen, for example, in the abolition of the standard Sunday and its replacement by a so-called movable Sabbath which is governed by the phase of the moon. (See *The New York Times,* March 20, 1967.)

38. Although the law was declared unconstitutional by the District Court of Colombo (*The New York Times,* April 26, 1964) and the Government was compelled to make concessions to the minority languages, the linguistic conflict has continued unabated. On January 8, 1966, a Buddhist monk was killed and 91 persons injured in a clash in Colombo between the police and rioters, who protested Government-sponsored legislation in Parliament to permit the use of the Tamil language for Government business in the northern and eastern provinces where the Tamils predominate. (See *The New York Times,* January 9, 1966.)

39. For background information, see *The Politics of the Developing Areas, op. cit.,* pp.65-153, *passim; Governments and Politics in Southeast Asia, op. cit., supra,* III, note 1,pp.75-169, *passim.*

40. See, for example, *The New York Times,* April 13, 1962; March 13, 1964.

41. *The New York Times* of July 24, 1964, reported the arrival in Madras, India, of a shipload of 1,580 Indian refugees from Burma, victims of the nationalist and xenophobic policies of the Ne Win Revolutionary Government and of about 100,000 other Indians who were left destitute in Burma. (See also the May 2 and May 6, 1967, issues of *The New York Times.*)

42. For background information, see Victor Purcell, *The Chinese In Southeast Asia,* second edition, New York, Oxford University Press, 1965.

43. See, for example, John D. Legge, *Central Authority and Regional Autonomy in Indonesia: A Study in Local Administration, 1950-1960,* Ithaca, Cornell University Press, 1962; G. William Skinner, *Local, Ethnic and National Loyalties in Village Indonesia: A Symposium,* New Haven, Yale University Press, 1959.

44. *Major Governments of Asia, op. cit.,* p.656.

45. At Bandung, China made a major concession when it concluded the first dual nationality agreement in her history to end her traditional claim on all persons of Chinese nationality, whether or not they regarded themselves as Indonesians. The Agreement provided that all persons of Chinese extraction who lived in Indonesia could hold only one nationality. *Ibid,* p.686; also, Purcell, *op. cit.* Part VI (1949.)

46. A great number of popular articles have appeared on the subject, but an authoritative statement on the so-called Red Purge is still unavailable. The estimate of the number of Communists and pro-Communists slain range from eigthy thousand to a million and a half. See for example, *Indonesia's Night of Terror,* an exclusive report from Jakarta on the Red Purge, by Horace Sutton, *Saturday Review,* February 4, 1967; Seymour Topping's dispatch to the New York Times of August 24, 1966. Items that have appeared in the Press in the aftermath of the purge speak of the increasing insecurity of the Chinese population in Indonesia and of the constant diminution of their rights and liberties. (See, for example, *The New York Times,* March 26, 1967.)

47. For text of the Agreement on the formation of Malaysia, see *The New York Times,* July 10, 1963. For background information, see Victor Purcell, *op. cit.,* Part V; also, Victor Purcell, *Malaysia,* New York, Walker & Co., 1965; *Governments and Politics of Southeast Asia, op. cit.,* Part IV.

48. See, for example, *The New York Times,* July 22, 24 and 25, 1964; also *Malaysia, op. cit.,* closing chapter.

49. For background information, see *Major Governments of Asia, op. cit.,* pp.522-523; *The Politics of the Developing Areas, op. cit.,* pp.158-159 and pp.369-454, *passim.* The reference to this question is relatively rare and much of the information is derived from the press in New York and London, which reported rather extensively on the diplomatic break between Afghanistan and Pakistan on September 6, 1961. See also *Afghanistan News,* a monthly published by the Afghanistan information Bureau in Washington, D.C., especially the August and November, 1961, issues.

50. For background information, see *The Politics of the Developing Areas, op. cit.,* pp.369-454, *passim;* H. B. Sharabi, *Governments and Politics of the Middle East in the Twentieth Century,* Princeton, Princeton University Press, 1962. On June 29, 1966, the Iraqi Government announced a plan for recognition of Kurdish nationalism side by side with Arab nationalism, including the recognition of the Kurdish language as co-equal with Arabic in predominantly Kurdish areas, and for the decentralization of provincial and district administrations necessary to insure local autonomy for the Kurds. Other concessions in the twelve-point program, referred to Kurdish representation in the national legislature and government, the civil service, political organization and national elections. To what extent this program, which reportedly issued from negotiations with the Kurdish insurgents, has put a final end to the historic struggle or produced but another peaceful interlude, time will tell. For the summary of the twelve-point program, see *The New York Times,* June 30, 1966.

For a statement of the Kurdish position and their aspirations, see Letter to Secretary-General U Thant, dated January 7, 1965, and signed by Mustafa Barzani, President of the Command Council of the Revolution of Iraqi-Kurdistan; President of the Democratic Party of Iraqi-Kurdistan, Commander-in-Chief of the Revolution; Letter to Secretary General U Thant, dated April 20, 1965, and signed by Ismet Cheriff Vanly, Envoy at large of the Command Council of the Revolution and spokesman for General Mustafa Barzani; Letter to Secretary General U Thant dated April 28, 1965, and signed by Ismet Cheriff Vanly.

In 1963, the Soviet Union and Mongolia made unsuccessful attempts to place the Kurdish question on the agenda of United Nations bodies. See Communication of the head of the USSR Delegation to the 36th session of the Economic and Social Council, requesting the addition of an urgent item on the agenda entitled: *The policy of genocide which is being pursued by the Government of the Republic of Iraq against the Kurdish people.* (*E/3809,* 9 July 1963); Letter dated 9 July 1963 from the Permanent Representative of the USSR to the President of the Security Council, calling attention to the situation of the Kurdish people. (*S/5343,* 9 July 1963); Letter dated 10 July 1963 from the Permanent Representative of Iraq to the President of the Security Council, protesting the Soviet Union's interference in the domestic affairs of his country. (*E/5346,* 10 July 1963); Request of Mongolia for the inclusion of an Item on the Provisional Agenda of the Eighteenth Session of the General Assembly entitled: *The policy of genocide which is being pursued by the Government of the Republic of Iraq against the Kurdish People.* (A/5429, 2 July 1963.)

51. For background information, see *The Politics of the Developing Areas, op. cit.,* pp.247-368 and 369-454, *passim;* George H. T. Kimble, *Tropical Africa,* II, *op. cit., supra,* I note 6; Rupert Emerson, *From Empire to Nation: The Rise to Self-Assertion of Asian and African Peoples,* Cambridge, Harvard University Press, 1960; William Hanc, *The Geography of Modern Africa,* New York, Columbia University Press, 1964.

52. *Statutory Instruments,* HM's Stationery Office, 1958, No. 600.

53. *Ibid,* 1962, No. 405.

54. For text of the Constitution of the Congo Democratic Republic, see *Revue Egyptienne de Droit International*, pp.113-181 (1964.)

55. *Monthly Newsletter*, published by the United Nations High Commissioner for Refugees, No. 27, November, 1963.

56. *Refugees from Rwanda*, a First-hand Account by Thomas Jamieson, Director of Operations, *Ibid.* No. 30, February 1964; *The Situation in Rwanda and Burundi;* Summary of reports to the Secretary-General by Special Representative Max H. Dorsinville, UN OPI, *Press Release SG/SM/24*, 3 March 1964. The racial antagonisms between the two tribes has continued unabated.

57. *Ibid.* On November 28, 1966, the four hundred year old Monarchy was finally overthrown at the hands of more radical Watusis who preached revenge against Rwanda and organized raids across its frontiers. (See *The New York Times*, November 30, 1966.)

58. *The New York Times*, January 1, 1965.

59. *The New York Times*, January 16, 1966.

60. For a summary of General Aguiyi-Ironsi's policy statement broadcast over the Nigerian radio; see *The New York Times*, May 25, 1966.

61. *The New York Times*, June 2, 1966.

62. *The New York Times*, July 30, 31, August 1 and 2, 1966.

63. *The New York Times*, October 22, 1966.

64. *The New York Times*, October 4, 1966.

65. *The New York Times*, May 31, 1967. For an earlier statement of the Eastern Province's demands, see *The New York Times*, March 10, 1967 (Advertisement).

66. Quoted by Hedrick Smith in his dispatch to *The New York Times*, August 15, 1965.

67. On February 9, 1964, Secretary General U Thant sent messages to Emperor Hailie Selassie and to the Prime Minister of Somalia in which he expressed concern over the border fighting between the two countries. (For texts of their replies, see *UN OPI Press Release SG/SM/8*, 10 February 1964.)

68. For a statement setting forth Somali views, see letter circulated at the Headquarters of the United Nations on November 12, 1963, and signed by Ahmed Nur Sheck Hassan and Abdulahi Mohamed Saad, representatives of the Provisional Revolutionary Government of Ogadenia (Western Somalia).

69. On February 14, 1964, the Extraordinary Session of the Council of Ministers of the Organization of African Unity adopted unanimously a resolution asking the two countries immediately concerned to settle their dispute and refrain from provocative actions against each other's border. (For text see press release dated February 18, 1964, issued by the Permanent Mission of Somalia to the United Nations.) Still the dispute has continued unabated. On June 21, 1966, Kenya was reported to have severed all trade relations with the Somali Republic in protest against the latter's tolerance of the Somali irredentist movement. (*The New York Times*, June 22, 1966.)

70. For text see *A/5763*.

71. For text of the Protocole d'Accord of July 6, 1961, between King Hassan II and Ferhat Abbas, President of the Provisional Government of Algeria, see Permanent Mission of Morocco to the United Nations, *Official Document*, New York, October 20, 1961.

72. *The New York Times*, March 4, 1967.

73. Tom Mboya, *Freedom and After*, *op. cit., supra* I, note 6, pp.107;110.

74. *The New York Times*, May 5, 1966.

75. *The New York Times*, August 29, 1965.

76. *A Preliminary Report of the Royal Commission on Bilingualism and Biculturalism*, Ottawa, The Queens Printer, 1965, p.133.

77. For background information, see Gerald Clark, *Canada: The Uneasy Neighbor*, New York, David McKay Co., 1965; see also Mortimer Schiff, "Separatism in Quebec," XI *Midstream*, March, 1965.

78. Thus a Federal-Provincial conference called by Ottawa for early 1968, which was intended originally to deal with a Bill of Rights to be entrenched by mutual consent in a revised Canadian Constitution, was broadened in October, 1967, to include all constitutional questions without limitation.

79. Among the specific measures designed to ease tensions between French-speaking Quebec and the rest of Canada, the most symbolically important was undoubtedly the adoption on December 15, 1964, by the House of Commons, by a majority vote of 163 to 78, of a new flag free of every reminder of Canada's link with England or France. The historic red ensign, which had the British Union Jack in one corner, was replaced with a new maple leaf emblem.

80. Detailed information on this former British territory may be found in the reports of the United Nations Special Committee on the Situation with regard to the Implementation of the Declaration on the Granting of Independence to Colonial Countries and Peoples, especially, *A/5800/Rev. 1*, Chapter VII; *A/6000/Add. 7*, Chapter IX. See also *Report of the British Guiana Commission of Inquiry: Racial Problems in the Public Service*. Geneva, International Commission of Jurists, October, 1965.

81. See the text of the closing speech by the Secretary of State for the Colonies, The Rt. Hon. Anthony Greenwood, M. P., at the British Guiana Independence Conference, London, November 9, 1965. British Information Service, Reference and Library Division, New York, T.89, November 19, 1965.

82. *The New Yorw Times*, June 5, 1965.

83. See, *inter alia*, Charles Wagley and Marvin Harris, *Minorities in the New World: Six Case Studies*, New York, Columbia University Press, 1958; George Eaton Simpson and J. M. Yinger, *Racial and Cultural Minorities: An Analysis of Prejudice and Discrimination*, New York, Harper & Bros, 1953; Arnold Rose, *Race Prejudice and Discrimination: Readings in Intergroup Relations in the United States*, New York, Alfred A. Knopf, 1951; Harold R. Isaacs, *The New World of Negro Americans*, New York, The John Day Co., 1963; E. Ginzberg and A. S. Eichner, *The Troublesome Presence: American Democracy and the Negro*, New York, Glencoe Free Press, 1964.

NOTES TO CHAPTER X

1. For text see, UNESCO, *Proceedings of the Eleventh Session of the General Conference*, Vol. 11 C/Resolutions, Paris, 1960.

2. For text, see *U.N.G.A. Res. 2200* (XXI), 16 December 1966.

3. *Report of the Sub-Commission on the Prevention of Discrimination and the Protection of Minorities, First Session, 24 November - 6 December 1947, (E/CN.4/52*, Section V.) Perhaps the best monograph to date on the subject of minorities and the United Nations is Felix Ermacora's *Der Minderheitenschutz in der Arbeit der Vereinten Nationen*, Vienna, Wilhelm Braumüller, 1964.

4. See Annotations on the text of the draft International Covenant on Human Rights, *(A/2929:183-188.)*

5. In a statement to the Third Committee on November 8, 1955, Hermod Lannung of Denmark, the Committee's Chairman, observed:

> In am aware that article 25 in the Draft Covenant on Civil and Political Rights does establish certain rights for persons belonging to ethnic, religious or linguistic minorities; article 25 provides that they shall not be denied the right, in community with the other members of their group, to enjoy their own culture, to profess and practice their own religion, or to use their own language.

Article 25 is valuable and should certainly be maintained. But it does not protect national minorities against discrimination in cases like those I have mentioned.

Consequently, article 25 does not rule out a provision to the effect that the rights enunciated in the Covenants should be exercised without distinction of any kind, *including* association with a national minority.

Bearing these considerations in mind I formally propose a small addition to the second paragraph of article 2 in the Draft Covenants on Economic, Social and Cultural Rights, and to the first paragraph of article 2 in the Draft Covenant on Civil and Political Rights, to the effect that no discrimination should be tolerated on the ground of association with a national minority. (UN OPI, *Press Release PM/3067,* 8 November 1955.)

The proposal was not adopted. Upon completion of the Covenants the Articles were renumbered. This accounts for the variation in note 2 above.

6. The relevant debates in the Third Committee of the General Assembly are summarized in documents *A/C.3/SR.1103* and *1104.*

7. It may be noted that the reaction of the Great Powers at the Paris Peace Conference in 1946 to the idea of international protection of minorities was decidedly negative. Speaking on behalf of the United States, Lt. General W. Bedell Smith said:

It is difficult for a citizen of the United States to understand the desire to perpetuate racial minorities rather than absorb them. If you are going to provide for a minority in one state, you should do so in all states. Joseph B. Schechtman, *op. cit., suppra* IX, note 5, pp.17-18.

England's Lord Hood remarked:

I agree that our aim should be to assimilate racial minorities in the countries where they live rather than perpetuate them. *(Ibid.)*

The result was that the attempts of Hungary to seek international protection for the Hungarian minorities in Roumania and Czechoslovakia ended in failure, as did Yugoslavia's attempts to secure international protection for the Yugoslav minority in Hungary. As already noted, the Soviet Union was concerned to eradicate all traces of a possible irredentism in her sphere of immediate interest. *(Ibid,* pp.15-16.)

8. *S/PV. 1088:70,* 5 February 1960.

9. See *Annotations, op. cit.,* Ch. IV.

10. Text was furnished by the Permanent Mission of Australia to the United Nations, October 28, 1955.

11. For text see Canadian Mission to the United Nations, *Press Release No. 20,* 27 October 1955.

12. *A/C.3/SR. 642:14.*

13. *U.N.G.A. Res. 1514* (XV), 14 December 1960.

14. *A/PV. 800:16,* 21 September 1959.

15. *A/4395,* 23 June 1960.

16. United Nations Treaty Series, Vol. 49, No. 747, pp.184-185. For the Austrian position see, Herbert Mischler, *Südtirol als Völkerrechtsproblem,* Graz, Verlag Styria, 1962, and the following literature issued by the Office of the Press Attache, Permanent Mission of Austria to the United Nations: (a) *Fact and Comment on the South Tyrol,* September, 1960; (b) *Austria States the Case for South Tyrol,* October, 1960; (c) *South Tyrol: The Meaning of Autonomy,* October, 1960. See also Dr. Bruno Kreisky's statement to the Special political Committee of the General Assembly made on October 18, 1960, *(Press Release No. 9)*, and his statement to the Special Political Committee of October 26, 1960. *(Press Release No. 12.)* For the Italian position, see *Statement on the Question Regarding the*

German-speaking Inhabitants of Alto-Adige, published by the Italian Mission to the United Nations, September 23, 1960; *Alto-Adige,* published October 13, 1960. See also, Summary Outline of the Statement by the Foreign Minister of Italy, the Hon. Antonio Segni, to the Special Political Committee, October 18, 1960; His Statement to the Special Political Committee of October 26, 1960, and the Statement by the Hon. Gaetano Martino, Chairman of the Italian Delegation to the General Assembly of the United Nations, on Item 68 of the Agenda, 31 October 1960.

17. See *A/BUR/SR. 128,* 23 September 1960.
18. *A/SPC/SR. 181:7.*
19. *A/SPC/SR. 177:8-9.*
20. *A/SPC/SR. 179:9.*
21. *A/SPC/SR. 180:3.*
22. *A/SPC/SR. 182:35.*
23. *A/SPC/SR. 181:11.*
24. *A/SPC/SR. 181:15-17.*
25. *A/SPC/SR. 182:31.*
26. *A/SPC/SR. 182:9.*
27. *A/SPC/SR. 182:26.*
28. *A/SPC/SR. 184:9.*
29. *A/SPC/SR. 181:1-4; A/SPC/SR. 182:2.*
30. *A/SPC/SR. 178:40-41; A/SPC/SR. 180:4-7.*
31. *A/SPC/SR. 179:15-17.*
32. *A/SPC/SR. 180:12.*
33. For text see *supra,* note 16; also *A/SPC/SR. 176:31.*
34. *U.N.G.A. Res. 1497* (XV), 31 October 1960.
35. *U.N.G.A. Res. 217* (III) C, 10 December 1948.
36. *Prevention of Discrimination and Protection of Minorities: Report by the Secretary General under Council resolution 414 B II (XIII) on the future work of the United Nations in the fields of prevention of discrimination and protection of minorities.* (E/2229, 23 May 1952, pp.35-36.) From time to time the question of international protection of minorities is raised in one context or another in various organs of the United Nations, but invariably without practical consequence. As an example, reference may be made to the discussion which developed in the Sub-Commission on the Prevention of Discrimination and the Protection of Minorities at its sixteenth session in January, 1964, and in the Commission on Human Rights at its twentieth session in March, 1964, over a clause proposed by the Sub Commission's British and Italian Members for inclusion in the then draft Convention on the elimination of all forms of racial discrimination which, as finally drafted, would have specified that nothing in the Convention implied the recognition or denial of political or other rights to groups of persons of a common race, color, ethnic or national origin which existed or may exist as distinct groups within a State Party to the Covenant. Nothing came of the clause, for the reason that the difficulties of arriving at a concensus or at a wording which would have reflected the various governmental positions proved too great to overcome. Many feared that the clause served to sanction special rights for minorities, while others thought that it prejudiced existing minorities rights. (For the debate in the Sub-Commission, see *E/CN.4/Sub.2/SR.425-427;* also Report of the Sub-Commission, Sixteenth Session, *E/CN.4/873,* January 1964, pp.41-42; For the debate in the Commission on Human Rights, see *E/CN.4/SR.802-804* and *808-809.*)

37. On the question of the collective aspect of the right to manifest one's religion or belief, see Arcot Krishnaswami, *Study of Discrimination in the Matter of Religious Rights and Practices,* E/CN.4/Sub.2/200/Rev.1, 1960, pp.17-22. (pp.20-21 in printed copy, UN 60. XIV. 2.)

38. This was the burden of the argument of the United States member of the Sub-Commission on the Prevention of Discrimination and the Protection of

Minorities, when in 1964 he suggested that the definition of discrimination in the then draft Convention on the elimination of all forms of racial discrimination would be incomplete if it did not take into account the possibility or group discrimination. Accordingly, he proposed the following formulation:

> 1. In this Convention the term "racial discrimination" shall mean any distinction, exclusion, restriction or preference based on race, color, national or ethnic origin (and in case of States composed of different nationalities discrimination based on such difference) which has the purpose or effect of nullifying or impairing the recognition, enjoyment or exercise, on an equal footing, of human rights and fundamental freedoms in political, economic, social, cultural or any other field of public life set forth *inter alia* in the Universal Declaration of Human Rights. (See *E/CN.4/Sub.2/SR.411*.)

The reference to group discrimination was omitted, on the ground, so frequently stated, that the United Nations had always followed a policy of proclaiming individual human rights, rather than the rights of groups. (See *E/CN.4/SR. 784-786, passim.*)

39. As in the case of the South Tyrol five years earlier, the debate on the question of Cyprus in the Political Committee of the twentieth General Assembly session in 1965 revealed a strong bias against the very idea of minorities. The representative of Ecuador articulated the feeling of the majority, when he stated:

> The Constitution of Cyprus, which was never accepted by an expression of the free popular will, recognizes the existence of two communities and all its provisions are made in terms of this dichotomy, which constitutes a sort of political strabismus; everything in it tends to paralize action. Instead of tending toward the rational integration of the communities in a national spirit, it maintains discord, encourages separation, and holds back the normal process of the development of nation-hood ...

> The crux of the problem is to determine whether the principle of separate development or integration should be supported—a problem which we know is common in various States of the African continent, as well as in various sectors of opinion in other states of the world. I should like to point out that, for those of us who are part of integrated communities, we have no doubt whatsoever but that integration is the only approach ...

> As my delegation views the problem, we support and have always supported the right to protect minorities against any form of discrimination, but we have never accepted the political self-determination of minorities living with the territory of a sovereign state ... Separate development of the communities appears not only dangerous but also an inoperable theory. (*A/C.1/PV.1410;* pp.26-27.)

The representative of Nepal declared:

> My delegation is in full sympathy with the problem of minorities in Cyprus. We consider that their rights should be fully protected. The traditional concept of the protection of minority rights through constitutional methods, as practiced in different countries where problems of minorities exist as political problems, should be rigidly enforced in the case of Cyprus. But my delegation is strongly opposed to the idea of viewing the problem of minorities in any country from an artificial angle, and we feel aghast if we find that the minorities are used for subversive purposes by external powers. Any attempt to reopen the issue of settled frontiers through the use of minorities of other countries is contrary to all norms of international behaviour and would only lead to disruption of international peace. This applies equally to the countries of all the continents ... (*A/C.1/PV.1410*, p.37.)

In the same vein, the Indian representative warned:

> Many states of Africa, Asia and Latin America are multi-racial, multi-religious and multi-lingual. What these countries consider to be of paramount and overriding importance is their unity and their territorial integrity. Nothing should or could bring into question this unity and integrity of the State ... *(A/C.1/PV.1411,* p.6.)

Speaking for African nations, the representative of Kenya declared that his country

> believes that all sovereign states should be supported in their endeavor to function democratically. The democratic process entails two fundamental principles. One, that in a given State, when a decision is to be made, the views of the majority should prevail provided that such views take into account individual liberty and the rule of law. Secondly, while the minority in such a State should expect that their views would be taken into account, it would be perverting the democratic process if such minority views were either to be equated with the views held by the majority or the minority views were allowed to prevail ... *(A/C.1/PV.1409,* p.32.)

The representative of Togo stated:

> It was about five years ago that Cyprus finally turned the page of several centuries of foreign domination. But, during those five years, the people of Cyprus, fully liberated from the colonial yoke, far from uniting to build a nation in an awareness of their rediscovered common homeland, have deliberately engaged in the path of division and of armed confrontation and disorder. This is because the two ethnic communities principally concerned have not agreed to cease to live in an atmosphere of suspicion and mutual distrust, because both Greek Cypriots and Turkish Cypriots have refused obstinately to renounce their respective origins, and because they have not become an integrated community in their new country, because both sides have endorsed the centuries-old antagonism which has divided Greece and Turkey and have willingly permitted themselves to be guided by the self-serving counsels of the leaders of their countries of origin ...
>
> In the light of the statements made by both sides, it would appear easy to fix the origin of the situation which continues to prevail in Cyprus, where everything happens as though the Greek Cypriots were more than ever determined to remain Greeks in Cyprus, and the Turkish Cypriots to remain Turks in Cyprus. Neither side apparently wishes to accept the overriding necessity of being pure and simple Cypriots, and nothing but Cypriots in Cyprus and in the world ... *(A/C.1/PV.1409,* pp.26-28.)

And the representative of Uganda had this to say:

> My delegation naturally understands Turkey's concern over the question of the Turkish minority in Cyprus, but we cannot seriously endorse the idea that any country can correctly speak of two separate communities or speak of the division of Cyprus into two separate entities. We have experienced the same thing ourselves in our country, where we have minorities groups from our continent. Although before independence the colonial Power tried to find a way to include in our independent Constitution some safeguards, which they described at the time as adequate and effective for the minority races, the minorities themselves did not raise this point, and after independence, and with no special safeguards entrenched in our Constitution, my Government respected the view that everybody should be protected equally under the laws of Uganda, regardless of his origin. And as a result, most of the minority groups have taken Uganda nationality and are living together happily ... *(A/C.1/PV.1413,* p.3.)

40. Report of the United Nations Mediator on Cyprus to the Secretary-General *(S/6253:158-173,* 26 March 1965.)

NOTES TO CHAPTER XI

1. See *supra*, pp.148-149. Under the title *Racialism is an African Sickness, Too*, George H. T. Kimble wrote in *The New York Times Magazine* of October 11, 1964, that there was a resurgence of racialism in Africa and that there was to it much more than antagonism and prejudice based on color. Color, he notes, of course, is part of the problem of Africa. But physical differences play an important part, too. To many Africans, differences of stature, carriage, facial features, texture of hair and "looks" generally are as provocative of prejudice as differences of color. The Watusi's height and patrician bearing, for example, have been in part responsible for the antagonism towards him of the smaller, coarser-featured Bahutu. In general, belief in the inherent inequality of people is encountered in many African societies.

2. See, for example, Emanuel John Hevi, *An African Student in China*, New York, Frederick A. Praeger, 1963, in which this Ghanian student shows that the Chinese could be as guilty of flagrant anti-black racial discrimination as any white imperialist or colonialist nation of the 19th century. And as in Moscow, Sofia and Prague, Communist professions of racial equality were shown to be quite empty in Peking, especially when African students began to associate with Chinese girls.

   Student demonstrations in Moscow in September, 1963, destroyed the myth that there were no problems of racial prejudice in the Soviet Union. Hundreds of African students battled Moscow's police following the death of a Ghanian student accused of "offending Russian womanhood." According to a dispatch to *The New York Times* of May 28, 1964, a series of articles by Nigerian journalist Geilbert Ofodile in *The Daily Times* of Lagos on student life behind the Iron Curtain, revealed the existence of official discrimination against African students. See also "Africans Don't Go to Russia to be Brainwashed," by Nicholas Nyangira, A Kenyan student and recipient of a Soviet scholarship at the University of Baku, *The New York Times Magazine*, May 16, 1965.

3. Sydney Collins, *Coloured Minorities in Britain: Studies in British Race Relations based on African West Indian and Asiatic Immigrants*, London, Lutterworth Press, 1957; J. A. G. Griffith and others, *Coloured Immigrants in Britain*, London, Oxford University Press, 1960. The first serious race riots in England took place in 1959 in Nottingham Hill Gate London. They revealed the existence of a race relations problem of no mean proportions and led to the enactment by Parliament of suitable legislation. For a brief review of measures taken to combat racial discrimination in the United Kingdom, see *E/4174*/Add. 3, 23 May 1966.

4. There have been many reports to the effect that Communist China had from time to time resorted to racial prejudice in her fight against the Soviet Union. Thus in July, 1963, *Izvestia* wrote:

> What can one say about the Chinese comrades who, announcing themselves as the first Marxists in the world, put out in a sneaky way the idea that the peoples of some definite region of the world are more revolutionary, more anti-imperialist-minded than others?
>
> This is indoctrinating the people of these regions (Asia, Africa and perhaps Latin America) with the idea of their exclusivity, their advantages over the white race.
>
> They blasphemously place an equal sign between the exploiting white upper classes, who suppressed the colored peoples, and the toiling masses of the West who have always fought against this upper class?
>
> Modern splitters are telling the people of Africa and Asia that the West is West and white people remain white. This drive is being camouflaged with many words, but it is maintaining that only the people of young revolutionary continents (whose skins happen to be colored) with nothing to lose can overthrow capitalism. (*New York World Telegram*, July 17, 1963.)

C. L. Sulzberger reported in his column in *The New York Times* of April 4, 1964, that Chinese publications in Burundi and adjoining areas carried as their principle message hostility to the white race, clearly including Russians and the West.

In May, 1964, *Izvestia* published a 2000-word statement the Soviet Government sent to all governments in Asia and Africa in which it denounced the "racist" policies of the Chinese, who sought to bar the participation of the Soviet Union in a Second Bandung Conference which had been scheduled for March, 1965, on the ground that the USSR was not an Asian power. The Soviet Union pointed out that she was not only the largest European, but also the largest Asian country in terms of territory and almost twice as large as China, and accussed her that under the pretext of "racial solidarity," the Chinese were trying to erect a great "Chinese wall" between the white, black and yellow peoples. (*The New York Times,* May 5, 1964.) On August 14, 1964, the Soviet Union notified all independent Asian and African governments that she was voluntarily withdrawing her bid for participation in the Second Bandung Conference in order to spare embarrassment to her friends, and repeated the accusation of Chinese racialism. (USSR, Mission to the United Nations, No. 51, August 14, 1964.)

5. For a brief history of *apartheid,* see L. E. Neame, *The History of Apartheid: The Story of the Color War in South Africa,* London, House & Maxwell, 1962; for more detailed information, see Julius Lewin, *Politics and Law in South Africa,* London, Marlin Press, 1963; Pierre L. Van der Berghe, *South Africa: A Study in Conflict,* Middletown, Conn., Wesleyan University Press, 1965. The South African Government's view of *apartheid* is succinctly stated in a pamphlet by John E. Holloway, *The Problem of Race Relations in South Africa,* distributed by the South African Information Office in New York. Current information regarding the situation in South Africa is to be found in the vast documentation on *apartheid* produced by United Nations bodies immediately concerned, as well as by the International Labour Organization. (See, for example, *Report of the Special Committee on the Policies of Apartheid of the Government of South Africa, A/6486,* 25 October 1966.)

The meaning of *apartheid,* as an immense human and personal tragedy, was explained with shattering clarity by Nelson Mandela, when on April 20, 1964, he rose in the courts of Pretoria in his own defense against charges of sabotage, which carries with it the death penalty. Said Mr. Mandela, who has been widely known as the Black Pimpernel:

> The lack of human dignity experienced by Africans is the direct result of the policy of White supremacy. White supremacy implies Black inferiority. Legislation designed to preserve White supremacy entrenches this notion. Menial tasks in South Africa are invariably performed by Africans. When anything has to be carried or cleaned the White man will look around for an African to do it for him, whether the African is employed by him or not. Because of this sort of attitude, Whites tend to regard Africans as a separate breed. They do not look upon them as people with families of their own; they do not realize that they have emotions—that they fall in love like White people do; that they want to be with their wives and children like White people want to be with theirs; that they want to earn enough money to support their families properly, to feed and clothe them and send them to school. And what "house-boy" or "garden-boy" or labourer can ever hope to do this? . . .
>
> Africans want to be paid a living wage. Africans want to perform work which they are capable of doing, and not work which the Government declares them to be capable of. Africans want to be allowed to live where they obtain work and not be endorsed out of an area because they were not born there. Africans want to be allowed to own land in places where they work and not be obliged to live in rented houses which they can never call their own. Africans want to be part of the general population and not confined to living in their own ghettos. African men want to have their wives and children live with them where they work and not be forced into an unnatural

existence in men's hostels. African women want to be with their men folk and not be left permanently widowed in the reserves. Africans want to be allowed out after 11 o'clock at night and not be confined to their rooms like little children. Africans want to be allowed to travel in their own country and to seek work where they want to and not where the Labour Bureau tells them to. Africans want a just share in the whole of South Africa; they want security and a stake in society...(Special Committee on the Policies of *Apartheid* of the Government of the Republic of South Africa, *A/AC.115/ L. 67,* 6 May 1964, pp.32-33.)

6. Special Committee on the Policies of *Apartheid* of the Government of the Republic of South Africa, (*A/AC.115/L.68,* 6 May, 1964, p.5.)

7. *A/SPC/SR.381:8,* 8 October 1963.

8. *A/SPC/SR.388:12,* 21 October 1963, p.6.

9. Australia, Belgium, France, Luxembourg, South Africa and the United Kingdom voted for the South African motion; Denmark, Iceland, Norway and Sweden voted with the Asian, African and all but four of the Latin American countries against the motion; while Argentina, Canada, the Dominican Republic, Greece, Netherlands, New Zealand, Peru, Turkey and Venezuela abstained. (*A/PV. 401,* 5 December 1952, p.38.)

10. All countries that voted against the establishment of the three-member Commission were Western European. The United States abstained. (*Ibid*, p.41.)

11. *U.N.G.A. Res. 1978* (XVIII) 4 December 1963, *S/AC.14/L.3/Add. 1,* 1 September 1964. This document contains the texts of all resolutions on racial discrimination in South Africa adopted by the General Assembly and the Security Council through August 30, 1964.

12. *Ibid*, p.28.

13. *Ibid*, p.35.

14. *Ibid*, p.33.

15. *Ibid*, p.28.

16. *Ibid*, p.33.

17. *Ibid*, p.29.

18. *Ibid*, p.40.

19. *U.N.G.A. Res. 2054* (XX), 15 December 1965. See also *E/4226,* 30 June 1966. This document brings together texts or extracts of decisions by United Nations relevant, *inter alia,* to the South African situation through the middle of 1966.

20. *S/5658,* 20 April 1964, p.9.

21. See *supra* Note 18. In a communication dated November 16, 1964, the South African Government refused to respond to the invitation contained in the Council's resolution, claiming that the resolution represented intervention in matters falling within the domestic jurisdiction of States. (*S/6056,* 16 November 1964.)

The Expert Committee was unable to reach agreement on its conclusions concerning the economic sanctions against South Africa, which required universal application and an adequate machinery to prevent the circumvention of the measures by States and individuals and to deal with problems arising from non-cooperation of any State. (See Letter dated 20 August 1964 from the Chairman of the Expert Committee Established in pursuance of Security Council Resolution *S/5773* addressed to the Permanent Representatives of Member States, *S/AC.14/ L.3,* 20 August 1964.)

22. *ECOSOC Res. 2028* (XXXVI), 30 July 1963.

23. See *A/5454,* 23 July 1963.

24. *UN OPI Press Release ILO/1399,* 16 March 1964. See also *Apartheid in Labor Matters: ILO Policy Statements and Reports concerning Apartheid in Labor Matters in the Republic of South Africa,* Geneva, International Labour Organization, 1966.

25. *S/5348*, 11 July 1963.

26. *Program for Peace and International Cooperation*, NAC-II/Heads/5, October 10, 1964.

27. *A/AC. 115/L. 68, op. cit.*, p.6.

28. *U.N.G.A. Res. 2054* (XX) A, 15 December 1965.

29. See, for example, *Question of Southern Rhodesia*, a working paper prepared by the United Nations Secretariat for the Special Committee on the Situation with regard to the Implementation of the Declaration on the Granting of Independence to Colonial Countries and Peoples *(A/AC.109/L.264*, 18 March 1966.)

30. *U.N.G.A. Res. 1514* (XV), 14 December 1960.

31. See, for example, Security Council Resolution of 23 November 1965, *E/4226, op. cit.* p.47, and General Assembly Resolution 2184, XXII, of 12 December 1966. On the question of South West Africa, see, for example, *Report of the Ad Hoc Committee for South West Africa, A/6640*, 7 April 1967.

32. In this connection, the following statement made by Guinea's former representative to the United Nations in the Special Political Committee in October, 1963, is illustrative:

> The present leaders of South Africa have been militant Nazis in the past, but the system they have introduced in South Africa is worse in every respect than the Nazism that Europe experienced. Indeed, whereas it was mainly ethnic and religious minorities that the Nazis persecuted, the neo-Nazism which prevails in South Africa oppresses the vast majority of the population. *(A/SPC/SR. 381*, 8 October 1963, p.8.)

NOTES TO CHAPTER XII

1. *UN, OPI, Press Release/SG/SM/488*, pp.6-7.

2. *World Bank Atlas of Per Capita Product and Population*, International Bank for Reconstruction and Development, Washington, D.C., September, 1966.

3. Exclusive of mainland China. See P.V. Sukhatme, "The World's Hunger and Future Needs in Food Supplies," *The Journal of the Royal Statistical Society*, Series A (General), Vol. 124, Part 4, 1961; also, *Progress Report by the Secretary-General on Multilateral Food Aid, E/4352*, 6 June 1967; *Six Billions to Feed*, World Food Problems, No. 4, Food and Agriculture Organization, Rome, 1962.

4. *E/3613*, 1962, p.59.

5. *The New York Times*, April 21, 1963.

6. Rene Maheu, Director-General of UNESCO, in a statement made at the Second Committee of the Eighteenth General Assembly, 1963. See also, *World Campaign for Universal Literacy: Report by UNESCO, E/3771*, 23 May 1963.

7. United Nations Statistical Yearbook, 1965, pp.106-107.

8. Report of the World Health Organization, 1966, *E/4197/Add. 1*, p.3.

9. *Ibid*, p.9.

10. *Provisional Report on World Population Prospects, as Assessed in 1963, ST/SOA/SER.R/7/1964*. For a summary see *UN OPI, Press Release SOC/3313*, 16 September 1964.

11. *Ibid*.

12. *UN OPI, Press Release ECAFE/344*, p.3.

13. UN OPI, Background Paper No. 20, September, 1966.

14. Rene Maheu, *op. cit.*

15. *The New York Times*, (editorial) , June 18, 1966.

16. *Children of the Developing Countries: A Report by UNICEF, (UNICEF/MISC.64/Rev. 1*, January, 1963, p.25;) *Integration of the problems of children and Youth in national economic and social plans in Africa. (E/ICEF/549*, 30 July 1966.)

17. *Ibid, passim.* See also, *The United Nations Development Decade at Mid-Point:* an Appraisal by the Secretary-General, *(E/4071,* 11 June, 1965.)

18. Economic Commission for Latin America, Tenth Session, 1963, *E/CN.12/686,* p.2.

19. See *Report on the World Social Situation,* 1963, *E/CN.5/375,* 4 March 1963, and Addenda 1 and 2. Add. 2 deals with social developments in Latin America, Middle East, Asia and Africa.

20. Report on the World Social Situation, *op. cit.,* p.32.

21. Octave Gelinier, *Morale de l'Entreprise et Destin de la Nation,* Plon, Paris, 1965.

22. *Social Change and Economic Development,* UNESCO, Paris, 1963; *Social Research and Problems of Rural Development in South East Asia,* UNESCO, Paris, 1963. See also, *Social Development in the Americas,* Eighth Conference of American States, Members of the ILO, Ottawa, 1966, Report I, ILO, Geneva, 1966; *Report on the World Social Situation: With Special Reference to Popular Participation and Motivation for Development, (E/CN.5/402/Add.1,* 7 March 1966.)

23. See, for example, *Basic Agrarian Structural Issue in the Adjustment of African Customary Tenures to the Needs of Agricultural Development,* Food and Agriculture Organization, *(RU:WLR/66/C.,* June 1966.)

24. *Review of the Implementation of the Recommendations of the Conference; Review of International Trade and Development,* Report by the Secretary General of the United Nations Conference on Trade and Development, *(TD/B/82/Add.2,* 20 July 1966, p.46.)

25. *Ibid.* pp.48-49; see, *inter alia, The Impact of Western European Integration on African Trade and Development, (E/CN.14/72,* 7 December 1960;) *Trade with Europe and Latin American Trade Policy, (E/CN.12/667,* 28 March 1963;) *Report of the Permanent Sub-Committee on Commodities on its First Session, (TD/B/C.1/21,* 26 July 1966.)

26. *E/CN.11/709,* pp.38-39. Addressing a joint meeting of bodies concerned with African trade of the Organization for African Unity and the Economic Commission for Africa in August, 1966, at Geneva, Diallo Telli, Secretary General of the Organization for African Unity asked that,

> without prejudice to science and progress, means should be sought to ease off the competition of synthetic materials with African primary goods. Developed countries are in a better position to effect some reallocation of resources thus resulting in the ease of competition on primary goods produced in Africa, without much difficulty. (*Report of the Extraordinary Joint Meeting of the ECA Working Party on Intra-African Trade and OAU Ad Hoc Committee of Fourteen on Trade and Development. E/CN.14/361,*29 August 1966, Annex I, p.3.)

27. *TD/B/82/Add. 2, op. cit.* Chapter IV, pp.96-136, *passim.*

28. *TD/BC.2/L.17,* 3 March 1966.

29. *TD/B/82/Add.2, op. cit.* p.73.

30. *Ibid,* Chapter III, pp.68-95; *passim.*

31. *The United Nations Development Decade: Proposals for Action,* UN. Publication, Sales No. 62 II B.2. *United Nations Development Decade: Activities of the United Nations and Related Agencies in the Immediate Future, (E/3776,* May, 1963;) *The United Nations Development Decade at Mid-Point: An Appraisal by the Secretary General, (E/4071,* May, 1965.) Perhaps the best guide to United Nations activities in behalf of the developing areas is the annual report of the Secretary General under the heading: *Work Programme of the United Nations in the Economic, Social, and Human Rights Fields and its Budgetary Requirements,* more particularly the Report for 1966. *(E/4179/Rev.1,* May 1966 and Addenda 1) through 18. For the work of the Specialized Agencies, see annual reports of these agencies to the Economic and Social Council. For a brief survey of United States foreign aid, see *The Aid Story,* a popular pamphlet published by the Agency for

International Development, Washington, D.C., August, 1966. For a brief review of the Colombo Plan see, for example, Summary published by the British Information Services in New York on January 15, 1965, (T. 47) of the 13th Report of the Consultative Committee of the Colombo Plan for Cooperative Economic Development in South and Southeast Asia. (P. 11646). For a study of Soviet Foreign Aid Operations, see Marshall I. Goldman, *Soviet Foreign Aid*, New York, Frederick A. Praeger, 1967. From time to time the Information Office of the Permanent Mission of the USSR to the United Nations publishes information on the foreign aid programs of other socialist countries.

32. *E/4196:301*, 5 May 1965.

33. The problem of anachronistic social structures has been pointedly illustrated in Latin America. While the countries in Latin America are not underdeveloped in the sense that the term is used for Africa and Asia, virtually all of them have no socially equitable distribution of wealth approaching the degree to which it is found in North America and most of Western Europe. The exceptions are Mexico and Chile, where serious attempts have been made to reduce the social imbalances inherited from the past. See, for example, Milton S. Eisenhower, *The Wine is Bitter, op. cit. supra* III, note 44; Tad Szulc, *op. cit.; The Politics of Change in Latin America, op. cit.* See also Irving Louis Horowiz, *Revolution in Brazil: Politics and Society in a Developing Country*, New York, E. P. Dutton & Co., 1964. In the Declaration of Bogota of August 16, 1966 (supra, III, note 45), the Presidents of Chile, Colombia and Venezuela, and the Presidents of Ecuador and Peru, through their personal emissaries, stated that,

> We are convinced that the strengthening of the institutions of representative democracy, through the active efforts of the people and their growing participation in the benefits of progress, respect for human rights and economic and social development are indispensable and inseparable conditions upon which the well-being of the American nations depend. (See also the Declaration of American Chiefs of State at Punta del Este, of April 14, 1967, supra, III, note 45.)

34. *A/6301/Add. 1*, p.6. See also Encyclical Letter of Pope Paul VI, *Populorum Progressio, The New York Times*, March 29, 1967.

35. *A/PV. 1414*, 25 September 1966, p.108.

36. See, for example, Barbara Ward, *The Rich Nations and the Poor Nations*, New York, W. W. Norton & Co., 1962; Robert L. Heilbronner, *The Great Ascent*, New York, Harper & Row, 1962; Herbert Feis, *Foreign Aid and Foreign Policy*, New York, St. Martin's Press, 1964; Frank M. Coffin, *Witness for Aid*, Boston, Houghton, Miflin & Co., 1964; William and Paul Paddock, *Hungry Nations*, Boston, Little, Brown & Co., 1965; Asher Brynes, *We Give to Conquer*, New York, 1967.

37. Thus, in his statement at the opening session of the Committee for Development Planning on May 2, 1966, Under Secretary for Economic and Social Affairs, Philipe de Seynes, told the newly created United Nations body:

> ... At a moment when we are setting up a new organ to promote industrial development—I refer to the United Nations Organization for Industrial Development, a body in which so many hopes have been placed—it would be somewhat disingenuous to tackle the problem of the industrialization of the under developed countries while continuing to turn a blind eye to the deficiencies of our present international division of labor ... Tariff systems and trade policies are not at present calculated to assist the accelerated industrialization of the countries of the Third World. Experience has shown us that it is somewhat sterile to discuss tariff systems and trade policies in the abstract and without having available a schema, even of a rudimentary kind, indicating what kinds and types of industries can develop most naturally in the varying conditions of the Third World ... (*E/AC.54/L.2*, 2 May 1966, p.6.)

Paul Prebisch, the Secretary General of the United Nations Conference on Trade and Development, told the GATT Committee on Trade and Development on January 17, 1967:

> ... Yesterday we listened with keen interest to an account of what has been done over the past twenty years to achieve the aims of liberalizing world trade policy on primary commodities. While acknowledging what has been achieved in that direction, it is plain that the developing world still has to contend with excessive protectionism, which aggravates instead of mitigating the adverse effects of technical progress on primary exports. Perhaps the most striking case is that of sugar. If there had been a deliberate intention to create a state of affairs that would disrupt the export trade of developing countries, nothing could have been more to the purpose than the situation that exists in the sugar market today, where extremely high-cost production in the industrialized countries is encouraged at the expense of low-cost production in the developing countries. *(TD/B/114*, 30 January 1967, p.2.)

Concerning manufactures, Mr. Prebisch declared:

> It has at last been recognized that trade policy must differentiate between developed and the developing countries, and that what is good for the one group is not necessarily good for the other. Fortunately, this principle of non-reciprocity, more aptly termed implicit reciprocity, has been recognized and it is to be hoped that it may have fruitful, practical results in the Kennedy Round ... Let us hope that reductions of 50 per cent or more can be achieved for the products of interest to the developing countries, without the condition of reciprocity. But I wonder whether, even on the most favorable assumption concerning the Kennedy Round, this will suffice to solve the serious problems of the external bottleneck which, in varying degrees, beset the developing countries. I do not think it will; I believe that, although a substantial cut in tariffs will certainly encourage some exports of manufactures from the developing to the industrial countries, it will not achieve the much greater results that would be produced by cutting the remaining 50 per cent, not for all countries—weak and strong—alike but only for the weaker part of the international economic system ... *(Ibid*, p.3.)

It would take us far afield to go into details concerning the economic and trade relations between the developed and developing countries. One has only to go through the proceedings of the United Nations Conference on Trade and Development, a permanent organization which convened for the first time in Geneva on March 23, 1964, to realize the depth of the feeling of the developing nations on the need for a new order of economic relationships, based on new attitudes and new responsibilities which would converge toward a new trade policy for economic development. (For a brief review of the Conference, see, *UN OPI: United Nations Conference on Trade and Development, Geneva, 23 March - 16 June, 1964: I-A Review of Action Taken by the Conference; II- An Appraisal of Its Impact on Public Opinion.*) Perhaps this is best illustrated by the adoption by the General Assembly's Second Committee on November 7, 1966, of a Bolivian amendment to a resolution on the Permanent Sovereignty over Natural Resources, which calls upon developed countries to refrain from placing non-commercial reserves of primary commodities on the world market when such action would adversely affect the foreign exchange earnings of developing countries. The amendment was adopted by a roll-call vote of 58 in favor to 2 against with 47 abstentions. *(Draft Report of the Second Committee. A/C.2/L.894*, 16 November 1966.) As the representative of the United Kingdom pointed out, the Bolivian proposal was completely out of place in a resolution of this kind. (United Kingdom Mission to the United Nations, *Press Release No. 60.*)

38. See Statement before the Economic and Social Council by George D. Woods President of the International Bank for Reconstruction and Development. Intei national Finance Corporation and International Development Association, on 2b February 1966. (*UN OPI Press Release/IB/1726*, 24 February 1966.) See also *UN OPI Press Release/ECAFE/438*, 30 March 1967, which cites the Economic Committee for the Far East Economic Survey, 1966, to the effect that the debt service ratio has reached disquieting levels in some countries. See also *International Flow of Long-term Capital and Official Donations, (E/4171* and Addenda 1 & 2, 23 May 1967;) *Problems of Debt Servicing, (TD/B/C.3/35, 36 & 37*, January-February, 1967.)

39. *The New York Times*, April 10, 1966.

40. *The New York Times*, September 4, 1966. In fact, one of the major projects of the International Labour Organization, launched in 1967, is a study of the causes of "brain drain." It calls for an inquiry into the migration of highly-skilled workers from developing countries, where they are scarcest, to advanced countries, where they are plentiful. The study also calls for devising measures to check this drain of manpower at a national and, possible, international level. (*UN OPI Press Release/ILO/1536*, 18 May 1967.)

41. *The New York Times*, May 19, 1966.

42. *Ibid.*

43. *TD/B/103/Rev. 1*, 31 August 1966, p.2.

44. See Proceedings of the General Assembly of the International Social Science Council under the auspices of UNESCO held in Paris 12-15 September 1961. (UNESCO, *Press Release NYO/24*, 29 September 1961.)

45. *The New York Times*, September 16, 1966.

NOTES TO CHAPTER XIII

1. *Dag Hammarskjöld: Speeches and Statements, op. cit., supra*, IV, note 9.

2. Anacharsis Cloots, *La Republique Universelle, ou Addresse aux Tyranicides*, Paris, n.p.1792. (Copy in British Museum). See also C. Richter, *Anacharsis Cloots: Ein historishes Bild aus der Französischen Revolution von 1789*, Berlin, J. Springer, 1865; Henri Baulig, "Anacharsis Cloots, Journaliste et Theoreticien," 41 *La Revolucion Française*, 1901; and G. Avenel, *Anacharsis Cloots*, Paris, A. Lacroix, Verboeckhoven & Cie., 1865, 2 vols.

3. Martin Buber, *Pointing the Way: Collected Essays*, translated from the German by Maurice Friedman, New York, Harper & Bros, 1957, p.166.

4. *Man and the State, op. cit., supra* III, note 21.

5. Peter Pavel Remec, *The Position of the Individual in International Law, according to Grotius and Vattel*, The Hague, Martinus Nijhoff, 1960, *passim*.

6. See, for example, B. V. A. Rölling, *International Law in an Expanded World*, Amsterdam, Diambatan, N. V., 1960; Carl Aage Norgaard, *The Position of the Individual in International Law*, Copenhagen, Einar Munskgaard Ltd., 1962; C. W. Jenks, *Common Law of Mankind*, London, Stevens & Co., 1958; H. Lauterpacht, *International Law and Human Rights, op. cit., supra*, VI, note 1. Myres McDougal and Associates, *Studies in Public Order*, New Haven, Yale University Press, 1960.

7. *Human Rights and World Order, op. cit., supra*, VI, note 8.

8. *The Nuremberg Trials in International Law, op. cit., supra*, VI, note 6; *The Crime of State, Ibid.*

9. In a pioneering decision in the case of N. V. Algemene Transporten Expeditie Onderneming van Gend & Loos *vs.* Administration Fiscale Neerlandaise, the Court of Justice of the European Coal and Steel Community ruled that the Treaty which brought that Community into existence did not exhaust itself in

the creation of reciprocal obligations of the member states; rather,

> it must be concluded from this state of affairs that the Community constitutes a novel juridical order of international legal character for the benefit of which the states, though only in limited areas, have limited their sovereign rights and the subjects of which are not only the member states but also their nationals; consequently, Community Law, independent of the legislation of the member states, creates not only burdens upon the individuals as such but, conversely, it also is apt to entail rights which enter into their legal patrimony.

The reporter adds that,

> The Court made it abundantly clear that it attached to the Community the character of an independent and novel legal order of international nature with sovereign rights of its own and direct operation upon its subjects, so as to vest them with individual rights and duties capable of being asserted before national tribunals. (*58 The American Journal of International Law,* pp.152-149, 1964).

10. See, for example, Gordon Lee Weill, *The European Convention on Human Rights: Background, Development and Prospects,* Leyden, A. W. Sijthoff, 1963.

11. See Carlos Garcia Bauer, *Los Derechos Humanos: Preocupación Universal, op. cit. supra* VII, note 6. Part II. Chapter VI.

12. The most important achievements to date are undoubtedly the International Convention on the Elimination of all Forms of Racial Discrimination of December 21, 1935. For an excellent analysis of this Convention see Egon Schwelb, "The International Convention on the Elimination of All Forms of Racial Discrimination," *The International and Comparative Law Quarterly,* October 1966; and the International Covenant on Economic, Social and Cultural Rights, the International Covenant on Political and Civil Rights, and the Optional Protocol to the Covenant on Political and Civil Rights, which were adopted by the General Assembly on December 16, 1966. (For texts, see *UNGA Res. 2200 (XXI.)*

13. Carl Aage Norgaard, *op. cit.* p.310.

14. *56 American Journal of International Law,* pp.1007-8, (1962).

15. For the Act of Athens and the other texts, see *The Rule of Law and Human Rights, Principles and Definitions,* published by the International Commission of Jurists, Geneva, 1966, Appendices B through G.

16. *The New York Times,* April 11, 1963.

17. On the fundamental importance of the right of so-called petition, see, *inter alia,* Carl Aage Norgaard, *op. cit.;* Carlos Garcia Bauer, *op. cit.;* and Moses Moskowitz, *op. cit.*

18. A broad survey of the contemporary scene in the world leaves little doubt that the universal functional standards of peace, human rights and human welfare are in the long run by far more salient than particular institutions and ideologies, whether liberal constitutionalism or Soviet Communism, Jacobinism or national statism which nations adopt in their pursuit of what they regard as their best interests. See, for example, C. E. Black, *The Dynamics of Modernization: A Study in Comparative History,* New York, Harper & Row, 1966; Adam Schaff, *Marxism a Jednostka Ludzka: Przyczynek do Marksistowskiej Filozofi Czlowieka* (Marxism and the Human Individual: A Contribution to Marxist Philosophy of Man), Warsaw, Panstwowe Wydawn. Naukove, 1965. This book by one of Poland's foremost thinkers of today is an analysis of Marxist philosophy, with emphasis on the early writings of Karl Marx that have been pushed into oblivion by his orthodox interpreters. In this connection, it is of interest to note that on the occasion of his 80th birthday, the noted Hungarian Marxist philosopher and critic, Professor Gyorgy Lukacs, declared on April 13, 1965, in an interview in Budapest that the renaissance of Marxism depended upon the recognition of the "humanist essence" of Marx. (*The New York Times,* April 14 1965.) See also Bertranm D. Wolfe, *Marxism: One Hundred Years in The Life of a Doctrine,* New York, The Dial Press, 1965.

Index